CU01019379

The Way Things Were

Stoke-on-Trent Libraries
Approved for Sale

A Potteries Tale
by
John Frain

With Illustrations
by Colin Lee

Stoke-on-Trent Libraries

3 8080 01618 9175

h 0001014735

STOKE-ON-TRENT LIBRARIES		
3 8080 01618 9175		
Author Supplied	7/1/08	
Six Towns Coun AF		£9.95

First Published 2007 by Appin Press, 14 Appin Road, Birkenhead, CH41 9HH

Copyright © 2007 John Frain

The right of John Frain to be identified as the author of this work has been asserted by him in accordance with the Copyright, Design and Patents Act 1988.

British Library Cataloguing in Publication Data.
A catalogue record for this book is available from the British Library.

ISBN 978 1 906205 03 4

All rights reserved. No part of this publication may be reproduced, stored in a retrieval system, or transmitted, in any other form, or by any other means, electronic, chemical, mechanic, photocopying, recording or otherwise, without the prior permission of the publisher.

Front Cover Illustration: The Old Town Hall and Market Place, Burslem, Staffs, 1947 (Colin Lee).

Love is enough

Love is enough: though the World be a-waning,
And the woods have no voice but the voice of complaining,
Though the sky be too dark for dim eyes to discover
The gold-cups and daisies fair blooming thereunder,
Though the hills be held shadows and the sea a dark wonder,
And this day draws a veil over all deeds pass'd over,
Yet their hands shall not tremble, their feet shall not falter
The void shall not weary, the fear shall not alter
These lips and these eyes of the loved and the lover.

William Morris

DEAR READER,
IF I MAY, I WOULD LIKE TO SAY A FEW PERSONAL WORDS TO YOU BEFORE YOU READ THIS STORY.

Much of the novel's action takes place just after the Second World War when the ceramics industry of North Staffordshire was booming. Frances Bromley, science graduate and daughter of a well-known pottery manufacturer, falls in love with Philip Hughes, a poor man employed as a plate maker. At that time, in that closed community, class distinctions were still rigidly observed. As you will see, this is only one of the obstacles in the path of Frances and Philip.

Perhaps I should explain that I was born in the Potteries and spent a lengthy part of my life working in the ceramics industry. We used to boast that our area had more artists per head of population than could be found in any other part of the country. Now there are very few. The streets which once buzzed with laughing paintresses and chirpy saucer makers are eerily quiet these days. I felt privileged to live and work in a city abounding with firms known all the world over - Wedgwood, Royal Doulton, Spode, Minton, Beswick, Johnson Brothers, Wade, Dudson and so many more. Tragically only one or two of them remain, for in the last few decades 40,000 jobs have been lost in our pottery industry. The Potteries reflects Britain's manufacturing decline. The "workshop of the world" has virtually closed down. Its traditional skills have perished.

Banished by technological progress and the Clean Air Act the bottle kilns, which once gave the "Six Towns" their distinctive landscape, have all been swept away. Some of the district's notable and finely detailed buildings, left to us by the self-confident Victorians have also been sacrificed - to accommodate the slab-like sheds of the grocery multiples, the do-it-yourselfers and the computer merchants. So the City of Stoke-on-Trent is cleaner but it has become amorphous and lacking in "soul". Which is why I decided to write about THE WAY THINGS WERE, before my generation vanishes and the memory is gone forever ...... but I mustn't get too tearful, for there are things to laugh at in my little tale as well as things to sigh over.

Now - the story is a work of fiction but it is set in a factual framework, like my merchant navy novel "Those In Peril". This means that the locations, and the technical and historical details I describe, are solidly factual but they only provide a setting for a fictional story peopled by fictional characters. So any resemblance to real organisations, past or present, or actual persons, living or dead, is completely unintended and wholly coincidental. Having said that, some of the story's more "colourful" characters are composites, drawn from the individual characteristics of a large number of people whose memory I still cherish. I wish I had a pound coin for every time they made me laugh. Also, readers who knew my late wife Pat will be able to discern her spirit in the "make-up" of Francis Bromley.

"Coming Home" these days and seeing how the place has changed is a bitter-sweet experience. One thing that hasn't changed is the kindness of the local folk. One of the district's most famous sons, Sir Stanley Matthews, once said "Warm hearts certainly beat in the Potteries". How right he was, for so many people were more than ready to help me to prepare this story for you, with their reminiscences and their trawling for information. I do, however, claim sole responsibility for any errors you find.

Thank you for reading what is, in essence, my version of an author's preface. I hope you enjoy the story as much as I enjoyed writing it.

Acknowledgements

As mentioned in the Preface, many people helped in bringing this story to publication. Here I would like to thank them individually.

Once again, Captain Colin Lee supplied the drawings for the book with incredible patience and good humour. Ruth Frain, inevitably, was the tower of strength she always is, both in preparing the manuscript and offering valuable advice along the way. In the final stages, she was ably assisted by Sybil Williams. Willing and important support came from Ian Shaw at The Potteries Museum and Art Gallery and Dave Harvey at the City's Directorate of Urban Environment. Kevin Roach at Liverpool Record Office also helped, as in the past.

Mention must be made of The Dudson Museum at Hope Street, Hanley. Mrs Audrey Dudson took a keen interest in the project and willingly gave permission for the famous Dudson Replica Clock to appear on the back cover of the book. Alison Morgan, the curator, was unfailingly pleasant and helpful. Jan Hamilton, cafe manageress at the Dudson Centre plied me with sustaining hot meals and ample supplies of Staffordshire oatcakes.

As well as offering constant encouragement Isabel Ferguson accompanied me on my walks to places relevant to the story and did so whatever the weather. Eveline Paulson was a patient and insightful reader, of every draft, as each section of the book emerged. Mary Fernyhough was a mine of information on the district and its culture and what she didn't know she found out at incredible speed.

Members of the Frain family who enriched my memory of things and offered valuable advice were Pat and Peter, John, Anna, Paula, Anne, Tricia, David, Arleen, John Laird and Eileen Ellis. Among those who sustain me in my writing I must mention Father David Morland OSB, Canon Bob Evans, Brian and Debbie Murphy, Therese de Rouffignac, Jean Lee and Martin Lynch. John Davies has been a faithful prop and stay to all my literary ventures.

I must also thank John and Jean Emmerson and the staff at Countyvise (Appin Press). Once more they spared no pains to provide a publication of quality.

John Frain,
Liverpool, March 2007

Glossary

In order to tell the story as authentically as possible I have used the local dialect from time to time. I have also incorporated some manufacturing terms used during the period the story takes place.

Set out below is a list of these types of word, which I hope you will find helpful. In the text, I have also described the production processes involved so as to complete the "picture" for you.

"abite the fost tarm"	: about the first time
"anner"	: are not
bat	: a flat, circular piece of clay
"baylermon"	: boiler man
"by thissens"	: by themselves
bung	: a pile of flatware (i.e. saucers, plates)
chittered	: clayware with an edge damaged by a fettling tool (see "fettle" below)
"conner"	: cannot or could not
crazing	: a cobweb effect of tiny cracks in a glazed surface
"demob"	: demobilisation from the armed forces at the end of the War and return to civilian life
dipping house	: the department where fired ware was given its coat of glaze – this dried to a powdery surface which produced a shiny coat on the ware after a further ("glost") firing
"doo-dees"	: terror stricken
dunted (ware)	: ware cracked during the firing process
"dust" (?)	: do you (?)
"enough on his plate"	: he has enough worries already

"fang owt of"	: take hold of
fettle	: to smooth ware using a sharp-edged tool
"green" saggar	: unfired saggar (see "saggar" below)
"hard lines"	: unfortunate
"he's got the wind up"	: he's frightened
humper	: a piece of misshapen flatware (hump in middle)
"Ah shill bost"	: I shall burst
lawn	: a sieve
"like a running bull"	: extremely angry
"lobby"	: a stew of meat, potatoes and vegetables (similar to "scouse" and "hotpot")
to "mash"	: to court or be firm friends with; also to make e.g. "mash some tea"
"mither"	: to pester ("stop mithering me")
"nate"	: night
"o'rate"	: all right
saggar	: a fireclay container for placing ware in an oven (see illustration on Page 81)
"snappin"	: food or a meal break
specking	: small spots on finished ware (usually kiln dirt)
stillage	: a system of racks to hold boards of ware
thixotropic	: the property of a viscous liquid to thin temporarily when stirred (e.g. Fred Knapper's tea)
"thunny"	: the only
"tickled 'im"	: made him laugh
"tripe hound"	: a scoundrel
"up, duck"	: pardon me, dear
to "werrit"	: to worry
"whay dustner"	: why don't you
"wonner"	: were not

Good reading!

Contents

Prologue		13-16
Chapter One	Back to Work	17-26
Chapter Two	The Visit to the Sliphouse	27-37
Chapter Three	Into the 'Top Shop'	39-52
Chapter Four	Laughter and Tears	53-68
Chapter Five	Exchange of Views	69-80
Chapter Six	Drawing Day	81-94
Chapter Seven	The Learning Curve	95-108
Chapter Eight	Significant Developments	109-121
Chapter Nine	The Works Outing	123-139
Chapter Ten	Sea, Sand and Smoke	141-162
Chapter Eleven	A Clue to Character	163-181
Chapter Twelve	A Walk to the Little Wood	183-205
Chapter Thirteen	Storm and Solitude	207-235
Chapter Fourteen	The Reckoning	237-259
Chapter Fifteen	Vale of Tears	261-286
Chapter Sixteen	Parting of the Ways	287-311
Chapter Seventeen	Love is Enough	313-336
Chapter Eighteen	The Testing Time	337-366
Epilogue		367-403

Prologue

Bradwell Grange

Before the land puffs itself up into the Pennine Chain, it sucks in its breath sharply. Now, here's the point.....the land's breath is sharp but not deep: there are no great features as a result of it, only those humps and hollows which lie between the peaks of Derbyshire and the plains of Shropshire and Cheshire.

The history of what went on in these hollows has rarely been recorded yet they have a far more individual character and a richer heritage than many other parts of these islands. Moreover, some of the most skilled and industrious people in Great Britain were to be found in what was originally a secluded rural area.

Potters lived in these North Staffordshire hollows. Their creations graced many a state occasion and added to the reputation of many a famous museum. "Staffordshire pottery" was to be found in the castles of kings, the cottages of labourers and even in the covered wagons of the settlers on the wild frontier. Yet the potters themselves toiled in grossly unhealthy conditions, lived in mean and crowded streets and were paid an insulting proportion of the prices their output commanded in the markets of the world.

There are six towns in the hollows – Tunstall, Burslem, Hanley, Stoke upon Trent, Fenton and Longton. Together they constitute the city of Stoke on Trent. Usually, each town has been allocated a particular hollow. The town centre is to be found sitting on a hump of land in its middle, an intriguing arrangement.

The story you are about to read took place in Burslem, "the Mother Town", birthplace of Josiah Wedgwood, prince of the potters. Just after the Second World War something happened there which generates intense attention even now and, at the time, gave rise to rumours of heroic dimensions. First, however, a little more about the setting......

The village of Porthill stands on the southern rim of Burslem's particular hollow. It governs the road to Newcastle-under-Lyme. Bradwell Lane runs in the opposite direction, towards the west. If, on that Monday morning in September nineteen forty-seven we had walked along the Lane for about a mile, set back from its right-hand verge we would have noticed two tall, wide brick pillars. On one of these pillars an ornate, well-polished sign announced that here was the entrance to Bradwell Grange.

The pillars had been built to support heavy iron gates. These had vanished – sacrificed to the "war effort". This applied also to the railings which once stood on the three feet high walls adjacent to the gates. Because of Britain's continuing dire shortages, gates and railings would not be replaced for some time.

Beyond the gates a five acre estate was well served by a network of well maintained roads made from a mixture of locally quarried red marl and finely sifted gravel. "Hoggin" is the term applied to the mixture but this is too prosaic, even vulgar, a word to attach to these roadways. They were a feature of the property, furnishing a link with North Staffordshire's brick and tile industry and providing perfect counterpoise to the lush lawns which, after six years of enforced neglect, were recovering their greensward quality.

Bradwell Grange had been developed from a seventeenth – century farmhouse. Its stables and outbuildings had now become garages, workshops and garden sheds. "The Grange", as it was known locally, had been built in 1882-3 by Enoch Bromley, Burslem potter and self-made man. Anxious to affirm his success in the world it had been constructed after the fashion of the Tudor brick and tile country houses which he much admired. With its shaped gables, tall chimneys and pedimented windows it might have been deemed over-fussy by latter-day taste.

This did not disturb Enoch, however, and did not prevent him adding an extra flourish to affirm the property as the home of a master potter. Flint was a fundamental constituent in the manufacture of Bromley tableware. So he stipulated to a careworn architect that on each side of the gabled entrance porch there must be a sizeable panel of knapped flints with elaborate flint-chip galleting.

The off-white knapped flints would present their flat, round surfaces to the eye as key points of interest. The gallets were razor-sharp slithers of dark flint placed carefully into the mortar bed around each knapped flint. This time consuming, elaborate ornamentation not only attested to the high status of the owner-potter, its irridescence in the morning sun provided "The Grange" with a unique, appealing character to glorify the art and practice of ceramics.

Immediately behind the house was a wide Yorkstone terrace. This was flanked by vases and urns – in Portland stone, no less. Beyond the terrace was a broad path of finely graded gravel. Next came the balustrading. This surrounded an elaborate parterre garden containing clipped box hedging, sculpted yews and conifers, a centrally situated fountain and randomly placed Victorian shrubs. One or two items of classical sculpture brought an already pleasing aspect to the margin of distinction.

Beyond the parterre, the improving lawns ran on to a thick hawthorn hedge. Here was the boundary of the property adjacent to Bradwell Wood. Altogether while Bradwell Grange fell just short of the description "mansion", in estate agents' hyperbole, "imposing gentleman's residence" was well merited. Our story begins here at Bradwell Grange.

Chapter One

Back to Work

A young woman was looking out of that window in the Grange's breakfast room which provided a clear, westerly aspect. But the parterre, the lawns beyond and even the Autumn colours of Bradwell Wood failed to hold her attention. As she crossed to one of the windows which revealed that hollow holding Burslem in its bosom, her tension was well concealed.

In the middle distance was the Old Town Hall: Italianate, solid, dignified and surmounted by its delightful bell chamber, clock turret and golden angel. It was reckoned to be "the most noble building in all the Potteries" but today this did not detain her. She lingered longer over those other features of the landscape - the bottles made of brick. Perhaps it was the Celtic strain in her formation for as a child she had liked to imagine that a family of giants had been responsible for these strange objects, left to litter the town. For food, drink and sleep they had sat astride the hollow. When, having been surprised by the lateness of the hour, they had hurried on, their brick bottles had been left behind.

Today, of course, she knew that the larger bottles were the "biscuit" and "glost kilns" of the potters - "biscuit" for baking the clay, "glost" for giving it a shiny surface. The smaller "hardening on" and "enamel" kilns were used after the pottery had been decorated. When she had made up stories for her brothers she got them to think of the large kilns as the bottles of the adult giants while their children had drunk from the smaller bottles.

"Frances, you'll be seeing that lot up close presently. Why don't you start your breakfast? Foley'll have the car 'round soon."

Ewart Bromley, master potter and grandson of Enoch Bromley, founder of Bromley Earthenware Manufacturers Ltd., was seated at the breakfast table. By now he was well through his meal. As he spoke, he was sliding an eighteen carat gold watch back into his waistcoat pocket. For its significance rather than its value, he had fingered the watch lovingly: it was a full Hunter by Waltham of Massachusetts, a present from his firm's agent for New York/New England. He often slid the watch back and forth from his waistcoat, being a man pathologically possessive of his time. Now, even a daughter he idolised could not be allowed to disturb the order of his day.

Frances Bromley turned from the window and walked slowly to the table. A little above the average female height for the time, she was quite beautiful. Her raven black hair was echoed in the soft curves of her eyebrows which, strikingly, had been left largely untouched. Big and lustrous blue eyes and an immaculate skin had an immediate impact, even on those who saw her frequently.

Like many of the "better off" women of the day she wore a cashmere "twin set" of sweater and matching cardigan. At her neck was a double strand of pearls. A Harris tweed skirt and brogue shoes in superb leather completed the stunning appearance of this twenty two year old.

She gave her father a small smile, sat down and stirred the contents of a cereal bowl. Bromley noted that she did this without enthusiasm. He spoke quietly:

"Eat up, sweetheart. It's going to be a long day for you. Better get a good breakfast."

Just then, Mary Ellen Foley, the cook-housekeeper and wife to Jack Foley, the chauffeur-handyman, came into the room. She carried a plate of cooked breakfast. The girl blenched at it. With a quick, concerned glance at the father, Mrs Foley decided how best to proceed:

"Oh, Miss Frances - you haven't started yet. I'm sorry. I'll just keep it warm for you and come back later."

"No, no....really... I'd rather not have that today. A cup of coffee perhaps, with this cereal. Thank you."

Before leaving, the cook darted another look at her employer.

Ewart Bromley was short and portly. In his dark blue suit and immaculate white shirt he looked very much the businessman. Since his father's death in nineteen forty he had been Chairman and Managing Director of the firm founded in eighteen eighty by grandfather Enoch. At its "Grange" pottery (yet another "Grange"), it had now become the second largest employer in Burslem. Bromley's dark hair was parted at the crown of his head and carefully brushed down to the short grey hair above his ears. A good-looking man in his sixties, he appeared older, for life's vicissitudes had left their mark.

For a second or so he watched his daughter:

"What's the matter, darling?"

"Nothing really. I suppose I'm a bit nervous."

"Nervous? Why?"

"Just wondering how people will feel.....whether they'll accept me."

"'Accept'?....'Accept' you!....I never heard talk of such a thing! 'Accept' you?.....you're going to be the boss!...well, number two that is."

The father leaned towards her, brandishing a knife to emphasise his words:

"Now don't you worry about 'acceptance' - just as if any of them had the option! I've already told Dempster and the departmental people - you're going to be in charge! In the meantime, while you're learning the trade, you're to be treated with the utmost respect. Anybody needing further instruction on that'll have me to deal with."

In ten more minutes, Mrs Foley was helping Frances Bromley into the smartly tailored jacket which partnered the Harris tweed skirt. Then father and daughter crossed the oak panelled hall. Its walls were unadorned but for a Staffordshire ceramic slip-trailed charger by Thomas Toft, an artefact of history and value. Fan palms in a pair of jardinières designed by William Moorcroft added their elegance and near the main door was a longcase clock with superb marquetry.

The clock waited until they were abreast of it before giving out its nine o'clock chimes. Yet the clock's guile did not startle them for it emitted only plummy sounds which dissolved in an exquisite perdendo. When the Bromleys stepped out beyond the porch there was a slight chill on the breeze so as to warn them that Winter was on its way.

"Mornin', Major!....Miss Frances."

Chauffeur Jack Foley was saluting briskly. He was a tall man whose livery did well to contain his broad frame. Ewart Bromley had been his battalion commander in the First World War. So far as Foley was concerned, Bromley's temporary wartime rank would always be permanent. Major

Bromley and Sergeant Foley had been bonded by their experience of war, by its hunger for men's flesh and bone, its unquenchable thirst for their blood. This fusion of hearts and minds was a silent but highly significant phenomenon of which the parades on Remembrance Sunday were only an element.

In the nineteen thirties, Foley had been "cod" placer at the Bromley pottery, which is to say he headed a team of men who placed the clay articles into refractory containers ("saggars") and carried them into the bottle kilns for subsequent "firing" - heat treatment at a very high temperature, that is. "Cod" Foley had been working at the top of a tall column of saggars and had fallen twenty feet onto the kiln floor. It was soon clear that he would never again work as a placer: placing was an arduous task and only for the fittest and strongest. The man's problems were compounded by the fact that "social security" was unheard of and the industrial legislation of the day offered him scant protection.

When Ewart Bromley learned that the Foleys were to be evicted from their "two up and two down" for rent arrears he offered them work as chauffeur and housekeeper respectively at Bradwell Grange. He had been careful to wave away any thanks and had tendered the offer in the most matter-of-fact manner, lest he be thought "soft".

"Smell that leather, Frances! by durs, there's something about a new car."

As the Humber Super Snipe went through the gate pillars of "the Grange" and moved onto Bradwell Lane, Ewart smiled to himself: the Bromleys might be "new money" but in the age of shortages he had wangled a new car while the "county set" owners of many other potbanks were still in the queue.

Then he frowned as he remembered another new car.... he had bought it in 1939, a Rolls Royce Phantom III which, when the marque was unveiled a few years earlier, had been deemed the most technically advanced car in the world. In fact, many believed that it was the best car ever made. His father Isaiah, had been amused when told it was for "state occasions". With rare emotion the father muttered: "Old Enoch would have been proud of thee for thy bloody cheek, lad." This was some compliment because Enoch himself had raised the cocking of snooks to the highest possible level.

Ironically, the car became something of a "phantom" in the real sense since petrol rationing ensured its immobilisation during the entire war. Its first peace-time appearance had taken place only a few months ago when it had followed the hearse bearing Ewart's beloved wife Alice to her interment.

The Humber purred its way through the morning traffic, down Porthill Bank and into Longport. As it crossed the bridge over the Trent and Mersey Canal Frances looked up. On the other side of the bridge and quite close to the canal stood a bottle-kiln belonging to a well-known teapot manufacturer. Since her childhood she had always perceived it as a sentry guarding the lower approach to Burslem town. In seconds they were approaching Trubshawe Cross. Here they turned right into Newcastle Street, a long throughfare which made its way up the southern face of the hump to the Market Place and the grandeur of the Old Town Hall.

The Bromleys were not seeking to go so far, however. While still in Dale Hall, the lower reaches of Newcastle Street, the Humber turned right into Furlong Parade. Frances looked out at the municipal building to the right. She thought it must once have been a school of some type and the large tarmac-surfaced area around it a playground. She especially remembered being driven down Newcastle Street on her seventh birthday in nineteen thirty two. She had asked about the crowds of men surging around the doors of the building. Her mother had smiled grimly:

"That's the Labour Exchange, dear. They're queuing up for their dole."

"But why are those women there, and the children?"

"To be sure that what little the men get doesn't end up in the pubs or the bookmakers."

And little Frances had been left to wonder.

Soon the Humber reached Lower Hadderidge, a terrace of cheap back-to-back houses. Like so many of the terraces in the town it provided homes for the potters and for the miners toiling beneath its streets. To mark their departure from this street and their entry into Navigation Road, a mongrel dog cocked its leg towards the nearest lamp-post and left a trickle of urine dripping into the gutter.

No sooner had they entered Navigation Road than they were making another right turn, this time into Pleasant Street. The Super Snipe glided imperiously into what was yet another grim terrace of two-up and two-down houses. Frances was saddened - whoever could have called this "Pleasant Street"?

However, the people on the pavements, obviously returning to work, lifted her spirits. At first they were in awe of the vehicle; then their nosiness won through and they leaned towards its windows nudging each other as they recognised the chauffeur and his passengers.

Two women peered into the rear of the Humber.

"Ooh, it's young Frances!", smiled one. "Isn't she lovely? Just like her mother!"

"Her mother?"

"Yes!....yer know Alice McLaren as-was, from the drapers in St. John's Square."

Crossing herself she added:

"She's dead now, poor soul. I'll bet Frances misses her."

The woman's smile became tender and compassionate. She waved and Frances smiled and nodded shyly.

Among the folk returning to work one man carried a pudding basin wrapped in a large, knotted handkerchief.

The knotted arrangement provided a convenient carrying handle for what the locals termed "a good bowl o' lobby".

Surreptitiously, Ewart Bromley was encouraging Jack Foley to increase speed when suddenly... .alarm! As they were passing a house on their near side its front door flew open. At lightning speed out came a little boy. On a parallel course to the car he ran along the pavement, his tiny bare feet slap-slap-slapping the bricks. Apart from a grubby jersey he was unclothed and must surely have been the dirtiest little boy ever to have emerged from Burslem's streets - from the World's streets to be sure, for no-one, not even Charles Dickens could have described adequately the dirtiness of this dirty little boy. It was the colossal amount of dirt in so tiny a framework which made its assault upon the vision.

Then came the piercing scream, a scream that overawed the Humber's engine note, a scream that could only have come from a mother bent on retribution:

"Ty..........rone!!"

Only the recording angel would know whether the child's given name emanated from Irish antecedents or the influence of Hollywood but no matter, the scream supercharged the boy's already considerable speed and he veered from the pavement and onto the roadway. Instantly, Foley swung the car away from the child so that Ewart Bromley in the front passenger seat found himself staring down at an enquiring face on which two trails of mucus, not unlike spent candle wax, were making their way from its nostrils to its upper lip. The curiosity of Tyrone the trouserless, and the starched indignity of the master potter had been brought into tense conjunction. It was too much for Frances who put her hand to her mouth to mask her amusement.

The mother caught up with the child and yanked him back onto the pavement. She swept him into her arms, on which the drying soapsuds of another washday were glinting like jewels. For an apology she clamped her front teeth onto her lower lip and shook her head. For a rebuke Bromley shook his head and motioned to Foley to drive on. For an expiation the mother brought her hand down hard on Tyrone's unprotected thigh. For a rejoinder Tyrone delivered a "fourpenny one" to his mother's astonished face. For the restoration of decorum Foley accelerated away from the wailing and counter wailing. He it was who broke the silence:

"I should hope Tyrone's the next thing in the dolly-tub!"

Frances still had her hand to her face but her shaking shoulders were giving her away.

Within minutes they were approaching an archway. A sign above it announced they were about to enter the premises of:

Enoch Bromley and Son Ltd
Grange Tableware
Established 1870

Ernest Biddulph, the lodgeman, peered out of his window and gave them a most polite nod as they went under the arch, over his weighbridge and into the factory yard, called colloquially the "bank". Foley opened the car doors briskly. On the "bank" were a number of potters who had returned from "snappin'" as they termed both food and foodbreak. Some of them were still queuing by the time clock to signal their re-entry. Several nodded agreeably, particularly to Frances Bromley.

One of the queuing potters, Sally Gratton, was thin and pale. There were faint blue rings under her eyes. She looked as delicate as a china figurine. Indicating the Bromley daughter she said:

"That's Miss Frances. They say th' boss wants her here now the boys have gone. It'll be a big change for her."

Her companion, Winnie Hood, was pretty, plump and rather short. Her eyes widened:

"Ooh, isn't she gorgeous!"

Then, exultantly:

"Who d'yer think she's like?"

A quick mental check down the list of cinema beauties, then Sally Gratton said:

"Merle Oberon."

Winnie was unimpressed:

"No!......wrong shape face..... I know!.....Linda Darnell!"

So it was agreed and Winnie chortled:

"'er'll find a rough lot, Sal - 'specially in the top shop!"

They watched Frances walk towards the office building, her stately progress contrasting with the rush and bustle around her. Then the two girls turned to each other and gasped in unison:

"Silk stockings!"

Chapter Two
The Visit To The Sliphouse

Ewart Bromley walked quickly down the dark central corridor of the office building. Frances followed.

As he was opening the door to his own office, Millicent Dean, an invoice typist, bid him a respectful "good morning, sir". He merely nodded and said:

"Ask Mr Dempster to come up right away, will you?" She scurried off.

When Frances entered her father's office she made for the worn leather chair facing his desk. As a child she had watched grandfather Isaiah wag words of advice to her father from this chair, so it had an iconic quality. Perhaps sitting in it would still her nerves.

"Come in!", shouted Ewart Bromley to the sounding door. Mr Jack Dempster appeared wearing a coat overall of Monday morning whiteness. He had removed his brown trilby hat and was holding it, obsequiously, to his chest. Dempster was tall and thin with round shoulders. His rimless glasses reinforced the impression of scholarly stoop. Frances knew him to be younger than her father but his receding hairline seemed to balance matters.

He was the General Manager of the Grange Pottery. She had known him for as long as she could remember. She classified her acquaintance with him alongside her first memories of such terms as "humpers", "dunted" and "chittered". He had not minded her childhood observation that "pottery talk" was "such a funny language" for he had remarked that had he spoken in the local dialect she would have found it even funnier.

The greetings over, Bromley nodded proudly at his daughter:

"Well, Jack......here she is and she's in your care till she knows as much about the thing as we do. I hope to find she's doing mixings by the end of the week."

Dempster nodded and smiled. Frances was in some awe of him. As she recalled, he said very little, but her father had declared on countless occasions:

"If you put Jack Dempster on a desert island and there was clay under the surface, he'd produce bigger, better and straighter ware than any other three managers, even if they pooled their knowhow."

The General Manager looked at the young woman he guessed would soon be a director of the company:

"Miss Frances, you'll need an overall to keep the slurry off your clothes. Let's see what Mrs Birks, in the stores, can do for you."

He let himself look at her more closely:

"You know, you've grown into a very smart woman, if

I can say that. You're going to be quite a distraction to the men."

Ewart Bromley tensed and, as if in sympathy, Dempster's smile vanished. Fearful lest her father might fly into one of his notable rages, she pursed her lips and shook her head to deter him, but it put him off only partially. He leaned towards Dempster:

"Now listen – Frances won't have much trouble with the technical side of things – her B.Sc'll take care of that. It's your job to see she gets the best possible grounding in the practical side. You must teach her to use her hands and to understand the use of their hands – so she's at nobody's mercy."

He paused. Frances knew this as the prelude to his crescendo. Still glaring at Dempster, the Master spoke menacingly:

"Your duties go further than that though – you're to see she gets the respect that due to her as my daughter. And that excludes the provision of nervous excitement for any man on this potbank!"

"Father I'm sure Mr Demp...."

Bromley silenced her with a wave of his hand and still looking at Dempster, he said:

"Just remember – I shall hold you responsible for her welfare as well as her progress. Do you understand?"

Then Bromley fished out his watch and looked at it. The meeting was over.

"Yes. Yes, of course..........Shall we go then, Miss Frances?", asked Dempster.

They walked across "the bank". She wanted to apologise for her father's outburst but the manager seemed preoccupied. Perhaps he pondered her systematic instruction and, in all probability, his years at the "Grange" would have provided ample experience of her father's vicissitudes.

"How's Gwen this morning, Mr Dempster?"

"Very well. Apparently, you had an enjoyable time

together yesterday but erm.....just before we go over to the stores, I want you to look at this batch of ball clay."

They were standing outside the sliphouse. Frances looked at the bays where the clays were stored. The potters called the bays "arks", she remembered. Standing there by the arks, it came to her again as in childhood – the dank, musty smell which comes from clays in storage. The particular faint odour had always, for her, been synonymous with potting.

Another significant smell came from the lithograph shop. This was the smell of the size which enabled the girls with deft hands to apply patterns to the plates. At University, whenever she thought of home the smells of clay and size would come to her, improbable though it may seem. She would recall how the size and oils smells permeated the girl's clothing so that when they passed her on the street she knew they worked on a potbank.

Room-mates had smiled condescendingly, suggesting that "Stoke-on Trent" was "not a very salubrious place". She had told them with pride about the people who conjured in clay and the people who, with consummate skill, decorated their output – the gilders, the printers, the lithographers, the banders, the freehand painters and paintresses. She had countered friends' cynicism with confidence, borrowing her answer from grandfather, Isaiah:

"All right – it is grim – but think of the things that come out of it. Next time you're passing through, slow down a bit – on every pavement you'll rub shoulders with an artist."

Jack Dempster interrupted her thoughts:

"We'll be back here presently but let's not forget Mrs Birks and that overall of yours. We must hurry. Stores are locked at ten and Florrie Birks won't open them again – even for us!"

As they walked he continued:

"About thirty years ago your grandfather told Mrs Birks

that the stores were to be open every morning from half-past nine till ten o'clock. From that time on they've never been open a minute longer."

Mrs Florence Birks and her stores were on the other side of the "bank" where the boiler hole, the engine house and the saggar-making shop were also located. Above the saggar-maker and the stores was one of the "flat" (that is, plate-making) shops. Known as the "top-shop" its dingy windows afforded some of the women working there a glimpse of Frances as she came across the bank. They smiled warmly.

Bent but bright-eyed, Florence Birks was sitting on a high stool totally enveloped in a woollen shawl. She looked like a perched bird. They found her in her best form. As they entered the dimly-lit stores, an exasperated potter was remonstrating:

"......but I can't get my work right with this sponge. I've used it till it's in bits! It's takin' me twice as long to make a job of anythink. Me husband says if it's going to take me this long to get any wages, I'd better pack it up!"

Though acerbic enough, the rejoinder came with a smile:

"An' how long has Frank been boss at your house, Phyllis Poyser?"
The dish-sponger turned on her heel, snorting. Seeing Frances she flushed with embarrassment and disappeared.

The old woman looked at her visitors:
"If spongers knew how to finish their work off properly, 'stead of pushin' and scrubbin' at it, sponges'd last longer an' dishes wouldn't come out of the ovens crooked." Frances was to learn that in having her own theories as to how factory loss was occasioned Mrs Birks was at one with all potters.

"Florrie – can you find a coat overall for this young lady – who, incidentally, is Miss Frances Bromley."

"I've got eyes, Jack Dempster! I can see who it is! While

you're down here you can go into my greenhouse and see some of the saucers that's comin' off the new machine. There isn't a good un in seven boards!"

Frances knew that the "greenhouse" was the room where the finished clay articles were carried for quality inspection before they were fired in the bottle ovens. The greenhouse was where Florence Birks held court except for thirty minutes every day when she visited this other part of her kingdom – the stores. Frances smiled as the old lady turned to her with all her attention:

"Hallo, duck. It doesn't seem long since a little girl came through my greenhouse on her way to see the bottle ovens. Now she wants a slop – I'd say about 'Woman's' size."

Pulling the shawl about her Mrs Birks hopped down from the stool. Frances noted for the first time the Victorian shoes with their side buttons. She went to a stillage marked "Staff" and drew from it a white coat–overall. The girl tried it on, drawing the tapes together at the back. To judge its length she made a half-turn and looked over her right shoulder.

"This is fine. Thank you, Mrs Birks."

"You're welcome, duck. Now I'm going to look out another one and when I go home for me dinner I'll iron it for you and leave it at the Office, at two o'clock. Let me have that one back on Sat'dee for the wash and it'll be clean and ready for you on Monday morning."

The bent lady climbed back onto her stool , withdrawing her feet within the canopy of the shawl. As she looked at the tall man her expression clouded:

"Don't forget them saucers, Jack Dempster! I haven't got time to come running all over the bank after you!"

Having seen the saucers some minutes later, he talked of the old woman as they returned to the sliphouse:

"She guards all the stocks in the stores as if they were her personal possessions and she took everything your grandfather said as absolute gospel. She still considers your father and I are a bit inexperienced."

"She's as bright as a button. How old is she?"

"Nearer eighty than seventy, I'd say and she'll never retire. That's O.K. by your father. He reckons it'll take two to replace her and her jobs won't be half as well done at that."

In a minute or so they entered the House of Noise. Motors, gears, belt-drives, blunger blades and the paddles in the blending arks all contributed to the cacophony. Here in the Grange's sliphouse, Dempster had to yell with all his power to make himself heard. When the men toiling there looked puzzled, gesticulations aided understanding.

Here was where the raw materials were blunged into "slips" of creamy consistency, then run down their separate channels into the great storage arks below floor level. Frances knew that the mixing of the earthenware body was supremely important to the "Grange" and all its workers. A mistake here and losses could result in nearly every stage of production. A "body" fault might take weeks to clear itself from the Grange's system.

It was true that soon great technological advances would reduce the significance of body differentials between "potbanks" but even as late as nineteen hundred and forty seven, the body composition of most firms in the hollows was the secret of the master potter shared only with his senior manager and his slipmaker. So to add to the lure of the craft, secrecy was part of the alchemy.

Only the members of this trio knew how many inches to mark on the mixing ark dipstick for each constituent – ball clay, china clay, flint and stone. The dipstick was to be thrust into the blend after each bubbling constituent had surged up the walls. Only one of the trio was to perform this operation having adjusted the mark for each constituent according to whether the slips of each one were actually over or under the pint weights stipulated by the secret formula.

Here the body was born. Here the approach must be faultless otherwise no subsequent process could cure the clay-child of its deformity. Ewart Bromley had deputed Jack Dempster to instruct Frances in the obstetrics of these roaring effluents until she was a peerless midwife.

The sliphouse men were agog. They watched as she picked her way over the pipes and across the puddles of Bromley's earthenware body. This was very much a man's world, which doubled, therefore, the impact of her beauty. So they stared, stupefied, until the manager's home-made semaphore signals set them shovelling again. From their spades, the clays flew into the hungry mouths of the blungers. These masticated, digested and when called upon ejaculated a particular slip, according to the material they had fed upon.

Frances stood above the great ark and watched while Dempster controlled the mixing. This was when she became aware that someone was watching her from the shadows. She did not want to look. Her father was bound to ask several questions about her reaction to the mixing procedure so she had to give it her close attention.

Until a few minutes ago her watcher had given his mind and heart over to a sublime memory - the first meeting of the "Flat" Racing Season last year and his one shilling treble which had netted him winnings of £8.4.6d plus the return of his shilling stake. Eight pounds five shillings and sixpence! While still coming to grips with the enormity of his fortunes it was decided – his luck was "in", he was "gambling with their money" and he had to commit all his winnings to secure his goal of becoming Burslem's first post-war millionaire.

Needless to say the winnings were lost before that particular meeting was over but the memory would always remain, would always motivate him to repeat the experience. So he had squatted, with his back to a blunger when he had been bumped out of his reverie by the beautiful vision now standing alongside Jack Dempster. His eyes still watched her and just as the mixing was ending she capitulated to curiosity.

It was an elf......an elf in baggy trousers which, in spite of their bagginess, still managed to paunch at the knees. Even gay patches in many colours could not break up the beautiful curves of the knee-paunches. Next came the shirt, a buttonless affair of cotton so thin it barely touched, rather than covered, a tiny chest. The slash that existed in the absence of buttons laid bare much of the chest. Dry, sorry hairs were struggling to grow there, within a coppice of ribs.

The face was an absurdity. Though only a slit, the mouth could not prevent itself from wriggling into a perpetual grin. The nose was a grog-blossomed, red disfigurement, but the eyes were a puzzle, for sadness and gaiety lingered there in equal measure. These red-rimmed, smarting things had a permanent conjunctivitis which could only have come from long years of committed insobriety. Altogether this projection of roguery had about five feet two inches in which to contain itself and was apparently called "Billy Hogan". Frances now knew this for Jack Dempster's calling of the name still rang in the rafters of the sliphouse. His imprecation had been:

"Billy Hogan! Are you going to stand there all day?! The Cup Shop's waiting for that clay!"

"Right ho, Mester Dempster!" called Hogan. Then with a grateful look at the manager and a nod towards Frances he added:

"....unny we don't have visitors like this every day, yer know."

And off he went, pushing his loaded truck of prepared clay, soon to become dozens of cups and bowls, big and small.

"Billy Hogan is the clay carrier and oven oddman."

"Oddman?"

"Yes he helps the fireman, topping up the firemouths with fresh coal. He's also a bookie's runner, though I'm not supposed to know that. Don't believe anything he tells you and never, ever, give him any money."

The general manager then resumed his technical tuition:

"When the body has been mixed in this ark, we sieve it through those 'lawns' over there to remove the coarse particles."

She followed his finger to the jumping sieves.

"Then it's passed over electro-magnets to get rid of any tramp iron before it goes into the finished ark, then over to the filter-presses."

They came to the great metal presses.

"The clay builds itself up on the filter cloths inside the metal chambers. You can see some of the press-cakes on that trolley, next to Billy Hogan's 'pug'."

They walked to where the elf had stood, watching her.

"When a press is emptied, he feeds the cake into this pug-mill. The pug takes the air out of the clay and slabs it up so it's a convenient form for the making-shops."

As a child, Frances had once watched as the mouth of a pug-mill sent out a great tongue of prepared clay. The tongue was some nine inches square and she had seen the clay carrier cut it into "wads" with a cheese-wire, each wad two feet or so in length.

The pug-mill was stopped now but from its mouth there was a six inch protrusion of clay. She bent to feel its texture. Just then, in the corner of her eye, an empty sleeve appeared.

She straightened up. Ernest Biddulph, the lodgeman, was smiling at her. She well remembered this tall, soldierly figure with his pink face, white moustache, blue eyes, brown "slop" and black Homburg hat. She especially remembered his copperplate handwriting, which appeared in his many great books. One day when she had asked him where his arm was, he had smiled and told her he had left it in "foreign parts". When she had mentioned this to her father he had muttered:

"He was in the Dardanelles and a damn good soldier apparently."

"Good morning, Miss Frances, would you excuse me please?"

The lodgeman turned to Dempster:

"There's a 'phone call for you in the Lodge, sir."

Dempster looked back as he hurried away:

"We're going into the "top shop" next. Please go up to the wooden steps outside the stores. Through the door you'll find about fifty boards of finished work. You might just look at them before we go into the shop. I'll be back shortly."

Chapter Three

Into the "Top Shop"

Frances climbed the steps leading to the "top shop". She was disconcerted to feel a sideways movement in them and saw a slurry of wet clay scraps lying on the treads in places. She wondered why the staircase was not covered from the weather.

In a few minutes she was looking at the stillage containing boards of finished clayware. As she glanced at various shapes and sizes of plates, round and square, plain and embossed, she remembered the collective noun for them was "flat". She noted also how the larger sizes were placed on short boards while the smaller sizes from six inches in diameter down to the saucers were placed on longer boards of about six feet.

She had the impulse to pick up some plates from the "bungs" of twelve in which they rested. She knew though that in the dry-clay state they had no more strength than the chocolate egg of a child's Easter. Only when the flat had been fired in the bottle ovens would it be safe for inexperienced hands like her own to handle it. She smiled in remembering how old Mrs Birks had shuffled a bung of clay saucers through her fingers as though they were playing cards. It was a skill Frances resolved to acquire.

At that precise moment, when a door opened behind her, Frances was bending to look at some boards in the lower rungs of the stillage.

"Come on, Vera.......boards!"

That much she heard. Then came the stinging pain across her thighs.

Pain and shock twisted her around at incredible speed. A young man stood there, alarmed. She wanted to strike him but his consternation was so genuine it abated her wrath.

The man was above medium height. His fair hair inclined to waviness but not so as to make him foppish. At the speed with which women register such details, Frances noted his broad shoulders, square chin and hazel eyes were attractive but because of her smarting thigh she did not dwell on the matter. What she could not care for was the way he kept his gaze averted.

Perhaps it was his embarrassment. And he did seem sincerely sorry but it had not dispelled her anger:

"Well?!"

He made as if to speak but at first there was nothing but a tightening of his mouth. During these seconds she noticed the rubber-bib and the slurry drying on his arms. He was probably a plate maker. When it came his voice was low and contrite:

"I'm very sorry, Miss. I thought you were someone

else."

"Oh ......and are you offering that as an excuse?"

Her words had come quickly and were too harsh she thought but she had been unnerved by the incident and did not soften her stare. He did not reply but, almost imperceptibly, shook his head. She noticed that in his right hand he held a length of broken vee-belt and realised it was the instrument of her discomfort. This revived her indignation.

"When Mr Dempster comes I intend to report you. What's your name?"

"Hughes, Miss........Philip Hughes."

He made no move. Sensing she would have to end the incident she made a half-hearted sweep of her right arm and said, ineffectually:

"Go on then......Mr Hughes."

As he left and she was irritated with herself for managing his banishment so badly, she noticed two men on the far side of the stillage. They had either seen the incident or grasped its import. Frances knew they were probably placers. They were grinning and, she decided, would soon be carrying the news to the four corners of Grange Pottery. For her part, she had already resolved to say nothing about it to Jack Dempster. So when he returned, they entered the top shop without more ado.

"This shop has eight jiggers, Miss Frances. Incidentally, a plate-making machine is called a "jigger". For making cups and hollowware the machine is a "jolley". O.K....well in here, the nearest six jiggers are rope-driven but we've just motorised the two at the bottom of the shop. We shall do them all, gradually, then start on the cup shops."

Frances looked down the long shop. Faces gazed up at her for a second and then returned to the spinning clay. Always, she recalled, there was intense preoccupation when potters were potting.

She watched the potter at the nearest jigger. Alongside the jigger-box was a thick, round plaster of paris wheel mounted on a spindle. This was the "spreader-block", she remembered. A large, pug-fresh wad of clay rested beside it. The plate-maker's strong fingers clawed a lump from it. The fingers knocked the torn clay on the side of the spreader block. The clay became a perfect ball. The perfect ball flew from the strong fingers and smashed itself onto the dead centre of the spreader-block. A rope-drive whirred under the benches of the long shop and now, under the goading pressure of the potter's knee, she heard the mechanism of the spreader-block click into contact with the rope-drive.

The block was now revolving. A little pressure from the potter's fingers helped to stabilise the clay ball in preparation for the descent of the spreader blade. The blade flattened the ball into a pancake, which the potters called a "bat" – another term Frances remembered without difficulty.

Now the potter took up the "bat" with his left hand. There was skill here because he held up the clay like a curtain before his face. Despite the pull of its own weight, the clay did not tear. Meanwhile, the potter's right hand was clawing more clay from the wad. In a second or so another perfect ball had smacked into the dead centre of the spreader-block.

The potter's right hand went up to join his left hand behind the clay curtain. He threw the "bat", perfectly centred, onto a plaster mould by the side of the jigger-box. So, already, the underside of the bat had become the face of a plate. Now he was about to jigger the back of the plate.

The mould went into the jigger-box. She heard a quick "clap" as it seated itself in the round, metal head of the jigger. Soon the mould was spinning. The potter brought down the steel profile which would cut out the back of the plate from the bat. From a bowl in the jigger-box water stole through the potter's hand onto the clay. This was the water to ease the dwell of the steel tool on the soft clay – water to help the potter's fingers glide the clay under the dominating will of the tool. The clay was thankful for the water and for the potter's fingers.

The complete process had taken, perhaps, less than a minute and another plate had been made in the hollow. Frances was sure it was a performance she would never tire of watching. In the meantime, the potter's assistant (a "mouldrunner") was taking the new plate into the dobbin-stove behind them. The dobbin (or "dobby", as the potters have it) was a series of shelves rotating on a giant spindle. As the girl-mouldrunner came out of the stove with two moulds bearing dried plates, Frances felt the moist heat of the stove on her back. She noted that the plates went onto a board while the empty moulds rattled onto the side of the jigger-box to await the touch of two more "bats".

The girl-assistant was speedy and dextrous. While they watched she placed the two dried plates onto an orderly pile (or "bung") of other plates. When these had numbered one dozen, she began another bung. When she had built up a whole board of bungs, an empty board would go onto the hooks to receive more bungs. Frances saw the perspiration now forming in the nape of the girl's neck and reflected that after five and a half days of this gruelling labour she would receive about two pounds, and possibly a few shillings, as her reward.

"I'll just go for some more boards", said the girl to the potter and Frances remembered the incident in the "greenhouse": the young man had been on his way to look for boards. As she moved down the shop behind Jack Dempster, Philip Hughes came into the shop with eight boards on his shoulder. A girl was with him, also carrying boards. She was rather small but pretty and her hair was blonde and long. Her features were also small and she had a slightly pinched expression but her blue eyes were attractively large. Frances noticed she wore a white coat overall like her own and knew, intuitively, that when they were in the greenhouse Philip Hughes had mistaken her for this girl.

As she came down the shop, she gave Frances a stare which was searching and somewhat hostile.

"Excuse me, please!", she called, still staring as she pushed past them. Philip Hughes came behind, the boards he was carrying hiding his face. When he drew up to Dempster and Frances she sensed he paused slightly as if expecting to be stopped but Frances' decision to say nothing about the incident was quite final, so he passed on. He and his companion went to the two jiggers at the bottom of the shop, the ones which had been independently motorised.

Jack Dempster turned to his protégée:

"Now everybody is here, Miss Frances, I want you to meet them. You'll be spending a lot of time here, in the top shop."

She couldn't remember all the names and faces but returning to Bradwell Grange that evening she had a clear recollection of the blonde-haired saucer-maker with a piercing stare named Vera Foskett. She also recalled going to Philip Hughes' jigger. When the introductions were made she was sorry for his embarrassment. Her introductions to the others comprised an exchange of friendly nods. She was anxious to reassure Philip Hughes the incident in the greenhouse was forgiven so, before realising her mistake, she offered him her hand when his own was gloved in a slurry of clay. He had hesitated before diving towards the water pot in his jigger-box. His toilet had been completed with some agitated drawings of his hand across the apron below his bib.

Frances had immediately liked his mouldrunner, Winnie Hood, though she wondered how long the girl's pink cheeks would stay so, there in the top shop. Little more than a child she had run from the jigger to the dobbin stove at great speed. The moulds for plates of ten inches or more in diameter are heavy affairs the more so when the tiny assistant had to stretch to her limit to fill the topmost shelves of the tall stove.

Yet, for all that, every two minutes or so she would skip into the steamy heat with two great moulds bearing heavy clay plates. Then she would reappear with two more moulds bearing dried plates made the previous day. The plates would go onto a board, the moulds would go to the side of the jigger-box and Winnie Hood would trip back to the stoves again singing:

"They say that fallin' in love is wunderful,

It's wunderful – so they say......."

Occasionally Winnie had to pause because one chamber of the stove would be full. Now the whole stove had to be rotated on its spindle so that the next chamber could be brought opposite the stove's entrance. Rotating a stove full of large moulds would be some task even for the heftiest man.

Winnie managed it by gripping the door frame of the stove and moving the stove itself with the weight of her body. Doing this brought her face to face with the photos of the gods from the cinema magazines she had pasted to the door of the stove. So, while thrusting her hips at the massive stove she would gaze at Robert Taylor.......

"I can't recall who said it, I know I never read it

I only know they tell me that love is grand....and......."

Frances was still smiling at the memory of this when other thoughts obtruded, about the visit to the "towing shop". Leaving the "flat" shop they had turned right into the parallel passage. This was where, with their metal tools, their emery cloth and their bundles of blond "tow" (prepared fibres of flax, hemp or jute) women worked upon the dried plates and saucers. Here the rough edges left by the moulding process were removed and the surface of the ware was made completely smooth.

The lives of the towers were in some danger from the

insidious build-up of clay dust in the lung. Silicosis was the killer but it was lumped together with the other industrial diseases of the potbank under the generic term "potter's rot".

Of the towers Frances Bromley particularly remembered a brunette with skin so pale she seemed to have been cut from wax. This was the girl who had been "clocking on" when they arrived that morning. Beneath her eyes were the faintest blue rings. She seemed such a quiet and kindly soul. Apparently, this tower with the china doll's face was Sally Gratton.

A feature of Bradwell Grange was its library-drawing room. This was a large rectangular space in which the drawing room element was divided from the much larger library element by Doric columns in marble. The effect was to combine easy access to either element with a clearly defined purpose for each of them.

The evening meal was over and the Bromleys were sitting in the drawing room before the neo-classical fireplace which was surmounted by an overmantle mirror extending to the ceiling. Across the hallway, Harriet Foley was to be heard leaving the dining room with the last of the dishes.

"I'm glad the first day was so interesting. When the thing really grips you, you'll never be happy away from the place. That's how your grandfather found it and that's how I've always found it."

Ewart Bromley paused and then mumbled:

"And that's how Denzil and Peter would have found it."

He looked at Frances:

"Still......it's up to us now......but it means you'll be doing the job of two men."

Another pause, then –

"Listen to Dempster. Find out all there is to know about the sliphouse, that's where it all starts. Keep asking questions though and once you've mastered the mixing formula and the dip-stick calculations you'll have the hang of things in there."

He made himself more comfortable:

"In the next three months, I want you to go quickly through the whole bank – bottle ovens, biscuit sorting, glost firing, decorating, packing house. Then I want you back in the potting shops for a more thorough grounding in platemaking, quality control, tool filing – everything. I want you to have so much know-how you need go cap-in-hand to nobody. And bear this in mind – knowing your onions is the only way you'll get the respect of craftsmen."

Frances looked at the flames in the hearth, silently. Ewart waited before saying quietly:

"I know you're a girl, Frances but I've every confidence you can do the job and do it well. In the next few years we're going to be busier than we've ever been in our history. The order books are full now for two years on....two years!"

He massaged his eyes with the forefinger and thumb of his right hand. The reddened eyes looked at her.

"I heard one of the lads in the "George" the other day say we're replacing the wastage of war."

Sardonically he smiled:

"I thought about that quite a bit. I suppose the war's wasted us more than most – five of us around that table in there – now there's just you and me."

He leaned towards her. His voice was low:

"I knew your mother wouldn't be with us long, but I kept it to myself. She'd never looked up since the boys went. Didn't seem to have the will to fight it anymore."

The fire danced on the tears in the girl's beautiful eyes. Suddenly Ewart Bromley straightened. His voice was strong, quick, determined:

"Now we must help each other, Frances. This family's scrimped and saved and worked all the hours that God sends to build what it's got today....and what's more this family's got the pluck to take things further."

He pointed towards the hollow:

"You can see the 'mushroom' firms, the 'ham an' egg' firms, the 'rag-timers', springing up left and right. What are they? A couple of cottages knocked together to cash in on the boom – that about covers most of 'em. They'll do this City more harm than good. But we shall see 'em all off!"

He thought for a while before adding:

"They'd give a lot to have names like ours and Beresfords, I tell you."

His pipe was brought out for lighting.........

"I can see the 'Grange' revolving around you in a year or two, sweetheart. To my knowledge, no woman has ever controlled a potbank – well, not one the size of ours certainly. If you don't watch out you'll be a monument in your own lifetime."

He laughed a little, then stopped suddenly:

"I'm building for your future and when I can see that you're ready I'll let go the reins, but not before I've planned the best layout in the industry for you."

His grey eyes narrowed:

"It's no more than a model yet and there's a lot more still in my head – but by nineteen fifty the "Grange" will make even Clive Beresford sit up!"

She smiled but did not reply.

"There's another thing I want to come to and it's this..... while you're learning it all, you'll come very close to the potters. You'll be responsible for their output, their quality and their wage bill. Now – because you're a girl, there's a bit of danger. Until they see you're no dud – they may try to take advantage of you. We've never believed in riding rough-shod over people – but they have always known who the bosses were and, furthermore, we've never had a strike."

Frances looked puzzled:

"Have any of the other firms had a strike?"

"Well, no.....least not for donkey's years. I suppose it's because potters are gentler folk than most. Still, you've got to keep a grip on things. Clive Beresford reckons you've got to let 'em see you're human – get to know their husbands' names, how many children they've got – that sort of thing. I've never been much for this 'human relations' guff and you'll work out your own approach – but remember – you can't put up with familiarity, otherwise your authority's gone!"

Over the stretch of carpet separating their chairs, he drew an imaginary line with the stem of his pipe:

"There's the dividing line. You're on this side – they're on the other. They must always understand – you're the boss!"

He looked up at her:

"Do you see that, Frances?"

The silence pressed in on them. The clock hesitated in its ticking.

"Yes", murmured Frances at last.

Bromley was re-stuffing his pipe. Since he felt the answer was indisputable he had already anticipated it.

A little later, Frances was at her dressing table. She brushed her hair with slow strokes – always, for her, an adjunct to concentration.

She was worried. Her devotion to her father did not blind her to his faults. She knew full well that the future of the firm weighed heavily on him now the boys were gone but resented his assumption that she would instinctively step into their roles. The matter had not even been discussed.

She didn't want to do "great things". If she knew anything about her aim in life it was that she wanted to do the "little things" and do them with love.

Naturally, she expected to work. Her graduation had been preparation for it. Yet while work might be her first duty she did not count it her highest duty. She was a woman, a fact her father found elusive. Supposing – just supposing – she wanted to marry and have children. Would her life now become so irreducibly complex she would have to shelve such a prospect? – permanently?

She thought about her brothers as her slow brush strokes continued. Peter – killed in Burma early in the war on or about his nineteenth birthday. So much to do with his death was still uncertain but one thing about him had already become apparent – the dreamy, lovable Peter would never have taken to industrial management. Drawing on the sustenance that music and the arts provided he would have become an outstanding natural teacher, given the opportunity.

His father had scorned his love of literature and harangued him about taking up, along with Denzil, the torch being passed to them by Enoch, Elijah and now himself. Her mother's remonstrations had been futile. Frances recalled her final pleas on Peter's behalf – she had emerged from a heated quarrel frustrated, tearful and murmuring:

"It's no use – he's just pig-headed obstinacy with a low boiling point."

Wednesday, eleventh of April, nineteen forty five. The day and date were now branded onto her brain. Less than one month before the end of the European war and Denzil had died on the north German plain. The spirited, laughing Denzil had been introduced to potbank work before his call-up. He had loved it and many a female at the "Grange" pottery had loved him. He had been the perfect foil to his father: competent but ever ready to smile his way to the trickiest decisions. When once his father had upbraided him for being "too casual" his pert response had been: "I'm not in favour of strategy reduced to personal tantrum." The spluttering Ewart had not had the guile to reply.

Frances sighed. She feared that her father's belligerent concern for the future now verged on the demagogic and she was determined to resist falling under its spell. Languidly she put down the hairbrush. Its slow strokes had produced a shining splendour.

A few miles away from Bradwell Grange, in a Burslem bedroom, Philip Hughes, platemaker, struggled with his feelings too. Ever since the "demob" and until that very day he had existed virtually in self-imposed isolation. Compared to the compelling horror of his wartime experiences everything now seemed trivial. Some party hack had said: "We need young men like you to get involved in local politics." Philip knew it was wrong and selfish, not to care whether the local authority closed a swimming pool or sold off some allotments for housing, but the misery and barbarism of Burma had rendered him incapable of engaging with such issues.

Also, the gap between his own and other generations had blocked any catharsis he might have gained through sharing his experiences – even had he been so inclined. The young did not want to know and the old seemed embarrassed by what their offspring had been forced to endure.

But today, something had happened. He had met a woman – a beautiful woman who was also beautiful, as the potters would say, "where soap and water don't reach". He trusted his instincts so knew, from the way she had smiled and talked in the "top shop", she was beautiful in mind as well as body. Now he acknowledged he was hopelessly, helplessly in love with her. If the impossible somehow became possible their coming together would make his Burma experiences worth the suffering.

That the prospect of gaining her was impossible only

fuelled his hunger. Why "impossible"?.......well for one thing Britain was still class ridden despite the democratising effect of two wars. For the likes of him there was no admission card to the upper classes, even to those upper classes recently arrived from the lower classes. But there was another impossibility, one which dwarfed the first: he knew something of great importance to the Bromley family, something he hated to remember, something he would never, ever, divulge. The keeping of the secret meant the less the contact he had with any Bromley, the better.

Yet_what a coup de foudre!_love at first sight!_ here in Burslem! Had those facts been common knowledge few in the town would have slept that night.

Chapter Four
Laughter and Tears

The Autumn weeks which followed Frances' arrival at Grange Pottery saw her systematic introduction continue. She had watched the placers carry and stack their fireclay boxes ("saggars") of ware into the bottle ovens. She had watched the ovens being sealed, then fired. She had drawn Bullers' rings from the oven trial holes and checked them on a ring-gauge to ensure the five-day period of firing and cooling proceeded along a satisfactory temperature x time curve.

She had watched an oven being drawn and had sat with the sorters in the biscuit warehouse while they scoured the ware and inspected it for quality. Then on to the "dipping-house" where the slip-form viscous glaze made no distinction between an egg-cup and a turkey dish, a butter-pad and a soup tureen - it covered everything.

Not that all the now-strong, handleable biscuit ware went into the dipping house immediately. Some, destined for under-glaze decoration, went into the printing-shop where delicate sheets of beautiful prints were peeled from engraved copper-plates then cut, fitted and rubbed down onto the biscuit ware. Frances was especially fond, and rather proud, of the ware produced here with its willow-patterns, country scenes and many combinations of leaves and flowers, all in rich cobalt blues and chrome greens. After a "hardening-on" lower temperature firing to fix these colours she watched the ware progress to the dipping-house for its protective coating of amorphous, unfired glaze.

Back to the bottle ovens for the "glost" firing from which it emerged with its gleaming, reflective surface en-route to the many markets around the world which prized it. A significant amount of the ware as yet undecorated now went onto the on-glaze decorating shops. Here were fitted patterns of pride in bright colours: floral motifs, chintz lithographs, gay wash-bands, Greek keys, bands and lines of "best" gold and most noticably, a range of *hand-painted* embellishment. Then off to the "enamel" kiln where the glaze was softened by another lower-temperature firing and the bright colours were trapped under a mist of volatilised glaze.

Frances had noted all this, and the skills and the many quality checks that went with it before Bromley products could safely be consigned to the packing house en-route to the customers. She was now beginning to know the people who had brought the clays and the colours to this fulfilment and they were beginning to know her. Potters are slow to form firm judgements but she seemed "o'rate" to them. "All right" was praise for sure.

Some had not always been kind. The two placers who had seen her that day by the stillage had informed others.

Some of these had smiled and hinted about the indelicacy of having "one's bottom smacked." It was her embarassment and genuine stupefaction which got under their guard. She had found a way to their gentleness so that they became dumb. It would only be mentioned in those gusts of high spirits which sometimes swept the shops and recounted occasionally for the benefit of a new face. Not everyone had heard the news though - mercifully Ewart Bromley was still happy in his ignorance.

"Well, Miss Frances, it's done. That's the biggest wage-bill I've ever seen at the 'Grange'. It's a good job we can show your father that production's up to an all-time high as well. We're getting there now, in spite of shortage of skilled people, fuel shortages and transport problems."

As Jack Dempster sighed contentedly, Frances reflected that she was always glad to see the end of "settle." She had now been working on the "potbank" for three months and since her stay in the "clay end" was likely to be lengthy, she had been made responsible for the wages "settle" of the cupshops, the flat shops and the sliphouse.

So, they had just finished the clay-end settle. As she tidied up the great pile of settle books she too felt relieved: sitting-in with the potters on the mutual determination of their earnings tested even her mathematical reach. Bakers were different with their dozens but added very little to the standard twelve units. Potters on the other hand, insisted on counting the dozen for some products right up to thirty six. Fractions of a penny were still in vogue for some settle rates. It was all part of the lore she had decided.

"Are you going back to the potting-shops now?"

She looked up from the sloping desk-top.

"Yes. I'm off to the 'top shop', Mr Dempster."

"Would you call at the boiler-hole and tell Fred Knapper to come here about his next load of fuel?"

She picked her way through a porridge of clay and

early snow down that slope of the "bank", between Number 2 and Number 3 biscuit bottle ovens, which led to the boiler-hole. She looked down at the Lancashire boiler. Although electricity was making some inroads into the potbank's processes, steam power was still at the root of its activity and the boiler where it all started.

There was no Fred Knapper so she opened the door to the engine-house. Here bedlam was unhindered for the monstrous arm of the engine was flinging itself at the far wall of the little building then always pulling itself back in the nick of time. Like all visitors, Frances reserved her first seconds of fearful fascination for this thundering giant of brass and steel.

Fred was sitting on the bench below the tiny, solitary, dirty window laughing without let-up. It was clear as they say in the hollow, "summat 'ad tickled 'im." His feet were splayed across the concrete narrows which extended from the bench to the guard rail of the engine. His left hand held his portly stomach while his right was occupied in wiping away the tears from his bladdered eyes. Frances was fascinated by Fred Knapper. She noted today that his perpetual accoutrements were all in evidence - the corduroy trousers worn so long they were more membrane than garment, the "yorks", famous lengths of twine which plucked the trousers from the atmosphere and girded them to oaken calves.

And there was the belt buckle, of fine clean lines and no nonsense but which was the envy of every horse in the town carnival for the way it shone so, thanks to the friction from Fred's fingers, from a sagging shirt-front and many an absent minded oil rag. The shirt was not noteworthy for from time to time it was changed, not so the blue 'kerchief' with the white spots worn on the throat - thoughts of change here were profane.

Fred's face could be described economically: the boiler man appeared to be a pudding with sense organs, but there was one intriguing detail for, a little to one side of centre, the front teeth of the lower jaw had thoughtfully depressed themselves so as to receive the stem of his pipe. Finally, Fred's cap was there, a cap of character. While growing out of his head, it had fed well on the oil and coal dust in the boiler-hole and these elements had been melded together by the soakings during the years of street tramping while its master had looked for work.`

Through the mist of thick-twist fumes Frances could also discern the "lobby" basin by Fred's feet and the shoes which bent their noses up to heaven, as the boiler-fires had told them to when once they had come to work wet through.

Fred was not laughing alone. He sat with the biscuit ovens fireman. When the oven mouths had been fuel-fed, when the trials had been drawn, when the atmosphere in the ovens was "sweet", this man would join his inflammatory intimate at the boiler hole. Fred would receive him socially with corrosive tobacco and thixotropic tea. All he asked in return was a good story.

The fireman was a bean-pole whose eyes had contracted from the fierce glare of the firemouths and the bottle-ovens innards. The lean man was a comedian though of that subdued type that the potters call "a dry 'un", one in whom boisterousness had been replaced by quiet, cogitative subtlety. He was known for a pretty fair thirst and carried some of the glow of his ovens in the tip of his long nose whose length and narrowness could hardly have been otherwise if the face was to contain it. Like Fred Knapper, he was a bachelor and this was completely understandable, married as he already was to his beloved bottle ovens. The fireman's name was Louis Dunning. The potters thought the Christian name out of character and had corrupted it to "Ludo". As was so often the case, Ludo Dunning was the cause of the boilerman's helplessness.

When they saw Frances Bromley they both stood up. Fred Knapper intimated he was regaining control by a painful gathering together of his fat body, a last flick at his eyes and a long "e-e-eh dear!"

"May I share the joke?," she smiled. The characters looked at each other.

"Dunner tell it agen Ludo, else I shill bost!"

Of course, if the boilerman had burst the displacement would have been tremendous and it was conceivable that, perversely, this appealed to the fireman for he began:

"Well, ye see, ah wuz jus' tellin' Master Knapper abite the fost tarm your father, Mester Ewart that is, 'ad th'ortermatic stokers put on this bayler. Anyroad, the nate baylermon was off bad so we exed Billy 'ogan ter cum on in his place."

Thinking she understood, Frances nodded. Fred Knapper's hysterics were returning.

"Nah... yer know Harry Billing's Boardeen Kennels on th'other side o' St. John's Church?"

There was no wait for an answer.

"Well - when any a Harry's dogs an died o' disease, he asks Mester Dempster if he kin put it in bayler."

He stopped to lick his lip, tiny eyes gleaming:

"Any road up, when Billy 'ogan comes on, Mester explains to him as how he munner put coal inter fire any more, but jus fill them 'oppers up, so's 'oppers erll feed it onter fire by thissens. He dunner tell Billy as Harry Billings ees comin' on that nate with a dog".

It was time for him to take a breath.

"So when Billy fills his 'oppers, he sets off rind shops ter see if steam's comin' through o' rate. Then Harry Billings comes on the bank, sees nobody, puts dog in bayler an' gets off up ter th' lodge.

"Billy comes back, decides it's time for rakin' out, opens fire doors an' sees this gleamin' red skull lookin' at 'im. Now ter tell the truth I think Billy'd 'ad a few that nate because yer lose a lot o' sweat on this job, yer know. An' his father, who could drink a sea dry, used to reckon, in the last stages of his complaint, he could see the pit of Hell an' other disturbin' things. So Billy's always bin worried about the 'dts' hissen, or the 'blue uns', as we say 'rind 'ere.

"Well - listen ter this - Billy's rooted ter th' spot see - conna shift an' he reckons from the skull there are these great teeth - white 'ot. He's terrified - then two lumps o' coal fall down through the fire an' two long curlin' green flames come from 'em and pop out through the eye sockets in the skull.

"He must have 'ad the doo-dees then 'cause all the night-men on the bank heard this terrible 'oo..oo...oo...oo..er' from Billy an' when he went past the lodge winder Harry Billings an' the night lodgeman reckon 'is feet wonner touchin' the ground. They all 'ad to 'ave a brandy with him out o' the Fost Aid box afore he were properly right!"

The telling of the tale had been a masterpiece of power. Dunning had contrived all the necessary accents and effects yet they had all been achieved at the top of his lungs in competition with the thundering engine.

Frances beckoned Fred Knapper to leave the engine-house with her. Her throat still hurt from the first time she had made herself heard. Now it was weakened by laughter so she knew she could never drown the din however momentarily.

Mr Dempster would like to see you in his office - about the boiler fuel."

As he waddled off, she could see that his strength was gradually returning.

She climbed the wooden steps leading to the top flat-shop, noting again their "whippiness", which she must mention to her father. This time she entered the shop from the end where Philip Hughes and Vera Foskett worked. Her smile had not yet vanished.

"Good morning, Vera."

"We've done nothing but wait for boards this week! It's about time summat was done - else I might as well go day-waged. How can you earn anything on piece-work when you're standing 'round all day?"

"I'm sorry about that, Vera. In a few minutes I'll see what can be done."

From the next jigger, Winnie Hood, the mouldrunner, smiled to compensate for Vera's bad manners.

"Have you been waiting too, Winnie?"

"No, Miss Frances. We went to the saggar-house early this mornin' an' got ours."

The indiscretion was innocent enough but Vera Faskett glared:

"Was that meant for me, Winnie? I come here at 8 o' clock. I don't intend to be here in the middle of the night, scrawmin' for money like some folks. That doesn't mean I'm not entitled to boards!"

Philip Hughes had been bent over his jigger-box. He cut its electric motor and turned to the blonde saucemaker:

"We've got a few spare boards, Vera. We didn't know you were waiting. Winnie didn't mean any harm."

There was silence for a second then Philip returned to his plate making.

At the side of Vera's jigger were several newly-made saucers. Frances moved to them. She cut one across its back and removed a segment half the size of a saucer. Vera suddenly stiffened and pointed to a faint line on the plaster mould:

"Would you mind askin' for the cuttin' mould when you want to cut one through?" You've cut about twelve of my moulds altogether and the tower spends half her time trying to fetch the marks off!"

Frances blushed with embarassment. She felt totally foolish for when the surface of a mould is cut, the article subsequently made on it comes from the mould with a ridge on its face where the clay has raced to fill the tiny groove made by the knife.

"I'm very sorry," said Frances at last.

It had become part of her duties that each day she should cut through and weigh an article being made at each jigger. When checked with a list of "clay-state weights" posted up in the flat shop, this helped to guarantee several things: firstly, that the weight of each article was in accordance with the list; that the articles nested with each other in their bungs of twelve with a minimum of strain and that a standard amount of clay was being used, per article, so that material costs were reasonably constant.

There was an ideal weight for each article. Many of these "standard" weights and settings in existence at the Grange on that morning had been agreed by Ewart Bromley, Jack Dempster and even Isiah Bromley with the potters concerned. It had now fallen to Frances to see that these standards were maintained but she had shown a little lack of savoir-faire and Vera Foskett had promptly informed the shop.

In the tense atmosphere a shaft of sunlight came through the window adjacent to her jigger box. It illuminated the particles of clay dust hovering in the air and fell on the blonde's head and the dark head of Frances as they bent to examine the saucer newly cut through.

Frances frowned. Lying on its mould, the saucer had looked well enough at first glance - a nice setting of uniform thickness, approaching on eighth of an inch deep throughout its width until, that is, it arrived at the scrap-edge of the mould. This edge was the point at which the potter sheared off the excess clay at the end of each clay making operation. Here, this particular saucer was too "proud", so that the tell-tale height of the clay at the mould edge signified that article was probably too thick all through its setting and was consequently overweight.

She took the two halves of the saucer over to the dairy-balance.

"Five and a quarter ounces, Vera. That's a full ounce overweight."

"There's a big difference in some of these moulds. Try this one!", bridled Vera, slamming down another freshly made saucer.

"But surely, if there's a big difference in the moulds, you'd have said so before now, wouldn't you?" And it would hardly be representative for me to take a sample from your cutting mould every day, would it?"

For once Vera was silent.

"Are they very bad, Vera? May I see the last full board you've taken from them?"

The question had been put politely.

The saucemaker turned quickly from her jigger box and thrust her hands into a bucket of clean water. She withdrew them rapidly and wiped them on the bottom of her bib. The atmosphere worsened.

"It's 'round 'ere!", she spat and the two young women followed her pointing finger around the dobbin-stoves and into the towing shop.

Frances examined a board of saucers which awaited the tower's attention. It was clear that the moulds used making these articles must have varied significantly. Some of the saucers were thick, others thin. Instead of a uniform space between each of the saucers as they rested on each other, the thick saucers touched each other while the thin ones stood further apart than they should have done.

"Look, Vera, how they kiss and gape! I'm sorry, you should have mentioned this sooner - though if there are others like this, perhaps Mrs Birks has managed to stop them before they've been sent to the oven."

From the start Frances Bromley had maintained a

reasonable tone. Most of the potters at "the Grange" now realised it was not in her nature to do otherwise. Vera was an exception, however, and was undoubtedly incensed. In a quite serious situation, for which she was responsible, she blustered to save face. Turning with a martyred look to the nearest towers she called:

"It's all right, isn't it? You teach people about pottin' and then they come and pick faults in your work!"

Defiant, hands on hips, she shouted back towards Frances:

"If I'm supposed to tell the mouldmakers how to make moulds as well as wait for boards, I can't see how I'm ever goin' to earn anythink! You'd better give me my cards. I can be working on an organised 'bank' inside an hour."

Ewart Bromley's daughter gave her an understanding smile:

"Look, Vera - let me just explain. We placed a very large order for new boards months ago. Everything is in short supply still, including boards. The saggar house is full of placed work, to release as many boards as we can... but there'll be some bottleneck till the new boards arrive. I promise to find some boards for you...I will...but in the meantime I think you'd better empty your stove. All of these other boards of yours are the same, so you'll get thick and thin work until you get a completely new round of moulds. I'll go to the mould makers now and I'll also see about some new boards for you."

"An' what am I to live on, fresh air?!"

"Note your time in making the change-over and in next week's settle I'll log in what you would have earned on the jigger."

Vera, fuming, returned to her jigger took up a large bench-sponge and hurled it into a pail of water.

"Know-all little pig!" she hissed, loud enough for Frances to hear. Philip Hughes looked across at her, then returned to his work without comment.

Frances, masking her feeling walked up the length of the towing shop. Nearing the top door, the waxen Sally Gratton smiled at her.

"Good morning, Miss Frances."

"Good morning, Sally."

When the door closed behind Frances, Abel Beardmore, a biscuit placer, nodded towards it:

"What a bloody gem she is. Who'd ever think she was Bromley's daughter?!"

En route to the mouldmakers, the young woman reached the "greenhouse" door. She could see Florrie Birks sitting on her high stool. In front of the old woman was a board of clayware lying across two trestles. It was there for her scrutiny. If she considered the board as a whole below standard she would tell its potters to take it back. It would then be deducted from the settle count. On the other hand, if only a piece or two needed improvement Mrs Birks would see to it herself.

There would be a flurry of the magic sponge in her fingers and a passing back and forth from the water bowl and soon its defects would be fully restored. Many were the articles born of the bent potter's own fingers when she had been the finest at her craft as a hollowware maker. She it was who made the well-known Bromley sugar bowls and butter dishes. Then those joints which propelled and manipulated the flying hands had stiffened and inflamed - driving the fingers together into crowded uselessness... for jolleying clay, that is.

Frances moved behind the shawled figure. She watched the old hands fondle a cream-soup cup and saw the lame fingers. She also noticed, surveying their malfeasance from the heights of the knuckles, the knobs of rheumatism. Jack Dempster had told her of how the cloud of unemployment had threatened to settle over Florrie Birks and of how grandfather Isaiah did not forget these almost impotent hands which had helped him to a fortune:

"Irrespective of what she does, tell Florrie she's to come here for as long as she's able and when she can't work at all - if ever that happens - she's to come and see me".

So now that she could make pots no longer she had to inspect and, where necessary, improve the pots of others. The job had lasted throughout Isaiah Bromley's lifetime and much of that of his son.

Suddenly, the old overlooker whirled on her perch:

"Oh... good morning, duck."

"Good morning, Mrs Birks. How are you today?"

"Mustn't grumble - a bit stiff but it passes off."

Then she smiled:

"I have to come downstairs a bit at a time these days but I'm all right when I've moved about for an hour or two, yer know."

Frances frowned:

"Don't you feel a draught from this door? ... it seems to be forever opening and shutting."

"Oh, no. I keep me shawl 'round me an' it's a good thick un."

A small silence, then:

"Mrs Birks can you tell me if the work carried out for Vera Foskett is all right. There seems to be quite a variation in her moulds."

Florrie had stopped smiling:

"She's known all about it for a week! I told er' about 'em kissin' an' gapin'. If the placers hadn't bin waitin' to set the oven in last Thursday I wouldn't have sent a board of her work! 'alf of it is still in the stillage 'ere, but I've told 'er, she'll stand 'em. When Mester Ewart looks at the oven on drawing-day I'm expecting 'im to send for me!"

Drawing-day was normally five or six days after the initial lighting of a bottle oven. Then the "oven" became thousands of pieces of fired ware carried to the biscuit warehouse to be brushed free of placing sand and sorted for quality. It was the unchanging rule at "the Grange" for one of the Bromleys to be in the warehouse on drawing-day to see the oven sorted and counted. The custom dated from when the potters were paid "good from oven" instead of "good into oven". In those times on many a potbank, workers had had to oppose "the Master" in the matter of the money they had earned, lest they be blamed for others' faults.

"Don't worry about tomorrow's drawing, Mrs Birks. I can explain it all - because I should've seen the problem sooner. I'm just going into the saggar-house now to look for boards then I'm off to the mouldmakers about it."

She began to leave, then half-turned, looking at Mrs Birks with wry curiosity:

"You know, I can't seem to get off on the right foot with Vera Foskett."

Florrie sniffed and gathered the shawl about her:

"Vera Foskett's one on her own then - that's all I can say! She's got some old buck that one...nothin's ever right for 'er! I don't know where Phil Hughes' eyes are."

"Pardon?"

"She's his girl friend...*least* she thinks she is."

"Oh."

As Frances walked to the saggar house she mused on why, for her, this last item had struck such a jarring note.

That evening, the potters from "the Grange" were threading their way through the crowds pouring from Burslem's many potbanks. Only Vera Foskett and Philip Hughes remained in the top shop. Standing among a mound of moulds, Vera straightened to ease her aching back.

"Just look at this mess, Phil. I could wish that Bromley wench far enough, I'll tell yer."

"I think you made that clear to her, Vera."

"Oh... an' what's that supposed to mean?"

"Well, it means that for some reason you can't bear her and you make sure she knows it."

"But... did you hear..."

"Vera, listen to me... the girl has a job to do, like you and me. It could be she's not doing the job from choice... she's here because of her brothers. Did you ever think of that?"

"I don't care, she..."

"Now we're on our own Vera, I'm going to tell you something. You shame us... do you know that? She's doing you a good turn getting the moulds changed. You wouldn't earn anything otherwise. She heard you call her a little pig..."

"I wanted her to..."

"Exactly, but she could have made things awkward for you, like she could have done for me a while back. In both cases she chose not to... we should bear that in mind."

"Anyway, I don't want to talk about her... Miss Glamour Pants... are you taking me to the 'Col'!"

"The 'Col'?"

"Yes, I told you... 'Odd Man Out'... James Mason... it's on at the Coliseum. You said we'd go."

"I don't think I did."

"You didn't say we wouldn't go."

"But that's not the same thing is it?"

"Why have you changed all of a sudden?"

Now Vera hesitated, fearing to put her next question:

"You're not getting sweet on her are you?" she sneered.

"If I was it would be my business, wouldn't it?"

"You stupid sod! Do you think the likes of her would ever waste two minutes on you? Her father'd ave you drummed off the bank in any case!"

"This conversation is about you, Vera - not me. There are barbs sticking out all over you just lately. You don't seem to be aware of your dignity as a human being. You despise Frances Bromley but you could learn something from her in that respect."

"You slimy b...!"

As she made to strike him he caught her arm and held it away from his face. Her arm shook, as she struggled against his strength. When he felt her relax he let go of her, gently.

"Go home Vera, and take it easy."

"Sod off."

Weeping she dragged on her coat and fled down the rickety steps outside the shop. Without clocking off she went under the archway trying to stem her tears. What she had known intuitively for weeks had now been confirmed for her: Philip Hughes was in love with Frances Bromley. The lodgeman, Ernest Biddulph, watched her impassively as she walked past Edward Street and into Pleasant Street. "Funny girl, that one," he thought.

In the top shop, Philip was carefully stacking Vera's old moulds, ready for the scrap collector. Before long they would be tipped onto one of the town's many "shord-rucks" - those unsightly heaps of potters' waste that so disfigured it.

Chapter Five
Exchange of Views

She knew that in addition to her father, Herbert Bancroft, Sales Director of Turnhurst Pottery; John Birch of Ellgreave Hotel Ware; Theo Moreton of Moreton Tiles Ltd; and Clive Beresford of Beresford Ceramics were now before that other close-coupled fireplace and giant mirror – the one in the library.

She was in the dining room at Bradwell Grange, having returned home about a half-hour before these gentlemen had arrived. They had gone into the library-drawing room without disturbing her. She knew the pattern of their evening well enough – they would have attended a late afternoon meeting at the Manufacturers' Association Chambers, fortified themselves at the North Stafford Hotel with as good a meal as could be contrived from post-war austerity and, before returning home, stopped at the Grange for a nightcap and an exchange of views on problems old and new.

Accompanied by Gwen Dempster she had seen earlier the film "Brighton Rock" and had been driven back home by Gwen who had now departed. Frances toyed with the remnants of a light supper prepared by Mary Ellen Foley, who appeared at her elbow just then:

"Will there be anything else, Miss Frances?"

"No, Mrs Foley. You can go now, and not before it's time either. We won't be long after you. I'm just about to interrupt my father. It's drawing-day tomorrow so we've an early start. You look tired – leave the guests to me now."

"Well, if you're sure, goodnight then."

"Goodnight, Mrs Foley and thank you."

As she watched the painful feet of the cook-housekeeper take her out of the room she decided the woman badly needed an assistant. Another matter to take up with her father.

Frances slipped quietly across the hallway and opened slightly one of the great doors to the library-drawing room. John Birch was talking:

"Just how we got through it I'll never know. We literally – literally, didn't have a scrap of fuel nor a load of clay for nearly three weeks."

Her father was cutting in:

"We were exactly the same - there was finished clayware waiting for the ovens all over the bank."

"At least we managed to eat and keep warm," said Theo Moreton. "What about the folks in the villages around Leek and Ashbourne?"

"Oh, yes!" they all chorused.

Encouraged, Moreton continued:

"No bread, no trains, no mail, drifts as high as telegraph

poles and as fast as they'd cleared a section of road – forty men working in a gang – the wind blew all the snow back onto it again. The farms couldn't even get the milk collected."

It was John Birch's turn, once more:

"Our glost warehouse manager lives at Longnor and he reckons that over two nights the householders in the village dragged four tons of coal on sledges from the dump at Hindlow twelve miles away!"

Next, Frances heard the urbane voice of Clive Beresford:

"The RAF Halifax crashing on Grindon Moor trying to make a food drop was a tragedy – six crew and two passengers – all killed."

There was a momentary silence. Frances decided to enter. They all rose to greet her.

As she came towards the library fireplace her father smiled:

"And here gentlemen, is my answer to horizontal combination and the industrial trust."

There was appreciative laughter.

"Forgive me for butting in, father, but I..."

"Not at all, darling. This gives us a splendid opportunity to find out how you're progressing."

He embraced his friends with a sweep of his brandy glass:

"It also gives you opportunity to pick some of the foremost brains in the industry."

There was more laughter but the idea had little appeal for Frances:

"No, don't let me interrupt – I think you were talking about the weather..."

Ewart Bromley was encouraged:

"Yes, well we were saying how grim it was to keep going through this last winter."

"And hoping we don't have another one like it!" added Theo Moreton.

Then Ewart Bromley again:

"You know we've had loads of problems since the War ended and have mastered them all! Think about it – when we shed the concentrations forced on us by the War and we were all back with our own firms, we thought it would just be plain sailing. And what have we had?... shortage of skilled people, because demobilisation was so damned slow, shortages of coal, clay and practically everything else and then that beast of a winter to make things worse. But do you know what? ..."

He paused, to ensure their full attention:

"I reckon at the year end, we'll be twenty percent up on our 1938 figures, how about that?!"

"Same for us," said Herbert Bancroft.

"We won't be far off," said Theo Moreton.

This pricked Bromley's balloon and when John Birch put the next question to Clive Beresford, Frances saw her father's frown deepen:

"It looks like you're re-started work on that extension of yours, Clive, is that correct?"

Bancroft smiled:

"Yes... when are you going to open that box of tricks for us to see?"

Frances liked Clive Beresford and was as anxious as the others to hear his reply. As usual, his tones were soft and matter-of-fact:

"There's no secret, really. At the first phase, that particular building'll house a tunnel oven for biscuit firing. When the trials are satisfactory we shall then take two or three bottle ovens out of commission. That will free up the space for us to build a works canteen. It's part of a general plan to reduce costs; anticipate the legislation on smoke emission, which is bound to come; improve working conditions and introduce new equipment."

There was silence, some of its admiring, some resentful.

Frances smiled:

"I shall be sorry to see the bottle ovens go."

"I shan't," piped up John Birch. "As well as being filthy they're notoriously inefficient. Do you realise, Frances, it takes ten tons of coal to produce one ton of ware?"

The discussion was not proceeding as Ewart Bromley had hoped but his curiosity plagued him and, after all, attack might be the best method of defence-

"How're you going to fire the tunnel oven, Clive?"

"Town's gas...which is now so commercially pure it carries no risk for firing ceramics."

"Mm. And what do you mean by improving working conditions and introducing new equipment?"

"Well, working conditions need improvement right across the industry. It's more than just canteens – it's anything that touches on workers' health and safety. We're going to look at the business of dust extraction, right across the firm. We shall provide lockers for outdoor clothing, so that our people won't have to take clay and glaze dust back to their homes. What's more this new Labour government is bound to have a point of view on this. Flint has now been prohibited for placing ware and lead can only be used in low-solubility glazes. We can all expect to see more of the Factory Inspector – but we shouldn't do these things because the law says so – we should do them because it's right."

Bromley seem immensely irritated. Beresford continued:

"Ewart – for the first time I can remember, we've all got full order books, and for a long time to come. This gives us a great opportunity to take the industry out of the low-cost, low-value, disease-ridden dark ages. And in the end, a fitter, healthier, happier work-force makes good commercial sense."

Ewart would not let up, discomforted as he was:

"You mentioned introducing new equipment, can you let us in on that?"

"It's no secret – the ideas are already out there – new methods for drying, glazing, even manufacturing and firing. They'll be tried out soon, then adopted, I feel sure."

"But you're talking about massive investment!"

"That's right – and the space and capital requirements may be such that the privately owned, family firm can't cope. We may need new forms of organisation..."

The other men were stunned. Not surprisingly, Ewart was the first to speak. Almost menacingly he whispered:

"My father and his father didn't work their tripes out so's I could dump the firm into the lap of investment bankers or onto the Stock Exchange!"

Frances felt that Clive Beresford sought not to patronise her father as he said:

"Well that's your decision, which you've every right to make but I think we need to look beyond Stoke-on-Trent. Very soon you'll see the Germans, the Japanese, the Italians, the French and even the Americans getting into our markets abroad. And in the case of the Germans and the Japanese they'll get financial support from their governments. I think we're baying at the moon if we expect the same thing. We'll need to make changes soon."

There was no improvement in Bromley's demeanour:

"We don't want financial help from anybody – but we are entitled to some protection of our home market. We're supposed to be the darlings of the politicians – the best of the country's exporting industries, little or no need for imports of materials or anything else, so everything we earn is net gain on the balance of payments - but if we want our market protected here at home, we can whistle."

Frances had originally joined a convivial meeting. There was now a sour silence. Cilve Beresford read her anxiety and smiled:

"Anyway, I was looked forward to learning how Frances was getting on and here we are ignoring her."

There was relieved assent.

"Are things going well, Frances? We all have tremendous admiration for the way you've buckled down to things at 'The Grange'," Beresford said encouragingly.

She looked questioningly at her father. When he nodded, she said:

"Obviously I'm making my way through a mass of detail at the moment, as well as learning a new language."

As the visitors laughed, Theo Moreton dug his thick thumb into her arm:

"Herbert'll help you with that – he's the expert!"

Herbert Bancroft nodded and winked at her.

"Anyway I'm probably too close to potting and it's problems to be detached about it. When I've covered all the ground, I'll possibly be able to give you a sensible answer."

She took a breath. They waited for her to continue.

"I'm fascinated of course. It may seem an airy-fairy notion but when I look at the things we make I wonder what other industry can produce such an intimate alliance of art and utility. So many personal skills are involved in the most ordinary piece of pottery. The material we work in is essentially simple yet its chemistry is so complex and its control demands such care. It's absorbing."

As her eyes grew brighter every man was made mute by her beauty.

"Now as far as the people are concerned, I could talk all night. I had some misgivings at first, and so did they probably, but their friendliness is almost overwhelming at times."

Ewart was pleased but anxious to affirm his reputation as the "hard" businessman:

"It does me good to hear you talk like that Frances but sometimes when you say they're "gentle" this and "gentle" that, in the end remember they're people. Give 'em an inch and they'll take a yard. Remember that 'dividing line' we spoke about. Don't let 'em get too familiar."

"Quite right, Ewart," beamed Theo Moreton, "tell 'em they mustn't make a *habit* of smacking your sit-upon, Frances!"

Now he beamed at Herbert Bancroft who only shifted his feet uneasily. Ewart's features clouded questioningly but Clive Beresford quickly took up the conversation:

"I think what Frances says is important. We shouldn't mollycoddle people, they'll wonder what we're at, but there has to be mutual understanding. They should be able to appreciate that, above all, we're human beings. Sometimes, when I'm pressed, I give the impression that it's a favour if I let someone speak to me – on what could be an important matter. And I think because they're craftsmen it can affect them temperamentally. I asked myself the other day – in spite of the fact that were still a private company, and there are three generations of some families working for us – how many of our people do I know by their first names? Precious few, I have to admit."

Bromley shook his furrowed brow:

"Oh, Clive – come off it. I pay a Works Manager to look after the 'human relations' side, as I suppose you'd call it. How else can I give my mind to broader matters? Remember this – it's the policy making the folks in the shops know nothing about that governs their future."

"It's not the same thing to leave it to a manager. We're the ones that set the standard."

Beresford looked at them all in turn, then added quietly:

"Getting down to the essentials, potters are like other workers, only more so – they've got to be happy in order to produce. We believe it will be difficult to keep skilled people in the future and we're finding it's the little things that make the difference. Besides, I don't think we're in the business just to make money, are we?"

He was manifestly sincere but John Birch intervened:

"On the whole I'm with Ewart. At 'Ellgreave' we'd say the biggest factor in keeping them happy is a full wage-packet. Organise things so it's possible for them to earn their money without snags, settle fair piece-work prices and provide the best working conditions you can afford – and they'll be happy enough – without applied psychology."

"I don't think Mr Beresford was suggesting that as a substitute for the things you mention – more a valuable addition."

Quickly, Ewart interposed:

"Yes – all right Frances – but I think it's time for you to be off to bed now – oven-drawing day tomorrow, you know."

His watch had appeared, but she smiled:

"As a matter of fact, that's why I came in here. When Doctor Emery called about your chest infection I promised I'd see to it you got as few late nights as possible."

In front of his guests, her solicitude irritated him:

"It looks as though it's you and Clive here who are bent on making a long night of it with all this talk about 'new thinking'."

She remembered from childhood that whenever a discussion was not going his way, he always recommended the efficacy of rest, as though his protagonists might awake of changed mind. Now he was looking at his watch again.

Theo Moreton rose, puffingly:

"I'd better be off, else Mrs Moreton'll give me what for."

The idea that he would quake before any other human would not have found credence at Moreton Tiles. By mutual agreement, they all stood up and in a few minutes Bromley and his daughter were seeing their guests through the hall. Clive Beresford turned towards Frances:

"Good night. Best of luck, and remember – stick to

your guns!"

He smiled and walked after the others who were chattering their way to the cars. Her father closed the great door:

"Frances – what did Moreton mean about you getting smacked?"

He had caught her off guard.

"Erm... I don't know, Dadder."

"Well, p'r'aps it's nothing. He always talks in riddles – same at meetings. I must impress on you though the importance of maintaining your distance and your self-respect. I know you'll come to see what I mean – but do take care."

"Can I get anything for you before you go upstairs?"

"No, I'm all right, darling – good night."

She kissed him:

"Good night then."

He reached the half-landing, then turned:

"Frances –"

"Yes?"

As she looked up he was fingering the carved head of a newel post. She thought how tired he looked.

"Salts have given me a thousand and one reasons why they can't organise a new car for you but they reckon they've got a used one in very good condition – few miles on the clock – laid up all during the War. Get Foley to run you over there and have a look at it with you. I'm glad you did your driving test while you were away. You can't always be hanging 'round waiting for me or the bus"

"Well, that's a wonderful present! ...thank you very much."

He was evidently pleased with her progress at the firm. This was the way he had always signalled his praise – no congratulations for examination results or good reports, just some gift they would find "useful".

"There was something else. I told Jack Dempster it's

time you got down to tool filing and tool setting. I know you're a girl but I hope you won't 'draw nesh' on that. The thing is, you don't completely know about clay production until you can do both jobs. If you can't, all the eloquence in the world won't help you – they'll grin when you criticise their mistakes.

As I say, I had a word with Dempster. He can't help, of course – got too much on his plate already but he suggests you get down to the bench and he'll have somebody in one of the shops to keep an eye on you."

His head was slightly inclined – something had escaped his memory momentarily, then:

"We talked about you working with one of the flat-makers. He mentioned one who files all his own tools apparently – fella called Hewitt – no, Hughes, Phil Hughes."

He was still remembering:

"We had a caster once named Lizzie Hughes – good, but very stubborn – you might as well argue with the Devil as try and best her. It's her son, apparently. You could do worse – anyway, I'm off – see you at breakfast."

"Oh, Dadder – you will remember about those steps outside the 'top shop' -"

His gorge rose again:

"I said I'd see to them! Now stop mithering me!"

In emphasis, he banged his bedroom door.

Because Frances was worried she resorted to another session of languid hair grooming before she got into bed. It was undoubtedly tragic that her father had been left alone to steer the firm and the family's fortunes. For this reason she had resolved for now to say nothing of her dismay at his growing expectations of her lifelong participation in the process.

Beyond this, however, she saw another issue. Would her father, himself, be able to stay the course? Physically, perhaps, temperamentally, she wasn't sure. She now doubted whether he had the internal strength to see things through, for he seemed not to get by on any of his days without tremendous outlay of emotional energy. The problem was intensified by the obvious professionalism and progress of Beresford Ceramics. Her father hated to be second best yet it was clear that, in the future, the gap between the two companies would widen.

Ironically, what Clive had said about new forms of organisation might be highly relevant to the future of the Bromley name. Yet she knew her father would never see this, constrained as he was, with almost mystical force, by the sacred role of guarding the legacy landed on by Enoch and Isaiah. Always dispositionally suspicious, he had now begun to treat any word or action running counter to his preconceptions as a threat to Grange Pottery. Would the need for change outlined by Clive bring pressures on her father which would finally break him?

She sighed with concern for him but did not forget to be angry. She had wanted to read English Literature. He had insisted she read Applied Sciences and, inevitably, had won. She had come down with a good degree and a bank of knowledge and skills which he now seemed determined to squander. In this day and age the idea of her being able to file tools was ridiculous. Did he intend for her to be a freak at some peep-show?

Then the thought of working with Philip Hughes brought a small smile with it. That would be interesting. She felt guilty for lying to her father about the smack he had given her but what was the alternative? ...the truth would have opened a real can of worms.

Chapter Six
Drawing Day

"I don't think we're in the business just to make money, are we?"

They were the first words her father had uttered that morning... in mocking imitation of Clive Beresford's comments the previous evening. Then there was more burlesque:

"We may need new forms of organisation."

This was followed by his own observation:

"Did y'hear him? If they could, that lot'd gobble up the whole of Burslem. Well, perhaps we're not as thick as he thinks we are. Maybe we've got a trick or two up our sleeves as well."

Frances felt the first faint glimmer of despair. He had brooded through breakfast and said nothing on the car journey. Only when the entrance arch of Grange Pottery appeared had he emerged from silence and even then his words were more to himself than to her. She did not reply but offered a silent prayer that all would be well when the oven was drawn lest some poor soul felt the dreadful impact of his anger.

When Jack Foley parked the Humber, Bromley called to her over his shoulder:

"You go straight to the drawing. Dempster'll send for me when they're ready in the warehouse. Be sharp - they'll have started."

As he stalked off she began to wonder whether he squandered his health and temper more to humble Beresford Ceramics than to safeguard the future of Grange Pottery.

She walked towards Number Three biscuit oven which had now fired and cooled. She drew near and could see the placers, besmocked and turbulent, who sang, shouted and cursed as they emptied it. Seeing her they became respectfully silent. Frances had learned that the special skills of these brawny men though not perhaps as subtle as the other skills of the potbank were nonetheless quite vital to it.

Others may work with clay, glaze or colours. The placer's raw material was the saggar, the fireclay container which made it convenient for them to fill and empty the oven and enabled them to protect the clayware from flames and draughts. Naked flames might "flash" the ware - "flashing" described the brown staining by fire ash deposits carried up from the firemouths of the oven by searing hot air. "Dunting" was the description when draughts of cold air shattered the white hot ceramics. The saggars saw to it that neither calamity occurred.

In addition to placing the saggars in the oven, Frances

had recently watched them place the ware in the saggars. The skill here was to place an adequate amount of ware to yield a satisfactory "pay load" per saggar. So these men, hired primarily for their physical strength must also have dextrous hands and nimble fingers.

She had admired how deft and quick they were as each placer would reach for a "setter" - a plate already baked hard - already "biscuit". He would place the setter on the bottom of a saggar and sand it. The first clay plate was "nested" on this sand. It too would be sanded. The rest of the bung of plates was placed on the sanded plate. Then sand was run up all sides of the bung so that the edges of the plates would not sag during the firing. But for the sand, when the clay was waxy soft at the firing climax, impelled by its own weight, the clay would surely do this. And the plates must never "go crooked."

Nor must the teacups "go crooked" which was why they were "boxed" by Florence Birks and the cup spongers. "Boxing" entailed sticking together, mouth to mouth, a pair of cups using gelatinous material. So "boxed" cups stood, on boards and in saggars, like so many oversized eggs. Thus, during the frenzy of the firing each cup helped its partner keep its perfect circular shape.

With a wry smile, Frances remembered that all the placers were "characters." They worked hard and played harder. They were the highest paid of the "Grange's" workers and the most impecunious. They worked in their teams on a contract basis, receiving a guaranteed sum from the company in return for setting and drawing each oven. Their chief, the "cod", divided this sum among them, reserving to himself a little extra for "codding" them. It was the "cod" who paid them each Friday. It was the cod who went to the "Office" no later than the following Tuesday to sound out the possibilities of a "sub" - the loan which ensured that, until next pay-day, all of them could imbibe sufficient ale to replace the sweat they lost in the torrid ovens.

"It's a hot 'un this mornin', Miss Frances. Would yer like ter go in an' send the tops out?"

Harry Birchall, the "cod", had asked the question. His men laughed.

"Her would'na be the first in the family," the giant Sam Rafferty reminded them all.

The older placers knew he alluded to the fact that, years ago, whenever the placers had disputed with either Isaiah or Ewart Bromley whether an oven was still too hot to enter, both men would strip to the waist, go into the ovens, scale the heights of the saggars and send out the "tops". These were the ones at the crown of the oven and consequently the hottest to handle. The Bromleys were happy to score their hands on the searing saggars in order to make a point. For her benefit, Sam the giant felt he must expand his statement:

"Ah kon remember Mester Isaiah gooin' inter Number One when none of us ud lewk at it. He sent the tops out then esked Billy 'ogan ter goo ger a gallon uv ale!"

The girl's eyes danced:

"And did it get here?" she asked. They roared and she added:

"I won't be sending the tops out or getting drunk. I'll go into the Biscuit Warehouse and wait to see how quick you are."

As they watched her go, Harry Birchall said:

"What a bloody bobby dazzler! Now I've seen 'er, tiddly winks 'as had it!"

"Aye," added Sam Rafferty, "an' she's got 'er 'ead screwed on an' all, surree!"

In the warehouse the women waited. Invested with their rubber gloves they sat poised for the arrival of the "flat" and the holloware. When the baskets came in they would be attacked with no second to lose. Before being sorted and scoured, the ware had to be stacked and counted. The flat would be stacked in its usual bungs, the cups would be stacked in "beds". The beds would have nine or ten dozen cups to every row with twenty rows to every bed. So many beds of cups, so many lolling whales.

The ware would be sorted for quality, checked for fired size, checked for porosity and the complete loss on the oven counted. The whole business would take a few days but the obvious loss - the breakages (the "pitchers") could quickly be calculated.

In a matter of hours, the warehouse would achieve some appearance of order and for a while the frenzy would wind down. Thousands of plates, cups, saucers and bowls would stand in silence awaiting inspection. It was now that Jack Dempster would appear. "Ludo" Dunning, the fireman, would come in quietly and take off his cap. Frank Eardley, the warehouse manager would have that last look to ensure everything was as it should be. Had anything been overlooked? Were all the women in their places? Were the count-cards in place for every type of article disgorged by the oven?

Soon it would be completely quiet, but only for a few minutes. Then there would be a few ringing steps on the yard outside followed by the bark of the latch. Next the complaining cry of the spring-loaded door as it moved out of his way. Mr Ewart Bromley had come to see the oven.

On this particular day, his mood was apparent to everyone. He prowled in front of his retinue - Jack Dempster, Frank Eardley, "Ludo" Dunning, and Frances, whose distance from her father was noteworthy. In front of his employees he treated her like a stranger. Bent from the waist, preoccupied, he suddenly snorted:

"Dunning - this oven is *easy!*"

As he said this he was unplucking his tongue from a ten-inch plate. This way he knew its porosity. When the tongue came away from the plate without difficulty the firing was hard enough. In this case it adhered stubbornly, so the oven was under-fired.

Bromley applied his gauge to another plate. The gauge was a steel rule with the standard fired sizes of various plates marked upon it. The plate stood well over its mark. What was true of the part was probably true of the whole, the oven was "easy". As the ware was insufficiently vitrified, it would be under strength. Nor would its subsequent glazing be ideal.

The master-potter questioned "Ludo" Dunning with his eyes...

"Ah'd've liked a bit longer with it, Mr Ewart, but ah understood as yer wanted it drawn to-day."

Bromley was not listening. They all followed his pointing finger to a bung of eight inch flat.

"Won't that lot stand higher than five dozen without scotching these days?"

Many other eyes were as practised as the master's. They did not have to count the bung to know there were sixty. Under the bottom plate two or three pieces of broken ware had been tightly fixed. They scotched the bung to stability. Without the scotches it seemed the bung might sway and fall. It has been said that to assess the efficiency of any potbank one should go into its biscuit warehouse to see how high its flat will stand without scotching. It might give warning signs about the bank's body composition, tool-making, jiggering, clay drying facilities, oven placing and firing control. Now Jack Dempster spoke:

"We usually have that size flat eight dozen high without any trouble, sir."

"Yes, and it should stand at least that high in a bloody gale!"

The unfortunate bung had all his attention:

"Let's have a look at some of it."

Expertly he shuffled a collection of plates, holding them individually to his narrowed eyes. His deepening disgust suggested each one was more crooked than the last.

"They're curled up like tin bonnets - and the bloody oven's easy!"

Bromley turned on Jack Dempster:

"Who's made 'em?!"

Frances noticed the man swallow quickly as he examined the back of a plate.

"There are two makers on eight inch. So we put this mark in the tool for Philip Hughes."

He had turned the plate over and pointed to a fine line, just inside the foot of the plate.

Ewart's eyes stabbed a question at the manager which Frances read and understood. He was querying the arrangement that she was to have instruction from someone producing work of this quality. Little Frank Eardley received the bidding:

"Bring Hughes down here!"

As he came into the warehouse drying his arms on his apron he looked, questioningly but unworried. His shy smile pleased her. Ewart Bromley looked at him for some long seconds...

"Have you seen this flat?"

The question was not a question but an inference that the flat was anything but good.

Philip bent towards the flat, then straightened:

"It's crooked."

Many heard the master potter inhale.

"And how did that happen?"

Philip, quite self-possessed, went to examine other items drawn from the oven.

"Everything else seems OK, except my flat, so the body'll be all right."

He looked at more items, still unhurried:

"The oven looks easy, so it isn't the firing. Vincent Hogan and Harry Birchall place all my flat so it'll have been settered and sanded properly."

Ewart Bromley's face was a study. He leaned forward slightly and whispered his next words. The warehouse women were leaning forward too, for all work had stopped...

"Are you being funny with me?"

"No. I'm here in front of an audience being asked about this eight inch, which isn't good. I'm trying to give you a serious answer."

Frances' skin prickled as she sensed her father's growing anger.

"Well, take your time - as long as we come to the same conclusion - that you're responsible for this rubbish."

The plate maker, still calm, looked levelly at Bromley:

"No... that's not true."

"And why the hell not?"

"Because I don't make crooked work."

Frances readily recognised the awful warning beneath her father's next words, hushed though they were:

"Listen, lad - you'd better make some sense with your next few words, else you're going to regret being so bumptious and cocksure."

She felt an explosion was imminent but then...

"I beg your pardon? I'm not being cocksure. I just know I make a special point of seeing that my moulds always run true. I've never had crooked work, but now I do think I know what's happened here... it's my mouldrunner probably, and my tower come to that."

Frances Bromley felt her heart stop in disbelief...

"- but that doesn't mean it's their fault. I had instructions that at least sixty dozen eight inch had to be ready for the next oven. I've only got six dozen moulds and they're being emptied too often - so the ware isn't properly dry. No tower or mouldrunner can handle ware like that without pushing it out of shape. It's probably crooked before it leaves the shop. They bung it up properly and do their best with it, but even if they pushed it back into shape, you know yourself it would only come out of the oven crooked."

Everyone breathed again.

Ewart Bromley fidgeted with frustration. His explosion seemed to have been muffled - but had it? The warehouse women, on their low stools, had been taking all in. Their mouths were open in wonder. While he was considering the platemaker's remarks his eye fell on them. In denunciation, he waved his arm:

"Get on with your bloody work!"

They brushed like beavers.

Now Jack Dempster came under observation:

"Why hasn't he got enough moulds?"

"They've been down in the mouldmakers' books for three weeks, but just at present all the mouldmakers are on that new range of jug moulds for the big South African order."

"Well see that he has some as soon as the jugs are out of the way. What the hell's the use of purging to get big flat into the ovens if it comes out like this? None of it can go into the decorating shops."

Bromley paused:

"All right, Hughes, you can go."

To the young man's back he said.

"And the next time you're asked anything, spare us the speeches."

The rest of the "oven" held little interest for him. He looked, looked again, grunted and grunted again. Inevitably, he took out his watch. Then he departed. In all, he had been in the warehouse for thirty minutes. Less than half his normal time.

That day there were two sequels to the incident. In the afternoon Ewart Bromley sent for his general manager. His immediate question was:

"What about that surly sod?"

Dempster was wary:

"Well, to be honest Mr Ewart, he was in the right. It's my fault really, I should have kept a close eye on the moulds situation."

"Whether he's in the right or not, he's no business talking to me like that! I'm not putting up with his old buck! Who does he think he is?... I'm trying to give you a serious answer'... I'll tell you what he is - one of the clever division!"

Dempster shrugged:

"The fact is, he's our best platemaker and an excellent worker. He's noted for it. He even goes down to the packing house to see his flat when its been decorated."

"Oh, does he?... well you can stop that! Does he think he's got the run of the place? Honestly... talk about brass neck! ... his face'd stand clogging."

Bromley searched the features of the tall, thin man:

"Are you absolutely sure he should be looking after Miss Frances? Think carefully about it. He's got enough edge on him now, what about when he's trained her? Be sure, because I'll hold you responsible."

"It's true, sir - he is his own man, but I don't think he'll ever overstep the mark, it's not in his nature. I've known him since he was serving his time. Miss Frances couldn't be in better hands."

The master did not relax his attitude:

"Well I'm not as happy about him as you are. There's something I can't put my finger on, but it's there all right - and it bothers me. Did you know he was in the war with Mr Peter?"

As Dempster's eyes widened, Ewart smiled grimly:

"Oh yes - he was in Mr Peter's platoon. I got to know that, so I sent for him and asked him if he knew anything about how Peter died. It would have helped my wife and I just to know. I couldn't get a peep out of him, but he knows something, I'm sure of it. He came out with some cock-and-bull story abut getting separated during the battle, so he couldn't say. But he wasn't so tongue-tied in the warehouse today, was he? I think the fella's as deep as a draw-well."

He crossed to the window of his office and looked down across the "bank". When he turned, his face was still a study:

"Remember - he's your choice and you're responsible for him, especially while he's with Miss Frances. We mustn't cut our nose off in spite our face though. We need him now - but we won't always need him! When the order book's run down and we're slack again I want him off the place. Keep your own counsel on this but when we're laying people off he's the first to get his cards and his coppers. Understand?" After a pause, Dempster nodded.

Later, the manager hung around the lodge until he saw Philip Hughes clocking off. He beckoned to him:

"I'm sorry about what happened today, Phil."

"Not as much as I was. In front of a warehouse full of people he made me a boke finger for what's really a management problem. You won't get the amount of work you want out of this place without more mouldmakers."

"Yes... but how things turned out was unfortunate and the boss has got a lot on his mind right now."

"Mm. I don't doubt that but I did keep my temper when I felt like losing it. He needs to know that Bromley Earthenware isn't the only bell that rings."

"Yes, well... it's a bit awkward to say this but I think things would be better if you showed him a bit more deference. I mean, I'm his works manager but to me he's always 'sir' or 'Mr Ewart'."

"Well, that's up to you Jack, but when I got demobbed I stopped saying 'sir' for good. One good thing about war

- it lets you see things as they really are - what's fact and what's fantasy. He gets good value for what he pays me. I didn't walk out of the Burma swamps to bow and scrape to anybody. Goodnight Jack."

Dempster sighed...

"'night, Phil."

He put down the "Daily Telegraph" and picked up the "Evening Sentinel" but it was no use, neither national nor local news had any significance for him: he wanted to talk to his daughter. So, when Mrs Foley had cleared away the last remnants of the evening meal he leaned forward at last:

"What about that pipsqueak of a platemaker today?"

"Dadder, I think you were hard on him. You seemed to hear a lot more in his remarks than I did."

"Oh I did, did I? You listen to me - when you've been dealing with labour as long as I have you'll know a sneer for what it is. 'Your question wants a serious answer' - smarmy bugger. He's too clever for his own good."

"All I can say is that in my dealings with him he has always been respectful and well mannered. I don't think it helped that you tore into him in front of other people, or that you swore at the warehouse women."

"You're pretty certain I was in the wrong aren't you? Well don't you make snap judgements and don't defend the workers against me either! I'd only hoped that today would have shown you what I mean about the 'dividing line'. Keep your own counsel and keep your distance. If you give certain types of people an inch, your authority's gone."

"You and mother brought us up to see things fairly, so I have to tell you what I see. You went for him immediately he came into the warehouse - which was demeaning and for something that wasn't his fault. But he didn't lose his temper. I think that says a lot for him."

Ewart was enraged but then his next words were full of concern:

"Look... I'm just anxious that you proceed to the highest job you're able to handle. That means my shoes. There are pitfalls that maybe you don't see. Your best insurance is to develop a sound judgement of character."

He looked into her lustrous eyes.

"You are a kind person, Frances - always have been. Kindliness can be taken advantage of, particularly by clever people."

"I think it's wrong to put Philip Hughes down as a smart Alec."

"Well I sounded out Jack Dempster about him pretty thoroughly. Apparently he's skilled enough and files his own tools - just don't let him get too big for his boots."

"I know."

"I told Dempster to put him on a fixed salary, up to the level of his piece-work earnings, so he can't grumble." To punctuate his next phrases, he prodded the air with the stem of his pipe:

"Now - if he's a good platemaker he's valuable to us. That means while he's training you, we shall be losing his production - and just when we need it most. Still, if he trains you to make flat and file tools properly, and bear in mind they're the nub of the thing as far as managing the clay end goes, then it'll be a good investment. We'll get the expense back and a bit more besides. You've got to show potters you want to bottom the job, Frances, and not just play at it. When they see that, they'll respect you and listen to any criticisms you have to make about their work."

He leaned back in his chair.

"You'll thank me a hundred-fold for getting you

started with first things first, especially when you feel your confidence growing."

He got up to leave but stood over her:

"Remember though - if he gets out of line, you're to shout about it. Got it?"

Peremptorily she nodded then cut in quickly:

"Before you go - two things - the Factory Inspector was in today. Jack was off the bank visiting the boards suppliers so I had to see him. He's writing to you but insisted I have a quick word about the steps leading to the flat shop - they need attention urgently."

Bromley frowned:

"Anything else?"

"A number of things apparently. Most of the doors in the clay end need turning so they open outwards in case of a fire. We're in breach of regulations and he could order a closure notice if we don't fix them quickly."

"Marvellous, isn't it? The Government's purging us to export as much as we can, then they send us inspectors to stop our gallop. I tell you - the right hand doesn't know what the left's doing."

"He thinks the steps are most urgent - if you remember, I told you about them earlier."

"Yes, yes, yes!" he grunted.

"And remember, you did say you'd see to some help for Mrs Foley."

"Frances - will you stop mithering me!"

He slammed the door as he left.

Chapter Seven
The Learning Curve

By May Day, another winter had left the hollow and the potters were looking forward to warmer times. The rising temperatures would only make the potting shops, with their steamy heat, that much more uncomfortable however. Yet that did not matter. They wanted the sun to become established and to show itself without fall on the great day of the "works outin'". So everyone looked forward with hope.

By the spring Frances Bromley was beginning to master the art of platemaking, even though her early efforts had been attended by all the usual preliminary failures. At the onset, the balls of clay had been thrown onto the plaster block well enough but they usually managed to escape before the spreader blade had descended to flatten them into clay pancakes (or "bats", as we have noted).

Even when the balls of clay, under the helpful, assisting pressure of her slurried fingers, had stayed on the block, they had not emerged from the spreader's touch as bats that were tight and round. Because the balls of clay had not been thrown onto the dead centre of the block they were elliptical or ovoid since the impatient spreader had flattened them while they spun eccentrically. If they were round they were not usually "tight", but ragged at the edges, for she had not knocked the balls of clay into solid shapes. Philip Hughes seemed to knock the clay to sufficient solidity in about three movements. She could use a dozen movements and still produce raggedy-edged bats. The clay was beginning to look apprehensive though on its behalf it must be admitted – it was used to better treatment.

In the actual making operation, Frances could not continue, at first, to throw down the bat centred exactly onto the mould. Rather was it half off the mould. When it was fully onto the mould this was only the prelude to other failures. At times, because she had sent the motorised drive racing away too fast and too soon the mould would jump nervously out of the jigger head.

When the fearful mould did stay in the jigger head she next faced the ordeal of running down the clay tightly onto its surface. With a watery hand she began to polish the face of the clay ready for the kiss of the tool. When she was too slow to do it properly a skirt of clay would raise itself provocatively and dance to the music of the motorised drive. At the climax of the dance it would fly from the mould entirely – into the water pot, onto her bib, onto her face, even, heaven forefend, into her beautiful mouth. As she extricated it from those exquisite teeth the empty mould was always there in the jigger head, smiling up at her stupidly.

Something Frances learned from all this concerned

Philip's nature – his patience was unbounded. On occasions she had seen some of the other potters smiling at her efforts, not a little patronisingly. They were as jealous of their craft as all other craftsmen and to see her failing at it so spectacularly did much to nourish their self-esteem.

Philip was quite different. He was in deadly earnest about her "apprenticeship". After every failure his brow would knit and there would be a careful appraisal of what went wrong and why. Then he would ask her, supportively, whether another approach to some particular operation would suit her better.

So she began to appreciate his supreme ability. He was a man immersed in his craft. Watching his arms and hands move over the spinning clay she recognised that while her touch was torture, his was a benefaction to it. And each separate article he made could only be made if he gave it his full attention. So each quantity of plates he made represented so many deep concentrations.

It was because she recognised his great capability that she began to be anxious to please him. So every failure now seemed shameful in its way while each success filled her, filled them both, with quiet emotion. She now comprehended how mastering the intricacies led to self-fulfilment. Because he possessed such sublime skill, she fretted at first lest he be scandalised at the treatment she meted out to the moulds, the making- tools and the clay. And one might surmise that with such a level of skill he might have proved a poor teacher. In fact he was tender with her and his quiet gentleness gave her hope. He exuded the unemotional confidence that time would move the miracle into her mind and hands.

And something more was happening to Frances. Feelings and an emotional attachment to him were beginning to materialise. The news that Vera Foskett regarded herself as his girl-friend had provided the first faint stirring. The manly way in which he had stood up to her father on that drawing-day had made her emerging fondness more profound. Now there was this other dimension to his character, compounded of his skill and his care and concern for her. So while it may seem fanciful to suggest that a woman's love could dawn in so mundane a setting, who is to say that the settings for such sentiments can ever be narrowly delineated?

Despite her deepening emotions, there were times when her faith was low. Yet, as she groped her way towards competence his solicitude kept her hope alive. What is more Winnie Hood, the mouldrunner, proved to be a great, good friend. After an isolated triumph Frances would turn: Winnie too was smiling triumphantly at the newly made plate. After a disaster and a sidelong glance at Winnie the words she read within the smile were:

"It's all right, duck – I can't make 'em either."

If she struck a particularly bad patch, Winnie was at her confidence – building best. For instance, after repeated attempts to produce one good plate, she might suddenly produce one that was almost good. Winnie would seize it eagerly and run to the dobbin stove. Then Philip's look would reproach her and with her back to Frances, she would slide the impostor plate unobtrusively into the scrap-box.

There was another factor hampering Frances' progress. Vera Foskett was working at the next jigger and across the intervening space flowed vibrations of resentment. Anyone would have been affected by the hostility, unspoken though it was. It was worsened, moreover, by another factor. Vera was a maker without a mouldrunner. Her piece-work earnings were reduced by having to run her own moulds to the dobbin. To compensate, she received a "mouldrunning allowance" in her weekly settle.

When she realised Frances was to work with Philip she was bitterly jealous. Then she saw how to turn this to advantage and explained to Jack Dempster that since Winnie Hood would be largely "unoccupied" (meaningful emphasis here) it would make sense for Frances to run her own moulds while Winnie was transferred to Vera.

Dempster and Hughes conferred. They agreed that if Frances was to learn the making techniques quickly it would be sensible for her to concentrate on them exclusively with Philip and Winnie in close, discussive support. Vera's face twisted with anger and frustration.

On the day of the decision Frances heard a snatch of conversation.

"Have yer brought yer tea with yer, Winnie?" Vera asked.

"Why?"

"Yer'll need it by the time she's made enough stuff to fill one side of your stove!"

Rarely do mouldrunners talk back to makers but Winnie straightened defiantly:

"You 'ad to learn, didn't you?"

"God bless you," thought Frances.

Before long, the successes were becoming more frequent, the failures fewer. The smiles the potters always had for her were widening. Winnie Hood, Sally Gratton, Florence Birks and Phil Hughes were especially glad.

Each day there were a few more plates for Winnie to run to the stove and for Sally to tow and smooth for the oven. The placers came up to the stillage and nodded approvingly to each other for each day there were a few more plates for them to carry away. Only Vera Foskett was miserable about developments. In fact her fury with Frances intensified when she was told about the Factory Inspector's stipulation that, in her interests of her own safety her long hair should be cut, taken up or turbaned. It would be grossly indelicate to report the words of her reaction in these pages.

Florrie Birks did not, as a rule, inspect "big flat" for quality but the placers had to cross the floor of her dominion when carrying ware to their own territory. With each successive board from Frances Bromley the joy of the shawled old woman deepened. She would tap her foot on the upturned saggar she used as a footstool. This was to keep time to the song – a song of her youth which she often sang, but which no-one else ever heard. As each day fresh boards went by she would tap a little faster and a little longer.

Of course everyone at Grange Pottery knew of Frances' progress. Exulting they said:

"Av yer 'eard? Miss Frances' makin' big flat an' warehus reckon it's comin' ite perfeect!"

The elfin Billy Hogan strode across the bank excited. He was all for making a bet that the "gorgeous wench" could make one hundred dozen big flat by the end of June. When Fred Knapper and Ludo Dunning laughed at the proposal he was bitter and dejected. If the sporting instincts were not entirely dead they were indeed on the critical list. Was there no-one left in all Burslem, other than himself, who could lose his wages with cavalier dash? He closed his eyes in anguish.

So, because her progress was now so marked, Ewart Bromley decided his daughter could be introduced to tool-filing. He was more than pleased with results so far because he liked an audience for his plans and outbursts. One outburst, in which he had stigmatised Philip Hughes a failure in front the whole warehouse staff had done him more harm than good. Now the situation was restored and once again coram populo, for the whole firm knew how well his plan to make Frances a "practical potter" had succeeded. However he was still acutely conscious of the cost of the tactic, so bringing his watch into view, as if the matter could be judged in hours and seconds, he told Jack Dempster, that the whole process should be concluded by the end of the month.

Because Ewart now needed his watch to the extent that others must have tobacco or alcohol, one or two of the potbank's cognoscenti, drawing on their knowledge of Lewis Carroll, had titled him "The White Rabbit". The sobriquet had soon become socially sanctioned. The hapless Jack Dempster, whose subservience to his master was likewise legendary, had earned himself the label "Little Sir Echo".

As for tool filing, the tools which cut the clay to shape were about 3/8" in thickness. They were made of mild steel and, just as water will re-shape the surfaces of stones, the non-plastic particles in the structure of the clay wore away the tools, and at a much faster rate. It was necessary then for the tools to be constantly filed back to the precise shape of the articles they were designed to make.

The cutting edge of the tool must be knife like. The non-active edge which lay away from the clay had to be filed down lower than the cutting edge. This produced a defined path up which the excess clay could slither away during the making operation. Frances knew that this gradient was called "the rake" of the tool. When she knew how to file the tools back to their correct shape and at the correct "rake" she would have become competent.

On the afternoon that her instruction began she walked out of the "top shop" with Philip Hughes. They passed the stillage they both remembered and entered the first of the Grange's two cup-shops. At the first making machine (a "jolley") they found Ben Brammer. Ben was the only male in the cup shop and he made one pint mugs. He had fought in the First World War and during the Second his mugs had gone all over the world with the Fighting Services. Now they were making their way to thousands of homes and hundreds of industrial canteens. Philip offered to file a couple of Ben's tools and these were readily given up.

They descended the steps outside the shop, walked past Number Two Glost Oven and into the fitting shop, which was empty.

"The fitters will be 'round the shops so you can have a bit of a practice in peace. By the time they come back you'll be filing tools with the best of them."

Frances laughed:

"I've already had a go at this. You couldn't have been watching!"

He grinned and pointed to a bench-vice under the far window of the shop....

"Look – this is the one I generally use for filing my own tools. You try it."

He put his arm to the shelf above the vice and withdrew a template for the tool of a one-pint mug.

"You see this tool?"

His finger traced its outline:

"See – no intricate pieces and apart from this round at the heel, just two straight lines – the shorter one for the bottom of the mug, the longer one for its sides. Good for a start – simple."

She smiled and nodded.

"Now – it'll give you valuable practice at using the file if you just try to restore the rake when I've scribed the shape on the back of the tool."

Having done this he put away the template. Then he set the tool in the vice and watched. In a second or so, he leaned down towards her:

"No – try not to scratch at it. Use the whole length of the file. Plenty of weight on the forward stroke – none on the back stroke. Then forward again."

He put his hand over her own on the handle of the file and she decided then she did not wish to make progress too quickly. He was struggling with the wondrous perfume wafting from her hair so did not know whether to be angry or relieved when they heard the bark of a door-latch.

They both gaped as a ghost made its way towards them, then they felt foolish, realising it was only a fog of thick-twist tobacco fumes sucking along Mr Fred Knapper in its wake.

In its surprise at finding them there, Fred's pipe jumped clean out of his mouth and into his hand. Fred had to think very quickly but his absolute artlessness only gave him away...

"Oh... erm... ah didner know there was anybody in. 'morneen, Miss Frances. Is young Phil keepin' yer at eet?"

As she smiled he looked at Philip:

"Er... 'ave yer got such a thing as a 'ommer?"

What a question! The fitting shop was an Aladdin's Cave of hammers – big, small, in an unbounded variety of shapes and sizes. They were in fixtures and drawers and out of fixtures and drawers, anxious to be taken away and used. There was only one other place in the whole of Grange Pottery boasting a similar number of hammers and that was Fred Knapper's own engine house.

Philip felt it best to say nothing – he moved over to a drawer lest Frances might see him laugh. He indicated a range of hammers:

"Better let the fitters know what you've borrowed, Mr Knapper."

While Frances returned to the mug tool, the boilerman moved speedily to the drawer:

"Has Billy 'ogan bin this road?", he whispered.

"I can't say I've seen him", advised Philip.

Then at that precise moment, the door-latch sounded like a rifle shot and the elf himself appeared.

Frances Bromley was the first to receive a grin but when he saw the thinning cloud of pipe smoke his own face clouded. Fleetingly it seemed he was concerned about Fred

Knapper's presence but now he was grinning again:
"'ow do all. Fitters 'ave sent me down for some pipe bends."

He went to a large fixture containing several types of bends, tees and unions for fitting electrical conduit. The fixture had its back to Frances, Philip and Fred, so Billy Hogan had passed from sight. Fred Knapper was following him.

Though Philip talked to Frances about the tool she was filing she could sense he was really interested in what was going on at the other side of the fixture. On the pretence of looking for something, he edged over to it and picked up the conversation.

Fred began cheerfully enough:
"Well Billy, thee cost treat theeself to a pint!"
A silence, then:
"'ow d'yer mean, Fred?"
The next silence was strained.
"Well... out er th'winnin's."
The third silence stretched the nerves...
"Wot winnin's?"
The fat man's voice grew louder and insistent:
"Your Vincent says the favourite won the two o'clock. Ah've exed him meself."
"Oh"
The final silence was fearful:
"Well... yer put eet on, didn't yer?"
"Who'd a thought eet? Givin' all that weight awee!".
"Wots (loud)... wot's (soft) that got do with eet?"
Billy's words were rapid now:
"Well, Fred – if yer must know – ah've put eet on 'Electrerstatic'. It seemed ter 'ave thë breedin', an' if eet 'ad a come in at sixty six ter one, ah know yer'd a bin pleased, now wustner?"

Behind the screen of the fixture, Fred Knapper's cap, neckerchief, buckle, trousers, shoes and pipe were straining to dance with rage. Ultimately, try as he might, Fred could not stop them:

"Billy – yer a bloody little varmint! Yer take no more bets for me. Ah've a good mind to tell Drummer Durber!"

"But Fred – who'd a thought eet? Who'd a thought eet? Eet wuz impossible ter give all that weight awee – on soft goin' as well!"

"Th'oss didner think so, did eet?"

They marched out of the fitting shop.

Through the window Frances could see them stalk across the cobbles. The boilerman, waddling off in his hurt, was trying to put down a smoke screen of thick twist between the elf and himself. On the edge of it, Hogan was remonstrating plaintively.

"Would you excuse me for a minute please?"

A worried Philip Hughes raced out of the fitting shop. The door swung open behind him and Frances was shocked to discover that in order to catch the words drifting in from the cobbles she had moved behind it.

"Suppose he tells Drummer?"

The question was Philip's and, of course, Frances was not to know that "Drummer" (Mr Absalom Durber to be more precise) was Billy's "other employer".

Absalom had been born of staunch Chapel people who dearly hoped he would always follow the path of righteousness. To set the seal on these hopes they had called him Absalom so that his very name would be a source of spiritual inspiration.

From his earliest days at the council school, however, "Absie's" name had been a constant embarrassment to him and the cause of many a playground scuffle. However, he had soldiered on and before long there was respite when, because of his prowess on that particular instrument in the Dale Hall Jazz Band, the precocious little boy had been re-christened "Drummer".

A lesser man might have been bitter about the derision

of his early days, but not "Drummer". He was one of rare creatures whose life was given over to the good fortune of his fellow men. Many a potter and many a miner in the hollow felt sure their ability extended beyond the jigger-box and the coal-face. They felt certain they possessed the skill, foresight and perception of those rare beings able to judge that equally rare breed of horse – the winner.

They could "beat the book" and the selfless "Drummer" decided to make the book they might beat. Well in advance of the enabling legislation that produced the betting shop, and Government assent to ready-money betting beyond the racecourse, "Drummer" conducted his philanthropic activities from the parlour room of his late mother's cottage in Amicable Street. It was not that far from the playground of the council school. But he had almost forgotten his early suffering and had even been known, when the mood was on him, to give his early tormentors lifts in his limousine especially if they were heavy losers.

"Drummer's" business depended on an army of "bookie's runners" who bore the money and the betting slips of the ever hopeful punters to Amicable Street. The most colourful, but sadly the least reliable, of these foot-soldiers was William Liam Hogan.

This information might facilitate understanding of what went on outside the fitting shop on that May afternoon as Frances Bromley leaned closer to the conversation Philip had taken up with Billy:

"Did you put Fred's money on any horse, Mr Hogan?"
No reply.

"How often do you think you can get away with this sort of thing?... Somebody'll be taking a cut at you one of these days."

"Ah wuz goin' put eet on, but when ah went for me snappin' this dinner-tahm, missus got on abite payments for th'wireless. Ah con deal with Fred better than with missus, so ah gis her th' money."

"...but you could've asked Vincent or me, instead of getting yerself into this mess."

"Ah owe Vincent a bob or two as eet is, an' how could you 'elp out on your bit o' pocket brass?"

As he returned to the fitting shop she saw Philip stroking his chin, lost in thought. Billy Hogan was racing after Fred Knapper in case he was racing after "Drummer" Durber. Frances found herself filing the mug tool again.

Back at the bench he was clearly embarrassed by the episode and as he feigned interest in her efforts with the file, a number of questions arose in her mind: why was he so anxious about Billy Hogan? Why had he shown such speedy insight into the man's failings? Why did Philip, a skilled potter and one of the best paid men in the firm, have to depend on "a bit of pocket brass"?

A pertinent conversation simply had to be contrived:

"Do you know Mr Hogan well?"

"We live next door to the family – in Hanover Street."

"Hanover Street?"

"It's about five or six minutes' walk away; turn right at the lodge and into Pleasant Street. Take the third turning right into Enoch Street and the second turn left into Hanover Street, opposite St John's Church. We live in the lower half of the street on the right hand side."

She nodded dumbly. He obviously felt enough had been said because he picked up the inch wide half-round file she had now laid on the bench. He began to file the mug tool himself quickly, still obviously put out because she had witnessed the confrontation. Nervously, he began to whistle. Mentally, she fitted the words to his tune:

"Loudly let the trumpet bray!
Tantantara!
Gaily bang the sounding brasses!
Tzing! Boom!"

It was the Chorus of Peers from "Iolanthe". Her lovely eyes shone:

"Are you fond of Gilbert and Sullivan?"

He smiled:

"Very fond – as Hanover Street knows to its cost."

He had a lovely smile. With her heart in her mouth she had to continue:

"Did you know that one of the amateur groups is doing a Gilbert and Sullivan week at the Hill Top Methodist Church?"

"I saw it in the 'Sentinel."

Her mouth became dry and she struggled with her next words:

"A friend of mine was going with me on Thursday to see 'The Mikado'. Unfortunately she can't come and I've booked the seats... Would you like to come?"

He looked at her and smiled again:

"Thank you. I would."

She was elated but did her best to conceal it. When he realised what he had done he became sick with worry. There was something about him the Bromleys must never know, so she was the last person in the world he should be seeing socially. He was furious with himself. What was he playing at?... it was simple, he loved her and it had blinded him to the consequences.

Chapter Eight
Significant Developments

He stood beneath the imposing portico of the Hill Top Methodist church. Frances walked up its broad steps towards him, appraising the Ionic columns above her. She wore a simple V-necked pale green dress flecked with dark green small-leaf motifs. Its attractive simplicity complemented her loveliness, though he qualified this impression by saying to himself:

"Mind you – she'd even look good in a collier's pit dirt."

She smiled:

"Hallo.....am I late?"

He was puzzled:

"No....but how've you got here?"

"By car, I've parked it just around the corner in Hall Street, by the Catholic church."

She looked up at the classical lines of the building:

"Imposing isn't it?"

"Mm, and it's worn well."

Philip stepped out from the portico and pointed to a plaque on the pediment:

"There y'are, 1837."

He added with a grin:

"And built as a result of a row in the family."

"How do you mean?"

"Well, a group of teachers, radicals I suppose you'd call them, fell out with the powers-that-be at Swan Bank, the big Methodist place. I believe they found the restrictions there too pettifogging. So they came here and built this. People got things done in those days."

The subsequent musical performance was most enjoyable. It was obvious they both found Gilbert and Sullivan fascinating and immensely entertaining. From time to time Frances watched covertly as Philip surreptitiously kept time with the music. His right hand tapped his right knee in perfect accord with every beat, every pause, every sweep and every crescendo. He knew the operetta to its last detail. The more she discovered about him, the more intrigued she became.

Between the Acts they were having coffee and seemed in agreement that "The Mikado" was the masterpiece of the immortal partnership. Having talked about the spellbinding selection of its songs, Frances said:

"But did you know it was nearly never written?"

"How was that?"

"They both felt the partnership had run its course – their work had become sterile. Gilbert was for breaking up the collaboration but happened to visit an exhibition of Japanese culture and costumes and it triggered off the idea of 'The Mikado'."

"Interesting."

"We had a Gilbert and Sullivan Society at University and in spite of the shortage of men, we managed to put on a production every year."

"Including this one?"

She nodded.

"I'll bet you were Yum-Yum."

"No, I was Katisha."

He feigned seriousness, then grinned:

"I suppose you could be a bit of a dragon."

As she gave him a playful push two observers saw them laughing. The first of these was the "cod" placer, Percy Birchall, who had been standing in the shadows with his wife. When Percy caught Philip's eye he could not help winking and giving the "thumbs up" sign.

The youth's irritated but appealing look seemed to say:

"No, you fool – it's not like that – I care for this girl."

Percy's grin only widened.

The other observer was better concealed. She had attended with a group of friends and took care to stay within the circle of their happy, chattering cacophony. Yet her stealth masked excited anticipation: "What a story for The Office in the morning!" thought Millicent Dean, the invoice typist.

The entertainment over, Frances and Philip left the church smiling. She was full of praise:

"Weren't they fantastic?! Every bit as good as professionals! Nanki-Poo was excellent "

"And Ko-Ko could sing a bit."

"They were all great", she concluded.

"Most of the chorus were from the Hill Top choir."

"You know, one of the things I'm proud of is our tradition of choral music."

"Well, a lot of that's down to the Welsh miners and

their families who came here when the coalfield was getting started. That's why we have so many Leeses and Reeses and Joneses and Edwardses around the place."

"And they brought their non-conformism with them," she added.

"Absolutely. I should think a good wack of all the Methodists in this country live in the Potteries. But, while the Church of England minds its own business we've got the Irish – the Catholics – to keep them both in order."

"Watch it!", she laughed, "I'm one of the Roman lot!"
She was telling him what he already knew, for he remembered that Peter Bromley was a Catholic, and a loyal one.

They had reached the top of Hall Street.

"Well, I'll say goodnight then – but please, Miss Bromley, do let me pay for my ticket."

"Don't talk such nonsense! But....where are you going? Surely you're not just about to walk away?"

He was uncomfortable and apologetic:

"No. No. I was forgetting my manners. I ought to walk you to your car."
As they went towards the car, parked in front of St. Joseph's Church, he thought it appeared to be a 10 h.p. Ford Prefect, probably 1938. She was offering him a lift home.

"That'd be a complete waste of your time. Just a hundred yards along the top and I'll be in St. John's Square. I live a few minutes away from there."
Uncertain what to say next, she motioned to her car:

"Look – get in, please. I want to ask you something."
As he opened the passenger door, he hoped his foreboding was unfounded but when they settled down she came to the point immediately:

"As you probably know Peter Bromley was my brother. I believe you were in the Army with him....."
Philip was angry. So this was the motive for the invitation to Hill Top! He decided to shield his reaction.

"Yes. Lieutenant Bromley was my platoon commander."

He had lied to her father and so must continue lying:

"Obviously I didn't know him personally but I was very sorry that he died. Please accept my sympathy."

Then he was silent and impassive but Frances persisted:

"We were very close you see. They've sent us some of his things.....one or two personal items, but we've had no official word of how he died. My father has even been to the War Office but we've learned nothing."

She turned towards him. Even in the gloom he sensed her eyes were searching his face. Almost defiantly he looked back at her:

"Your father has already asked me if I can help, but I'm afraid I can't. I'm sorry."

Vehemently he hoped that would end the matter but she came back quickly.

"It's so odd. When we learned nothing through official channels, my father went to the Drill Hall. By chance, a man there knew my brothers and he also knew you. He said you were with Peter and could probably tell us more. You see, all we received at the time was a telegram – "Missing, presumed dead." Later we got the official confirmation but in spite of father's efforts, and connections I might add, we've met a blank wall. I just want to find out as much as I can, especially about how he died and where he's buried. I'm really very sorry to bother you, but you're our only hope it seems."

She sounded about to cry. He composed himself:

"There really isn't anything I can tell you. At that time, your brother was in charge of our platoon. What I've said to your father, and it won't be news to him, is that you can start in a battle with someone right next to you and finish up all over the place. Eventually, when we pulled out I....I heard he'd been killed. Then we were given map co-ordinates and told to move back rapidly. The Japs always infiltrated our lines at an incredible speed and you sensed you were in danger of being surrounded. So none of us ever had the chance to go back and look for Mr Bromley. It was really hard lines."

Again he turned away. His duplicity almost made him gag on his words. He hated himself and he hated the situation she had put him in.

"Is there anyone else who might know?"

He waited, then said bitterly:

"I was the only one of that platoon to get back here. We left hundreds out there, thousands for all I know."

She felt sorry for him but it was important to continue:

"Will he be buried there?"

"Where?"

"Where you said he'd been killed?"

"I've no idea. If they've recovered his body and they put a War Cemetery at the site of the battle then that's where he'll be I would think."

"How can we find out?"

"I'm afraid I can't say. You have the connections and better access to the information than I could possibly have."

In the half-light he saw her head drop and sensed her sorrow. He tried to continue feelingly:

"You see, the Authorities won't have properly established their Cemeteries yet. The War's not been over that long and it might take quite a while to recover all the bodies from their temporary graves. And.....if some aren't recovered, their names will be included on a memorial inside the Cemetery. That's how they did it after the First War anyway."

"And whom do I contact about that?"

"I expect it would be the War Graves Commission – I've heard it does a wonderful job."

"It's funny – we know every last little detail about where

and how Denzil died but in Peter's case all our efforts lead us nowhere."

Though he should have stopped himself, he said:

"Well, now you know why we're called the 'Forgotten Army'."

So, at this point, not only was he lying, he was using the indifference of the nation to his comrades to cover his lying. Brimful of self-disgust, it was time to move. He opened the car door quickly. She leaned across, alarmed:

"I was taking you....."

"No. No. There's absolutely no need. I live around the corner, practically."

As she protested, he was pointing:

"St. Paul's Churchyard is at the bottom. Just before you come to it, turn left into Riley Street – which is the third down. Go along to the very end then turn right into Newcastle Street. You'll be well on your way home. Goodnight. Thank you for a very nice evening."

Before she could respond he closed the door.

At the top of Hall Street he turned right into Liverpool Road and threw back his head in exasperation. He had fallen for her hook, line and sinker only to discover that, however elevated her motive, she was using him. Maybe she was too good to be true after all. Whether she was, or wasn't, the future was clear – he would be giving her a wide, wide berth.

A nearby bottle oven, at the first stage of its firing, was sending forth a billowing cloud of black, acrid, smutty smoke dense enough to threaten any star daring to venture out.

The next evening was sunny and warm. Philip was at his jigger-box "doing his kale", which is to say he was stripping his machine, and the box itself, of every trace of clay scrap and slurry. Then he would sponge them down carefully until they were "as clean as a new pin." He was looking forward to a walk in the last sunny hours – perhaps up to Burslem Park or down to Westport Lake.

The door opened at the far-end of the shop. He looked up and his lip tightened. Frances Bromley was walking towards him. How glib a liar would he have to become to keep the manner of her brother's death a secret?

"Hallo, still at it?", she smiled.

He nodded: "Yes – trying to finish before the scrap collector arrives."

"Well, I don't want to keep you but I thought you'd be interested to see this......"

Because he could not take it into his slurried hand, she held a photograph in front of him:

"Recognise anyone?"

"Of course, it's your brother with his platoon."

"See anyone else?"

He pointed, among the group, to himself.

"That's me.......a very nervous lance-jack."

"How do you mean 'nervous'?"

"I'm no hero. I spent most of the war terrified out of my wits. They gave me that stripe to save to save me from being beaten up."

"I'm sure that's rubbish."

She searched his face:

"I know I'm being an awful pest, but could you tell me when it was taken?"

"Yes......in Calcutta, before we moved into Burma."

She hesitated:

"Do you remember anything after that?....anything?"

He sighed and continued to do his kale. This was not lost on her.

"As I've said, there's not much to tell. He was our platoon officer. We were trying to take back the Arakan. That's a sort of coastal area. Unfortunately, it didn't come off. So we were asked to act as rearguard to our Division. We were withdrawing to a pass called Ngakyedauk. We managed to hold it for six days – don't ask me how. Then we carried on retreating, to a place called Bawli Bazar."

His mouth was dry. He ran his tongue over his lips. She waited.

"After that we got separated – our mob was all over the place. When we re-formed I heard that Mr Bromley had been killed."

She leaned forward:

"And you don't know how he was killed?"

He turned from the jigger-box and looked at her. She was watching intently. He turned back to the jigger-box.

"I don't know. I can't say. At one time we were completely surrounded. It didn't look as if any of us would get out. As I said last night, that's what the Japs were really good at – infiltration. They would come through our positions like a knife through butter and we'd never see them come. Even if we weren't completely cut off they could make us believe we were. We underestimated how tough they were and how determined. And they could live on practically nothing. They had more armaments and equipment – more of everything – and they really slaughtered us. Most of the time I was as nervous as a kitten."

He seemed forlorn at the memory of it. It saddened her but she nerved herself to continue:

"Will he be buried there?"

"Where?"

"Where you said.....the Bazar place?"

In spite of his exasperation he tried to be calm:

"It's impossible for me to say. I mentioned the War Graves Commission – they're your best bet. If there's a cemetery at Bawli that's where he might be, though I can't swear to it."

He was dejected and it touched her. Then, strangely, he seemed to want to say more:

"It wasn't only that they had more men and more stuff – they were better at using the jungle. They could eat things that'd make you heave – rats, snakes, porcupines. And they were a vile enemy: I can't speak about some of the things they did. In the monsoon period we were sodden and everything was bogged down. Daytime in the high summer was baking – one hundred degrees at times. We weren't used to any of it and in the early part, when your brother died, we were completely demoralised, though later we got the measure of them. You were fighting in a hell-hole all the time – leeches, yaws, beri-beri, the stench of the jungle; get a nick and the next day it was a suppurating ulcer. Anyway, when we got back here, nobody had the slightest interest in us. So like the rest, I've decided to keep my mouth shut. We just want to get on with things."

She looked at him – this old young man whose recollections had brought back sorrow, horror and exhaustion into his eyes. The wish to hold him tenderly welled within her. If she held him she would also be holding Peter and all the others. But her natural reserve won the day and she was able just to say:

"That's been really helpful. Thank you very much."

Her emotion was not quite extinguished though:

"Philip, I wonder whether we could have a cup of tea somewhere before you go home?"

His tension returned:

"Look, Miss......please don't ask me any more about it. That's the first time I've spoken of it to anyone. I can't tell you any more."

They faced each other. She was sorry for forcing him to relive his experiences. His self-revulsion had returned and within he cursed himself for being a "lying toad". Still she stood there until he nodded towards the far end of the shop:

"Here's the scrap collector. I must finish this now."

He turned to his jigger-box and she walked slowly away. It seemed that a psychological distance between them was now emerging. Yet fate decided otherwise. Nor did it delay.

"Boards!"

The cry rang from one end of Grange Pottery to the other. Jack Dempster's visit to the suppliers had achieved results. A large quantity of new potters' boards, both long and short, now lay under the entrance archway. The news flew through the clay end. Makers, particularly those on piece-work, together with their mouldrunners, came dashing down the steps outside the top flat shop.

Frances Bromley was among this surge – feeling she had to conduct an orderly and fair distribution of the treasures. To counteract the wobbly motion of the steps she steadied herself at the handrail. Many others were doing the same thing. When she was six feet from the bottom the rail gave way. In her fall, she twisted a little to save herself, landing on her side. Her head cracked on the granite setts of the factory yard – the "bank".

She lay moaning, her skirt flung up by the fall. Within seconds, Philip Hughes, who had been following, knelt beside her. His swift hands restored her modesty. Dazed and oblivious to the cries and the sympathetic consternation around her she opened her eyes. Gently, he passed his hand through her hair but could feel no bleeding. He tore off his apron and made it into a makeshift pillow.

She looked up as, tenderly, he put it behind her head. He was frowning:

"Are you all right?"

"Fine I've just jarred my back. It'll be O.K. Help me up please."

Other willing hands were put out to her but the youth held them back:

"Give her some space."

Satisfied she could move her legs he put his arms beneath her and lifted:

"Better not put any weight on your feet until one of the first-aiders has seen you. Let's get you to the lodge."

The sight of him carrying her was thrilling and moving to the many onlookers. For the present even the boards were forgotten. A group of jug casters watched, enchanted, as the couple passed them. The most senior of them, Phyllis Eardley, folded her plump arms and registered her verdict:

"That lad's got feelin's for her. You mark my words."

There was a tender mumbling – the judgement was endorsed.

In the lodge, the initial commotion had died down and Jack Foley, first-aider as well as chauffeur, was tending carefully to the protesting Frances. Philip Hughes was helping.

Ewart Bromley appeared, drawn by the sound of rushing feet in The Office corridor. Even before he enquired about his daughter, he glared at Philip:

"What the hell are you doing in here?"

Quietly, but with contempt, Philip said:

"Slumming," and walked out of the lodge.

Bromley, now in full charge, conferred quickly with Frances, dismissed her remonstrations and decided:

"Foley!"

"Major?"

"She needs an X ray! Run her up to the Haywood!"

When the verdict was announced: bad bruising to the hip and lower back, a small swelling on the skull but nothing worse, the master potter relaxed enough to send for Jack Dempster:

"Remember – first opportunity – I want that monstink off this place!"

When he had seen the damaged steps, cod placer Percy Birchall gave an unmirthful laugh:

"Well, it's happened to the right one."

Vincent Hogan was appalled:

"Hold on, Percy – she's a nice wench."

"I know that – and I'm sorry about it. What I mean is 'cos it was his own daughter he'll do summmat about the bloody things. If it'd bin one of us he'd just have the rail knocked back an' we'd still have ter take our chances. Yer know what he's like – he'd skin a bloody gnat for its hide."

Chapter Nine
The Works Outing

Within the "world" of Grange Pottery, there was a smaller world. It was bounded by the same confines as the bigger world though as far from it as the Earth is from the Sun. The smaller world was "The Office". It encompassed many Sections, such as "Wages", "U.K. Sales", "Export Sales", "UK Invoicing", "Export Invoicing", "Costing and Statistics" et cetera. Each Section was an organ of the Body Administrative.

All in all, potters are gentle folk, humble even. They looked to the cloistered confines of The Office in open-mouthed awe. The workers in The Office were a master-race in their own bright world. They wore their worsted and linen with happy disregard of the expense for in that bright world every day was Sunday. In fact each worker in The Office could have walked with aplomb straight from their desks into church or chapel.

Little wonder then that many a mother in Burslem nursed the aspiration that her own son would eventually become the white collared cherub who licked the stamps. She would cuff him for his present pecadilloes, reasoning that suffering was necessary on the way to the hallowed place lest he realised, too late, he had seen and spat upon Utopia.

It is understandable then why the girls in the potting shops and yes, even the paintresses and lithographers, copied their clothes, shoes and coiffure from the goddesses they had glimpsed bearing a letter-folder, an ink pot or even a cup of tea down the Utopian corridors. If any of The Office spoke to a potter it conferred distinction on that potter. For a potter to know any of The Office set that potter apart. The other potters would wait for every declaration, every prophesy and even false rumour uttered by any potter who authenticated the information with the statement: "Ah've 'eard eet from The Offeece!"

So that is how the potters saw The Office and it was another drop of easing oil making for concord at "Bromleys" for that is how The Office saw itself. And just as the bigger world had its V.I.P.s, the smaller world had its own V.I.P. She was the queen who ruled there, however unofficially, and her name was Lucy Pelham.

Neither too tall nor too short, Miss Lucy Pelham had seen some fifty-five summers. Her hair had once been as black as night and now, when it struggled to stay so, in her compassion, she helped it. For Lucy, time had stood still since her thirty-fifth year so she strove to keep everything as she remembered it. Her face powder stood proud on the eye bags and when it was joined by the sundry droppings of mascara the effect was a perfect simulation of the gritstone ridges near Mow Cop, where the potters could often be found on a Sunday.

She still retained the figure of her youth and chance how her structural trappings protested she would always retain it, despite her passion for cream cakes. The waist was the thing so it mattered little if, at both ends of her trunk, she swelled dangerously.

Her clothes were impeccable. Be it a tailored two-piece (and she had many), a smartly cut dress, or a mere skirt and blouse, they stamped her immediately as a creature of taste, refinement and, as she herself would put it - "breeding". Her shoes were always elegant. They might puff up already bladdered feet but, as she winced happily along, they reminded her she was securely "in fashion".

Everything about her was contrived not merely to make her smart - that would have been a milk and water thing. Vivacity was the prize and so she ate and slept vivacity as did the tradespeople who clothed her with their raiments, petted her with their gliding silks and pampered her with their powders and perfumes.

It is immensely distressing to record however that in spite of the tireless efforts devoted to the project, Lucy Pelham was not the least bit attractive because, quite simply, she had never learned how to bestow a warm, genuine smile on any other human being. Old Jabez Pelham had kept a fruiterer's shop in Burslem and daughter Lucy had perfected her haughty stare from when, as a four year old, she had sat on top of the apples as Jabez had toured the streets of the town with his little cart and emaciated donkey. Though he was now deceased, Jabez's cry of "apples a pound pears" was still remembered in the hollow as was the response of all its little boys:

"Shan't be 'round agen tomorrer, donkey's peed on the strawb'ries!"

By dint of hard work, earnest application and persistent short weight the Pelhams had been able to leave the hollow for High Lane which was almost as far from Burslem's smoke as was Bradwell Grange on the other side of the valley. They lived on the reverse slope of the hill a short distance from the area known as Smallthorne Bank. The lawns and rose trees girding their abode and the residence itself had a sheltered importance about them which satisfied the Pelhams' self-righteousness perfectly. As an added bonus they were able to gaze towards Norton-in-the-Moors, that first stirring of the hills and moorlands leading eventually to Buxton.

Aristocratic in her bearing though she was, Lucy was not the power behind Ewart Bromley's higher throne. He considered her an "unmitigated fuss-pot" and her station no more than that of Senior Invoice Clerk. True, she took down his occasional dictation (he did not set much store by letter-writing) and when it was unavoidable he consulted her on the day-to-day running of The Office. This was unfortunate because his "I can't be bothered attitude" created a fallow situation for cultivating her empire. It is interesting how some men though decisive in weighty matters and courageous in risk-taking display only cowardly acquiescence when dealing with manipulative women. Fortunately for the good of Lucy's soul, Frances Bromley was not lacking in appropriate resolution, as we shall presently see.

For as long as anyone could remember, and except for the War years, on the third Saturday of every June a long line of motor buses left the precincts of Grange Pottery for Blackpool, on the Lancashire coast. "The Works Outing"

was the high spot of the year for the Bromley potters and was always eagerly anticipated from March onwards. It was a Pelham rule that one bus would be reserved for The Office. Lucy oversaw all preparations and arrangements for the Outing combining the several roles of esteemed personage, researcher and planner, route guide and refreshments supervisor.

So The Office bus looked forward annually to taking its polished self off to sea and sand, smug in the knowledge that its plush insides housed the most elevated company "the Grange" could provide, even including the Master Potter himself.

With a break for the Second World War, Ewart had sacrificed himself to the ceaseless chatter of the Pelham cohort every June since 1930. He considered the yearly trip and the lunch-time speech he had to make at Sankey's Restaurant near the North Pier the high point of his abundant commitment to the firm – this one day's work fully merited his director's fees. Naturally, he had to try to look happy but, as we have seen, his captious make-up had produced a man with some limitations.

His sense of foreboding took hold of him on or around each April Fool's Day when Miss Pelham would gushingly enquire where he would like to sit within The Office bus. He was even asked to mark the spot on the pen-and-ink plan of the seating provision she had thoughtfully drawn for him. He feigned interest in the exercise though he knew it made little difference for even if he designated the luggage compartment as his preference Lucy would engineer a seat beside him.

He felt that every cow in the Cheshire countryside leered at him in his predicament but when the outskirts of Warrington had been achieved Ewart had usually fallen into a miserable, fitful, twitching sleep from which he only emerged to look at his watch before slumbering on.

His head would nod in drowsy dejection as Miss Pelham went ecstatically on, his seeming agreement stirring her to demonstrate that each of her statements was even more incisive than the last.

In 1948, however, Bromley decided the torture must come to an end - henceforth, Frances would represent him. She had rested at home for a week to recover from her fall and on the night before the trip he carefully outlined his expectations. She was to travel in The Office bus. She was to make the speech at Sankey's Restaurant. It would be founded on such phrases as: "good fellowship", "mutual understanding", "thank you for your part in a bumper year", "have an enjoyable time" et cetera. She was to deport herself at all times in keeping with her name and position because, as he vigorously affirmed; "if you once relax your grip, over-familiarity can be rife on these occasions."

On that sunny Saturday morning she left Bradwell Grange knowing her performance would be assessed by over five hundred people. She also knew her father would require a full report when she returned. For her it would be as much of a working day as if she had been going to the sliphouse to do the bodymixing. When she arrived, however, she smiled warmly at everyone she met, complimenting the women on their appearance. They smiled warmly in return and asked concernedly if she was recovered from the fall. She assured them all was well. It increased their hopes for a delightful day.

Fourteen red buses were drawn up, extending along the length of the factory and beyond. She walked down the sparkling line noting a card in the front window of each bus. She read the titles – "Cup Shop No 1", "Cup Shop No 2", "Flat Shops", "Biscuit Warehouse", "Casting Shop", "Glost Warehouse", "Under-Glaze Decorators" and so on. Impressive enough, but it disturbed her that the Bromley workers were not free to choose the bus they travelled in or their companions for the journey. It would also have helped to break down barriers between the departments and between The Office and the Works. It appeared though that they must travel according to the Pelham diktat.

When she came to the last bus in the line her disappointment ascended to anger. It was labelled "Miscellaneous" and was the oldest, shabbiest and no doubt least reliable of all. Frances had little difficulty in finding Miss Pelham for as she herself had moved from bus to bus that lady had shadowed her, hoping for commendation on the effectiveness of her arrangements.

The simpering Lucy was suddenly chilled by the stare from Frances as she pointed to the "Miscellaneous" sign.

"What does this mean?", she enquired forcefully.

Pelham was rattled but rallied well. Favouring Frances with the most expansive of her synthetic smiles she explained:

"Oh, it's quite simple – these are the workers who don't belong to a specific department."

"Such as..........?"

"Well, erm....the boiler fireman, the oven fireman, the saggar maker...."

"I see.....some of the most important people in the firm."

Sweeping her arm in the direction of the other buses, Frances added:

"On whom all these other departments depend."

Lucy was bewildered, simply not knowing how to respond. Frances decided to help her: she went inside the "Miscellaneous" bus, detached the identification card and returning, handed it to her. The dazed Lucy accepted it submissively.

"Miss Pelham, as you think about it, wouldn't you feel it's rather demeaning for the people on this bus to find themselves described as 'Miscellaneous'?"

"But they're just...."

Frances would not let her continue:

"Miss Pelham, I'm sorry to be overfrank but let me give you my view.....in the end, people like you and me are expendable. On the other hand, are good firemen and good saggar-makers ten a penny? I think not. In fact, if you had to replace them you might have to look from one end of the Potteries to the other and still be unsuccessful."

By now, in order to hear these exchanges, a crowd had gathered, as crowds do. Lucy was polite – too polite – for in her tone there were undercurrents of malice and competitiveness which she now felt towards the young lady who had usurped her own position of premier female personage on the Outing. Covering her hatred with the broadest of her sham smiles she pointed to The Office bus at the distant head of the line. Her condescension was unmistakeable:

"Miss Frances, I do believe we're now running rather late. If I might just show you to your seat......"

"I've found my seat, Miss Pelham. Thank you."

Frances then mounted the steps of the former "Miscellaneous" bus. Billy Hogan followed her. From beneath the considerable canopy of his new cloth cap he turned and gave "Ludo" Dunning an ultra-outrageous wink.

"What's think o' ma wench now, surree?", was his triumphant question.

After the initial roaring of fourteen bus engines, which could be heard in all the surrounding streets, the great expedition set off. In "The Office" bus Lucy Pelham, alone and livid, rehearsed for her own comfort the grave shortcomings of the Bromley family. They were nobodies. They had come from nothing and they would return to nothing. The way of the latest of them – a mere slip of a girl, who consorted with a platemaker – was a sign – that was it – a sign of the misery she would eventually bring to Mr Almighty Ewart Bromley. Give some people half a chance and they would betray their origins.

In the seats behind her, Lucy's acolytes, though not yet knowing the full story, sensed their beloved leader had received "one in the eye". It sent them into ecstasies. They struggled to keep the lid on their joy which did not in the least abate until well after Holmes Chapel.

On the former "Miscellaneous" bus Frances also sat alone but only because her presence mesmerised her fellow passengers. At last one man went forward to her. He was the man who knew himself to be possessed not only of the necessary savoir faire, of just what to do and how to do it, but beyond that, of the necessary savoir vivre, that grasp of polite usages required to serve a lady of such distinction. Billy Hogan gulped at the sight of her beauty and as his first act of obeisance he took off his new cap:

"I 'ear yer've bin in the wars, Miss Frances – with yer back 'n that. Are yer all right now?"

"Oh yes thank you, Mr Hogan. It was just a bit of a strain and it's cleared up O.K."
She gestured for him to sit down. As he did so he shot a look to his companions – part joy, part triumph.

"Miss Frances, I 'aven't 'ad the chance ter say this before but I want ter tell yer 'ow sorry I was about yer brothers."

The words moved her, the more so for being unexpected. She could only nod her head in thanks.

"Luvly lads they were. I knew 'em both yer know. They used ter come inter the sliphouse. Peter wanted me to show 'im how the pug worked. An' Mester Denzil was gob struck by the bottle ovens."
Frances was on the verge of tears, but Billy pressed on:
"D'yer know – he tried to look up inter the firemouth o' Number 2 ter see how the firin' worked and 'e singed 'is 'air! I told 'im I'd cop it and 'e said "don't worry – I'll comb it out'.....an' 'e did!"
Then, realising Frances' distress he changed tack quickly:
"Now.....wor about some refreshment?"

"Yes....thanks. Do you have a tonic water?"

His resilience fully matched the unexpected question:

"Sorry. Yer see, we don't do shorts on 'ere. They're all ale drinkers. Bur I tell yer what we 'ave got.......'ow about a nice glass o' dandelion and burdock?"

"Mm......is that good?"

"It's champion.....you'll see."

He made for the back of the bus and its ample supplies of intoxicants knowing there was at least one bottle of mineral water if only he could find it. Subsequently, as Frances nodded her appreciation of the dandelion and burdock, he beamed with pleasure.

The early part of this journey to the sea was then taken up with an incident which, though indelicate, should be recorded for the sake of this chronicle's completeness and authenticity.

Cecil Durber was a saggar-maker's bottom knocker. His role had nothing to do with the anatomy of Levi Scarratt, the saggar-maker. Put simply, it meant that, using an oval shaped metal frame, Cecil knocked out a flat saggar-bottom made of fireclay. From this same material, Levi crafted the walls of the saggar on a wooden former. Then Levi joined the walls of the saggar to the bottom made by Cecil. This "green" saggar was then fired in the biscuit oven and the resulting strong saggar was subsequently used to fill and empty the oven, along with hundreds of others.

Cecil was the brother of "Drummer" Durber, the street bookmaker mentioned earlier. "Drummer" was strangely sensitive about his brother for Cecil was "puddled", one of the then local expressions for feeble-mindedness. The brothers rarely met. When they did, their conversations were short, but Cecil did not mind this for he knew "Drummer" to be a busy man. When their parents passed on, there being no other relatives, Cecil was quite alone. Yet his perpetually smiling countenance refuted any notion his existence was dismal. He was thought, by the whole community, to be the happiest man in the hollow and the potters loved and protected him.

Latter-day apostles of political correctness would find this impossible to understand given the description the potters attached to him. Yet while they would never use for Cecil such anodyne descriptions as "mentally challenged" they did undoubtedly love him. Moreover they felt that he gave them far more than they gave him and they were encouraged by his friendship on their own tomb-like days. As Percy Birchall, the "biscuit" cod placer said:

"I come in 'ere of a Monday, 'specially if Port Vale 'ave lost, with me chin on me chest and Cecil comes up grinning and says: 'how do, Perce!......how are yer, mate?' an' I feel champion."

But to get back to our narrative - the potters believed it was impossible for Cecil to be any happier but when he met and married Agnes Leach, he confounded them. The pair had an understanding that was blissful for "Aggie" was also "puddled". So, while neither of them was "all there", there were hundreds in Burslem of abundant sanity who envied them their pure, sustained joy in each other.

Cecil always felt he received more from each Works Outing than he could possibly return. With friends like Billy, Fred, "Ludo" and Levi the atmosphere was always one of bonhomie, cordiality and light-hearted banter. More stories were swapped than would ever be believed and, in fact, very few were believed. What is more, fortunes were made and lost with a happy indifference which would have shamed Monte Carlo.

Cecil had had sixteen of these "holidays", each with its own special memories. He was not the type, however, who milked each adventure of all its happiness without troubling to reciprocate. So, a few nights before the 1948 outing he glanced across the cracked face of the table in the dingy rooms they rented in Velvet Street. Aggie returned his adoring look. They had little food and less domestic equipment so that, portentously, some items had to perform double duties. Nevertheless it was decided. This year the couple would give Cecil's companions a pleasant surprise.

Earlier on the day of the trip while Frances exchanged significant words with Lucy Pelham, Cecil had moved respectfully past her. She had heard the cheers as he had entered the "Miscellaneous" bus holding a gift that was rich, nourishing and oozing with affection. He unpealed several pages of the "Evening Sentinel" to reveal a currant cake, already thoughtfully cut through into thick and thin slices.

It was while the bus made its way bronchially past Haydock Park racecourse that the distribution of the cake was accomplished. The warriors of the ex-"Miscellaneous" troop soon munched appreciatively. "Ludo" Dunning observed that Cecil had married a "good wench" indeed if the cake was typical of the "snappin'" Aggie provided. Cecil was much too modest to concur directly. Suffused with quiet pride he contented himself with these remarks:

"Oh aye. An' d'yer know what.......her made eet in th'chamber!"

Now his hearers were seasoned men but even to them the concept of chamber pot as mixing bowl was too great an assault on their sensibilities. Scandalised by Cecil's indiscretion, the cake leapt from every gullet. Surveying the air, by now full of flying cake, Cecil bellowed in defence of his wife:

"Well!.......it were bloody clean, anyroad!"

Philip Hughes walked from the coach park to the seafront. The potters were not pleased that the coach park was so near to Bloomfield Road, the home of the Blackpool Football Club. That club had recently signed Stanley Matthews, football genius and Potteries lad. He had left Stoke City F.C. with a heavy heart and left many heavy hearts behind him. Their anguish did not abate until the return of the native some years later.

As Philip walked, Vincent Hogan, son of Billy and a placer at "the Grange", accompanied him. Young Hogan was making a name for himself in local soccer and cricket. Strangely this disappointed his father for late in his young life the lad had put on several inches destroying Billy's secret hope that he would become a jockey. In that role he would, of course, have been privy to vital information from racecourses and training establishments.

Vincent had a fitness mania dating from the time he had almost decapitated his father with rusty chest expanders given to him by Fred Knapper. The boy had prised apart the expanders a mite too far for him to control. To save his arms, legs and trunk from being corkscrewed irreparably he was forced to let go of one handle. As Billy lay unconscious at his feet the boy feared for his father's life. Thankfully Mrs Maggie Hogan and her rough mercies had worked wonders and by and by the elf was walking and talking again, though having to defend himself for having "stood in the lad's way." So another violent quarrel had ensued between those bosom pals Fred Knapper and Billy Hogan, this time because of the chest expanders.

During his army service Vincent's quest for health and strength had escalated. Now he was a fully paid-up student on a body-building course. As they neared the sea-front, Philip was receiving his progress report:

"Yer see I reckon that when I've finished all the lessons I could pick up about a dozen of your long boards and walk around with 'em all day if I wanted. I wouldn'a know they were there. This bloke's marvellous. He's got it all weighed up. Won plenty of cups an' medals himself. But as he says in every lesson – 'clean living's the watchword!'"

Vincent felt no need for tobacco and alcohol, declaring "me dad's had my share." Girls were anathema, especially his sister, Teresa. He was a good-looking boy and his father's roguishness was there in his face. It was an irresistible combination but Vincent neither knew nor cared that many a Bromley girl pined for him. Even now he was oblivious to the admiration of the girls from the "clay end" and the decorating shops as they laughed their way to the promenade.

The youths emerged there just a few paces south of the Waxworks. They were held up as an elegant landau, its top neatly folded down, clopped by. Its single passenger was Miss Lucy Pelham. Unbelievably, her haughty stare had even managed to penetrate the dark glasses she wore. Vincent Hogan shook his head despairingly:

"She always looks as if she's sittin' on summat with a jagged edge."

As they crossed the broad road towards the rails by the Central Pier, a question came from behind them:

"In a hurry, aren't yer?"

It was Vera Foskett.

Philip nodded courteously and Vincent grinned:

"Hallo, Vera – got your bathing suit?"

She ignored the question and the three of them looked down at the sands below. Vincent was thoughtful: he sensed Vera had decided Philip was her Blackpool outing and she meant to hang on to him.

This was confirmed when, for the next few minutes Vera talked, not too artfully, about the things she wanted to see and do......"Pleasure Beach", "Tower Ballroom", "Up to the top of the Tower", "Stanley Park", were the main items emerging from her fast breaths and excited chatter. Vincent knew what he had to do. As if on impulse he took hold of Vera's hand, whisked her back across the pavement and into the opening doors of an arriving tram.

"Right......I'll show you the town, Vera! Be seein' you, Phil!"

Open-mouthed, Philip watched them go. As the tram doors closed Vincent seemed to be pointing to the far side of the promenade. The tram moved off. Standing beside the red telephone kiosks on the other side of the road was Frances Bromley.

She smiled and began to cross. He walked towards the edge of the pavement, watching out for her safety. In her light dress she looked cool and lovely. His mouth tightened - it was there again – that conflation of joy and apprehension.

"Good morning."

"Hallo Philip. I saw you standing here but didn't like to intrude."

He laughed:

"It looks like Vincent's taken care of that."

Conscious of the press of people now building up, they began to walk, rather aimlessly. When they reached a spot where the crowd was thinner she moved over to the rail:

"It's a lovely day."

"Yes. Blackpool's not my cup of tea but it looks well enough on days like this."

"I'm told the people at the 'Grange' always choose to come here every year by something like ninety votes out of every hundred."

"Oh, it's perfect for a day trip."

He laughed again but then fell silent, conscious of the exquisite importance of her presence but still on his guard.

"Is the other young man your friend?"

"Yes.....in a way. We live next to the Hogans in Hanover Street. Vincent is Billy's younger son."

"Oh yes....I've seen him from time to time at the works. I thought there was something familiar about him."

"Once seen, never forgotten."

He was encouraged by her amusement.

"He's a very steady lad. Mad keen on sport. I don't think he's going to follow in his father's footsteps."

"Oh, poor Mr Hogan – everybody has a dig at him."

"Not without reason."

"No, be fair. I travelled up here with him. He insisted on looking after me and did it very well."

"I beg your pardon?"

"I came up on the bus with him."

"On the 'Miscellaneous' bus? You?"

"Yes, except that it's not called the 'Miscellaneous' bus now, nor will it be in the future, but that's another story." Completely puzzled, he had come to a halt:

"Look, suppose we stop awhile, in this shelter. I'm walking your feet off and I've no idea where we are going." Alone in the shelter they sat facing the sea. She looked at him:

"Did you say he was Mr Hogan's younger son?"

"Yes, he had another son, Terence. He was killed in the war."

Frances looked bewildered:

"Oh no. You know, he made a point of telling me how sorry he was about my brothers. And he never mentioned his own loss. I'm really upset by that."

She hesitated:

"Do you know how it happened?"

He was also silent for a second or so, then decided she had not asked the question with guile.

"It was in Egypt. I was never there but I believe one of the drawbacks of fighting in the desert was you were never totally sure of where you were or where you were going. There aren't any signs – just hundreds of miles of trackless waste.

So, as a guide, our drivers used to try to pick up marks of British tyre tracks. Jerry knew about this so he'd strip a tyre from one of our abandoned vehicles and roll it through the sand – right up to where he'd sown Teller mines. The Teller is about as big as a dinner-plate and powerful enough to blow a truck to smithereens. Terry was in a truck full of Catholics going to Sunday Mass. They picked up a tyre track, ran over a mine and the lot of 'em were killed."

He saw the tears fill her eyes and decided to change the topic quickly. As a tram arrived on the other side of the shelter, he stood up.

"This tram goes to Cleveleys. It's quite nice there and not as crowded. Would you like to see it?"

"Fine."

He held out his hand and helped her board the tram.

Chapter Ten
Sea, Sand and Smoke

At Sankey's Restaurant they had waited for Frances Bromley until twenty minutes past one. Due to Frances' absence the caption on the "Miscellaneous" table had not been removed. The men there were becoming restless. And, in addition to his concerns for Frances' well-being, Fred Knapper was wrestling with his hunger. Miss Lucy Pelham on "The Office" table had fired upwards of twenty "tut-tuts" into the air, each one dripping with meaning.

Only Billy Hogan seemed reasonably at ease, having learned from Vincent of his ploy to ensure Frances and Philip were together. So, because it was not in him to be less than enterprising he had began to apply himself to the delights of the feast. The cheese and biscuits had been thoughtfully laid and the cheese had taken an instant liking to Billy for it had already made three trips to his mouth.

The various potting-shop tables had noted Philip's absence long since and their glee had extended as far as the "Biscuit Warehouse" table, so their end of the room was in a constant buzz. The decorators lent the Restaurant a county town coffee shop atmosphere, and not being completely conversant with the emerging reason for Frances' absence as well as being near to The Office table they took the opportunity to appraise Lucy Pelham and her lovelies most carefully. What a wonderful way to pass the time.

"The Office" table itself suffered the whole situation with its hallmark air of polite boredom. It switched on its mechanical smile whenever the other tables looked at it, except for the "Miscellaneous" table, of course, whose wicked grin it completely ignored.

"Hey up, it's Little Sir Echo," breathed "Ludo" Dunning. Jack Dempster got up, and barely audibly, raised the curtain on the proceedings. Despite the impatient rattle of crockery from the kitchens, the tables heard: "Miss Frances Bromley......unavoidably delayed.....wonderful to see you here....enjoy yourselves.....buses leave at 7p.m." The tables decided to give him a thin clap.

Lucy Pelham was like a cat on hot bricks. She trusted her suspicion and with good reason, it being such a practised thing: the Bromley girl's absence was the harbinger of momentous happenings. She just knew it and it was confirmed for her in the next instant when Vera Foskett, on the "Flat Shop" table, caught her eye. Vera looked towards the empty chair of Frances Bromley, then towards the empty chair of Philip Hughes, then back to Frances' chair and finally to Lucy. How beautifully expressed thought Lucy, then looked quickly away from the blonde girl so as not to endanger the Pelham barricade of breeding. Ah! Millicent

Dean, the silliest of her temple slaves had been right after all... she had seen Frances Bromley with the platemaker at a Gilbert and Sullivan concert. Well, well!....the outcome would surely be interesting! The whole jumped-up edifice might come crashing down!

When the meal was well under way, the annual ceremony was being performed on the "Miscellaneous" table. Each year it was the custom of Sankey's to provide for "Grange" Pottery a main course centred on roast beef and Yorkshire pudding. It was also the custom for the roast beef to gird itself in a fair amount of fat. Most of the "tickle-stomached" Bromley employees left the fat alone. It was the unswerving practice for any plate containing unwanted fat to make its way to the "Miscellaneous" table and the great girth of Fred Knapper. Cecil Durber, "Ludo" Dunning and Billy Hogan were among the shepherds who guided the lines of happy plates towards the smiling boilerman.

As is typical, each waitress had charge of one table and hence a given number of plates. At each Bromley visit the waitresses, who usually glided along in their orderliness, became a frenzied mob hunting down their quota of plates. Exhausted they would finally present themselves to Fred Knapper. He then looked at their black-and whiteness in ecstasy, explaining through a full mouth that:

"Fat......greases the lungs and sticks to the ribs!"

Admiring agreement rose from his legionaries and his pipe would look up from the table, smiling smokily. Never did any master know so much about everything.

When Frances and Philip had reached Cleveleys they had lunched in a little Victoria Road café which sported many crests and coats-of-arms. They had just started the meal when Frances suddenly remembered her commitment to the Sankey's lunch, and the welcoming speech. She was alarmed and nothing Philip said helped to lighten her gloom. Finally she murmured:

"I'm sorry. I'm ruining your meal – do forgive me."

They left the café and walked to the sea front which by now was crowded with children, parents and donkeys, thanks to the sun. They turned left and walked down the promenade, with Frances gloomily preoccupied: it was an appalling oversight and she could judge her father's reaction very clearly.

"Is it so bad? It's just one of those things, surely(?)"

"No, it really bothers me. I came to enjoy the trip but principally I'm here to stand in for my father."

"Then it's my fault. I whisked you away. Tell him that please, and let him take it out on me if he has to...."

She shook her head dismissively and walked on slowly, threading her hand into his arm. He indicated a stretch of sand free of people and pebbles.

"The sun's really warm now. Would you like to sit for a while?"

In a minute or two he had persuaded her to sit on an empty bench. He sat a little distance away supporting himself on his elbow.

She looked at him:

"It's difficult for you to understand perhaps, but my father sets a lot of store by what I promised to do today. He'll want a full report of what I said and how it was received. It's extremely important to him that I make good at this job. He was like that with my brothers and it's easy to see why now, with me, he's even more concerned."

Philip looked out to sea, shading his eyes from the sun. He said quietly:

"You say what's important to him. What's important to you, Frances?"

She was surprised by the question but glad that, for the very first time, he had spoken her name. Yet she was unsure how to answer. He continued:

"O.K. Your father has big responsibilities, but is it so terrible that you missed the lunch? How much harder do you have to work?....as it is you're in at the 'Grange' all the hours that God sends."

His comment stirred a number of thoughts but still she felt unable to speak.

"Don't think this question is out of place, but I'd like you to be frank....are you worried because you are with me instead of at the Restaurant?"

She could not look at him and as she lowered her head her beautiful hair fell over her face.

He sighed and gazed out to sea again. Then he turned to her and said quietly:

"Look – I don't like to see you upset like this. Let me go to see your father and explain everything....."

She looked up, alarmed:

"Oh no, no...."

"Mm. I think that answers my question."

Neither of them spoke for a long time, though she was glad for his tranquil reaction to her oversight because it steadied her. Then she decided that a complete change of subject was the way forward.

"You know, I'm disappointed in you."

"Why?"

"The other day, when I fell, you were very kind. Thank you for taking me to the lodge by the way. Then you disappeared and since then you seem to have been avoiding me. Why is that?"

"I left the lodge because your father ordered me out of the lodge."

She was bewildered and embarrassed:

"I didn't realise.....I suppose I was still muzzy..."

"I think you were, and in one way that was no bad thing....because you evidently didn't hear my reply."

She looked at him, saying nothing though obviously disconcerted. He decided it was time to be frank. Each time they met brought on mixed feelings: the joy of being with her then the sinking sensation that, once again, she might probe into the Burma campaign and her brother's death. Also, the undercurrent stemming from her father's attitude towards him added to his uncertainty.

"Frances, apart from the fact that we've worked together closely over these last weeks, why do you want my company?"

He had half expected her to be coy but she did not hesitate:

"Because I like being with you."

"Well that's fine, because I like being with you but I don't want to cause trouble for you and you must realise that your father doesn't like me at all. Now as far as I'm concerned that's his problem but it could become your problem. I hope you understand what I'm saying."

She nodded her head.

"Do you think we should carry on seeing each other?"

Again she nodded and he smiled tenderly:

"Well I would like that too but you have to understand that I want to see you because I like you. It has nothing to do with who you are and whether or not you're well off. I'm Phil Hughes....I'm a platemaker...the people picking coal on the colliery tips know me, because I've done it myself when we had nothing in the grate. Money doesn't interest me. I've never had much and what I've never had I'll never miss."

He searched her eyes for understanding and saw them moisten but he had to continue:

"There is another thing. Please don't ask me any more

questions about the war. I don't want to talk about it. Lots of men who've come back feel like I do....it's better left alone."

At this, he filled with self-disgust once more. What he had just said was true enough but what it concealed was his ulterior motive in wanting the subject closed. After that, they both stared silently at the sea for a long time. It was Frances who reopened the conversation:

"Tell me about yourself, Philip."

"It's all very commonplace. I went to school, then to "Grange" Pottery. I ran moulds for my mother and when she started casting I went onto her saucer jigger."

"Why did your mother leave?"

"Health – silicosis."

She stirred uneasily:

"I'm very sorry."

"Anyway, I was called up when the war started and when I got back I started making six-inch flat and coupes. After a few weeks Jack Dempster put the lines in I'm making now."

"Tell me about the rest of your family."

"I was an only child, so there are just the two of us."

Frances hesitated:

"What about your father?"

"Dead. We lost him while I was still at school."

"Oh Philip, I'm sorry."

"No need to be. It happened quite a while ago so we're more than used to it by now."

"Was he ill very long?"

"No...he was killed. He worked in the pit and a roof came in on him."

"I can't say how...."

"Look, don't fash yourself. As I say it was a long time ago and this is beginning to sound like a sob story."

"Not at all....you were merely answering my question, and I had no idea...."

Now she remembered the snatch of conversation between Philip and Billy Hogan outside the fitting shop. Billy had said something like: "how can you help, out o' your bit o' pocket brass?" Her curiosity outweighed her discretion and prompted her to say:

"Obviously it could never make up for your father but at least you'd know that you were both financially provided for....."

If he felt the question out of place he concealed it. He was quite dispassionate:

"Well no, it didn't happen like that. It's a long story but the big thing was he pulled out a roof support without putting in a temporary one to take the strain and that's against the book, so there was no compensation."

"Why did he do that?"

"I don't know – I wouldn't blame him. When the inquest was reported in the paper it said he was one of the most experienced men in the pit."

Intently, he stared out to sea again before turning towards her. His voice was low:

"I was just a kid yet I do know that he never talked about his work as a rule. I think that's a miners' thing. But in the week leading up to the accident he said there was a lot of water in the place where they were and there was a big sandstone intrusion towering over them. He didn't say as much but he was obviously worried that water seepage might bring down the sandstone. Some of the men who worked with him said he was trying to get the job done quicker because of the danger. He asked them to leave the place while he took out the post. There was a great rumble, they heard him cry out and when they came back around the corner he was under the sandstone."

She was too stunned to speak for a moment or so. Then she was quite intense:

"But if the conditions weren't safe anyway, how could it

be his own fault?"

"Well, in legal language, that's 'the moot point'. The inquest 'found against him', as they say."

Frances persisted:

"But why didn't his union take the matter up?"

He laughed without mirth:

"We did have a visit from a union man. It was to tell us that as there was no longer a miner in the house, our concessionary coal would have to be stopped."

"What's concessionary coal?"

"Well, when we ordered a full load of unbagged coal – about a ton – which is a helluva a lot when you've got to get it off the street and into the coalhouse – we'd get a bit of discount."

"I can't believe anyone could be so callous."

"Oh – it's true enough. He could see my mother was still grieving and I got so angry with him I ordered him out of the house,"

He laughed:

"I was eight at the time. I shudder to think what would've happened of I'd been nine. It wasn't his fault though – he was just a mouthpiece for the coal owners though why the union should've done their dirty work is beyond me."

"Oh Philip – what a dreadful experience. I really am sorr...."

"Hey – can we get off this subject? We weren't the first sad case in Burslem and we won't be the last. My dad used to say the price of coal was high because its cost was mens' lives. It's just hard lincs."

Again they were silent for a while and it was Frances' turn to look out to sea.

Eventually, she turned to him:

"What do you intend to do for the future?"

He thought:

"Try and stay in work, I suppose – making big flat."

"Anything else?"

He grinned: "Filing tools."

He sensed she thought the flippancy out of place:

"Well I don't know. I suppose if I wanted to move up the ladder the next job would be potter's manager."

"Why not works manager?"

"Why not build a potbank of my own?"

"No, don't laugh at me. You'd make a good potters' manager, I can vouch for that as your first pupil. And I think you're capable of going further."

"I'm not sure I want to be a manager. In any case, there's more to it than knowing how to make plates and file tools. You have to know all about clay bodies, mixings and firing. And look at how scientific it's becoming. It's no longer a pinch o' this and a bucket o' that. It's all about controls isn't it? When Vin Hogan came out of the Army he worked at Moreton's for a few weeks an' reckoned there was a swarm of B.Scs around the place."

"Does that worry you?" After all, I'm a B.Sc and look what a hash I've made of being a platemaker."

"You got on well. It's a pity you stopped because I was thinking of telling Jack Dempster you were ready to go onto piece work."

She laughed but only momentarily:

"We're on the wrong track again. What you said just now I agree with – improved technical control is a 'must' but you're intelligent, Philip. You'd cope with all the technical problems once you'd mastered the basics. What about the ceramics courses at Stoke Tech?"

"What about them?"

"They're among the best in the world. Staffordshire has that reputation. Highly qualified people come there from other countries for the tuition."

"Exactly. Highly qualified people. I'm from an elementary school."

"I see you very much as your own man but about this you're quite hard to follow. You were saying just now you want to stay in work. Taking qualifications is the best insurance. You'd learn about the manufacture of everything from fine china to bricks and tiles."

She looked at him and smiled. This stirred his feelings for her.

"Are you afraid to fail, Philip?"

"No, I don't think so.....but I believe in being realistic and only fighting battles I can win."

"Mm. Once I disappointed one of my tutors by taking the easier option in answering a question. He said he'd given me a mediocre mark because I'd seemed afraid to fail. He taught me that disappointment can be valuable because it makes us work harder at seeing and understanding things and learning how to express things. I don't think you would fail the course but even if you did at first, even the disappointment would be providing you with the education you say you lack. So the maxim should be – have a go!"

"I think it would all be way over my head."

"Nonsense. Look, you have the greatest asset a pottery manager can have, there in your fingers. Ask yourself, if you spoke to any of the potters about the quality of their work and I did the same, who do you think they'd be likely to listen to? Your interest in the industry is as plain as a pike staff and you're bright. A little sacrifice of your leisure time for a few years would see you well qualified."

"Is this a leg pull?"

She looked at him earnestly:

"It's nothing of the kind – and if you'll enrol I'll give you all the help I can with the chemistry and other technical subjects."

"Would you do that?"

"I would."

She glimpsed an eager expression that gladdened her, then

it vanished:

"Won't that make things.....difficult for you?", he wondered.

She looked at him, quizzically.

"I mean, how would your father look at it?"

"You know he might not like it at first, but that would change."

"We're from different worlds. You aren't doing yourself any favours as it is, spending time with me. Supposing I enrolled for this course and people saw us together all the time – they'd ask me what it was all about and I'd say you were helping me out with my homework – that'd get a laugh wouldn't it?"

"Does it matter what people would say? We would know and understand exactly what it was all about, wouldn't we?"

"It wouldn't matter to me at all, but you stand to lose a lot."

"I stand to lose nothing. You've helped me to make a good start at the 'Grange'. Now there's an opportunity for you to make progress and for me to help. It would be unreasonable not to help because I live at Porthill and you live in Burslem."

He scooped up a handful of sand. It took a few seconds to run through the slits between his fingers.

"You make it sound very simple."

"If there are problems they can be solved and when you start passing examinations that will silence the gossips."

"Don't you think it needs more thought - from both of us?"

"Hardly....but take as long as you like to think about it. My offer to help will still be open."

"I'd like to stew over it tomorrow. If you were free on Monday evening perhaps we could talk about it again."

"Yes......that would be all right, I think."

"Well if you've no objection we could meet at Trubshawe Cross and see where our legs take us."

She laughed:

"Do you know, I'm ashamed to say this - I've never been to Westport Lake."

"Well that's easily remedied. If we met on the canal bridge opposite Trubshawe Cross at 7 o'clock, you could leave your car in Bridgewater Street and pick it up later."

Presently they walked back into Victoria Road and had an evening meal before returning to the coach park in Blackpool. On the tram Philip suggested it might be sensible if he joined her on the former "Miscellaneous" bus for the return journey. Frances laughed and nodded.

Now it was goodbye to sea and sand and back to the smoke. In the coach-park the buses coughed and tried to shake off their torpor. A day in the sun had sapped their energy and soon they would have to leave the broad Fylde behind and be running south-east in search of Burslem. Only the former "Miscellaneous" bus was not caught up in the preparations. It dozed contentedly.

Inside "The Office" bus concern was creeping into the constant speculation. "Where could she be?" "Could anything have happened to her?" "Ought the police to be notified?" Miss Lucy Pelham meditated, formed theories, dismissed them and was speculating further when the cry went up: "She's here!"

All the buses, except the former "Miscellaneous" bus of course, turned to look. Then they rubbed their eyes and looked again – it was Miss Frances and she was with one of the platemakers! – Philip Hughes! Yes, Philip Hughes! Wide-eyed with the wonder of it, the buses gibbered madly as the young couple, smiling at each other, made for the former "Miscellaneous" bus.

Inside "The Office" bus Miss Pelham would not look. This dared anyone to look. The juniors squirmed, then one of them was immature enough to giggle. This set them all giggling. Jack Dempster left "The Office" bus and followed Frances who explained she would be returning on the bus that had brought her to Blackpool. He smiled his understanding and returned to "The Office" bus which then left in a huff.

The snake of buses left Blackpool gabbling to each other that not only was Frances Bromley a good potter, she was mashing a good potter! The "Flat Shop" bus was saying "He's a bit of a lad all right!" though the sentiment was hardly unanimous as Vera Foskett looked decidedly uncomfortable.

When the former "Miscellaneous" bus did get started, the annual concert began. Nearly all the occupants were expected to do a "turn". Ludo Dunning was the master of ceremonies and first he exhorted every one to "give order please!" Among the long list of contributions culled from the Victorian Music Hall, the Jazz Age and the Swing Era were "The Legion of the Lost", "Jealousy" and "Run, rabbit, run", this last provided with just the right touch of levity by Fred Knapper. All musical contributions were accompanied by saggar maker Levi Scarrat on the harmonica. He blew and sucked for almost three hours with no slackening of pace or volume – a prodigious feat.

Not that the programme was entirely musical. Recalling the days of the British Raj and his own service on the North West Frontier, Ludo Dunning himself, gave an insightful rendering of "The Green Eye of the Little Yellow God", a poem by J. Milton Hayes. Other poems followed though not of such epic quality. There were two sequences of funny stories though by unspoken agreement and acknowledging Miss Frances' presence, neither of these was of the "colourful kind".

The passengers felt their return journey was nearing its end when the bus left the smooth roads of Cheshire for the peaks and troughs of the roads in Staffordshire. With the vast stocks of Parker's Pale Ale now virtually depleted, the concert was moving to its climax. This was the moment Fred Knapper had awaited. He was highly conversant with the whole canon of sentimental songs which paid homage to motherhood. He was also discriminant, prizing one song above all others and beyond that, the one performer who did it justice. Because Billy Hogan's voice was a slender, silver thing, Levi Scarratt toned down the harmonica to a perfect accompaniment. And so the elf began to weave his spell:

"Just an ole fashioned ladee....with ole fashioned ways
An' a smile that says welcome to youuuuuu
Just an ole fashioned bedside where she kneels and prays,
When the toil of a long day is throu..ou..ou..ou.....gh"

It was already too much for Fred Knapper. Between the great, shuddering sobs that caused his roly-polyness to reverberate, came the blubbering exclamations:

"The lad's an arteest. An arteest!"

Of course Billy could easily have been carried away with the brilliance of his own effort but he was objective at all times – which was why in spite of the abandoned cheering and the delirious applause, he kept his head. When he was handing the bumper collection to the driver, as the bus came to a halt, he saw two half-crowns jump from his voluminous new cap and make for his pocket. He did nothing to stop them. Call these his "performance fees" if you will.

Burslem was mightily relieved to see the former "Miscellaneous" bus. For some time the bottle ovens had been peering anxiously westward. Now it was here, cats howled, dogs barked, lights went on, windows flew up and heads came out. St. John's Square and the whole of Dale Hall would have been ashamed to slumber. Even the town police force seemed to have added to its numbers. Now the prodigals had returned to the hollow, all was well.

Philip walked Frances to her car:

"I hope you enjoyed your day, Frances."

Even in the acrid gloom he could see her wondrous eyes were shining:

"Philip, it's been wonderful – thank you for everything. I hope I'll be able to drive, my sides are still aching!"

They confirmed the proposed meeting on Monday evening and he waved her goodbye.

Outside his own home Billy Hogan was finding it hard to open his front door. Every time he tried to insert the key the door seemed to move away. Trying at the same time to hold on to several large sticks of lettered rock compounded his problem.

Philip arrived on the scene and volunteered his services while Billy gripped the rock. When the door was opened Billy proudly displayed the rock including, improbably, one packet in which the confection had been fashioned into the shape of a bunch of radishes:

"I bought this for the missus," said Billy proudly.

"Great. And what sort of a time have you had, Mr Hogan?"

"O.K....O.K....quiet, yer know....but I enjoyed it. G'night me ole Phil."

And with that he fell into his premises.

Frances had returned to Porthill. The hall was dark and she decided to leave it so. A few more steps and she might have gained the stairs; then came the roaring voice:

"Frances!"

"Yes?"

"Come in here!"

As she went towards it she saw the door to the library/drawing room had been left slightly ajar. She did not close it behind her.

"Good evening, Dadder. I didn't know you would wait up."

He faced her, in tailored vest and shirt sleeves, holding a whisky tumbler. His eyes seemed to have depressed themselves into ovals. The potters knew this look, so did his daughter. He pointed to one of the fireside chairs. Not altogether passively, she sat down.

He moved to close the door. Still at the door but without closing it he looked across at her:

"Can you explain yourself?"

"What do I have to explain?"

This brought him striding towards her:

"Are you trying to be clever?"

The question and her father's tone reminded her of that day in the biscuit warehouse when he had confronted Philip. She shuffled forward in the chair joining her hands at the edge of her lap:

"You make me feel I'm about to be gobbled up. Why?"

She emphasised her next question:

"What is the matter?"

Breathing heavily, he came forward towards her. She pulled back from the whisky on his breath.

"I'm in no mood for joking and I won't stand for you acting half-soaked!"

An instant's pause, then he cracked his next enquiry like a whip:

"What did you do in Blackpool today?"

"I'm sorry but it's a case of what I didn't do. I'm afraid I didn't make the speech. Really, I mean I didn't attend the luncheon at all."

'It's a case of what you didn't do and what you did do isn't it?"

Now he was leaning over her. She felt mentally as well as physically confined.

"And tell me, what did you do?"

"I went to Cleveleys."

"Yes – to Cleveleys with that know-all platemaker, the chap in the biscuit-warehouse that day."

He saw that he had surprised his daughter and, to turn it to full advantage, he continued quickly:

"What the hell were you playing at? Did the sea air affect you?"

"There's no need for your attitude, Dadder. I'm grateful to Philip Hughes. He's helped me a lot."

"What's that got to do with it? Did he do it free of charge? Wouldn't you have got the same help from any other potter?"

She could no longer bear the way he hovered over her, oppressively. So she slithered out of the chair and they turned to face each other:

"Possibly, but....."

He interrupted her quickly, pointing in emphasis:

"I told Jack Dempster I wasn't keen on you working with the chap. I've never liked him – not since he snubbed me when I asked him about Peter's death. 'course Dempster can't see further than the end of his nose."

He breathed:

"Do you know what you've done? Probably more damage than you realise, to yourself, to me and the firm. I know his type – he'll boast about 'his conquest' on and off the 'Grange'. You'll come in for a lot of grinning small-talk from the men and evil speculation from the women."

Frances was baffled:

"But....you're completely wrong about this! We haven't done anything shameful! We came back to the bus park together quite openly. This morning we went to Cleveleys. I forgot the time. So we had lunch and tea together and between times talked – mostly about his career."

"His career? His career?"

It was Ewart Bromley's turn to be stumped. France came back strongly:

"He's a good potter – and he's also got a good head on his shoulders. I think that, underneath, he's anxious to improve himself. I mentioned the courses at Stoke Tech. He's thinking about them. I've worked with him and learned something about him. You seem to think he's got a lot of loud-mouthed companions. I don't think that's true. I think he is serious minded and solitary. All he needs is a little encouragement. I'm sure he'll get somewhere."

"'Serious minded and solitary'....you talk like 'Peg's Paper'. All he's interested in is the fact that you don't exactly look like Nanny Goon and sooner or later you'll come into money."

Now Frances was infuriated:

"That's an appalling thing to say! You're so unjust!"

"All right! All right ! ... but you make me wonder whether you've been learning the trade or reading his soul."

"I just became interested in....."

"Well you can just stop being interested! You think he'll make something of himself and you've given him some advice. Now – leave it at that."

Sighing he sat down, looked at his watch and began to talk quietly:

"I've laid great stress on what I call the 'dividing line'. Why? Do you think I want you to live according to my plan; do you think I want to dominate you? You mustn't be familiar with people who work for you. I've drummed that into you and what do you do at the first opportunity? You go gadding about Blackpool with one of them, in the full sight of everybody."

Then his voice began to rise again:

"Haven't you any sense?" Can't you find any young men of your own type to interest yourself in?"

"I've tried to explain to you, it's nothing like that."

"Friendships between youngsters are nothing else but that, or if they don't start like that, they finish up like that. And even if there's nothing serious in it, don't you know that's how people are going to see it? You can't stop 'em thinking the way they do about such things?"

"I don't care what people think."

Now he lost control:

"Well I damn' well do! Where the family and the firm are concerned I do! My grandfather took butter pots on a pack horse to the markets of Yorkshire in all weathers. That's how the firm started and my father and I have sweated ourselves to develop it and it won't cave in for want of protection. You take too much for granted my lady but we've had to make it what it is and it's not going to be thrown away because you've interested yourself in a fella from the flat-shop!"

"I've not interested myself in him."

"I'm not the fool that you think. The pair of you have started something and it's clouding your reason."

She brushed her hair back in exasperation:

"Dadder – this is being blown up out of all proportion. I spent a few hours with a quiet, steady young man. How can that possibly jeopardise the future of the 'Grange'?"

Ewart Bromley's fists tightened and he was red with fury:

"Frances, I've told you not to be clever with me. Your carry-on is beyond me and I'm bitterly disappointed. I've been patient because you're a girl. If this had been one of your brothers – hell fire – I'd have gone for him. You try to make it strange but you know very well what I'm driving at when I talk about the firm. I just hope that the chin-wagging and head-nodding you'll have to put up with about today will just show you how right I am."

"I don't feel the least bit disloyal about the matter and that's the absolute truth but I do feel sorry about missing the lunch and not making the speech. Philip Hughes hasn't got any lurking desires about the 'Grange' - I'm sure of that. He's not had it easy and I'd feel miserably self-centred if I didn't give him a word of advice."

"You're sure he's decent and sincere but when you've been in business a bit longer you'll find that people aren't always what they seem. And what I'm saying is that even if he is all you say he is, it wasn't a discreet thing for you to be with him! Can't you understand that?"

"Please, please don't go on so. I feel basically right about what I did and I'm sorry for what I didn't do. When I try to explain my point of view it sets you off in a tirade. I wonder if you'll excuse me now – it's late."

She crossed the floor to kiss him briefly, then turned towards the door, bidding him goodnight. Ewart opened and closed his hands then grunted self-consciously but Frances was gone.

Having closed her bedroom door, she stood with her back to it. Thought followed thought: how did he know so quickly what had happened in Blackpool? Was someone in the firm determined to make trouble for her? It was amazing. In such a short time how could she have aroused such enmity? Whoever was reporting to her father was certainly making her miserable and frightened.

Later, as her head went to the pillow she had one comforting thought: it had been an enjoyable day and Philip's company had had much to do with this. The truth was her present life provided nothing but tedium. Her days were leaden, except when she was with him. So she would see him on Monday evening, as planned. In time perhaps when he saw she was resolved, her father might view things differently.

In the kitchen below Jack and Mary Ellen Foley sat facing each other. The chauffeur-handyman was grim. He idolised Ewart Bromley, the man whose leadership and courage had brought them safely back from the pit of hell. He and so many others would be lying in the ooze of France and Flanders but for this man. But fate had rewarded his boss with further afflictions. It was determined to rob him of the peace he had earned.

"You know, Mary Ellen, I care for young Frances as if she were one of my own. But the Major's got enough on his plate and if she brings him more trouble she'll have a hard pillow to put her head on. She'll realise that when it's too late."

Despite the hour his wife was still sewing. She did not look up as she said:

"The girl's entitled to a life of her own, potbank or no potbank."

Chapter Eleven

A Clue to Character

The following Monday was unique - all Grange Pottery employees actually looked forward to returning to work. Obviously there was the Works Outing to discuss but it was something beyond that which stirred their excitation. Evidently Miss Frances Bromley and Philip Hughes were courting! The impact on Burslem's socially sanctioned rules of conduct was simply staggering. It would give grist to the grinding out of hundreds of discussions. With sublime anticipation the Grange folk were making for work as fast as their legs would carry them.

By the time that "clocking on" had finished, Lucy Pelham had already held a full Cabinet meeting at which every scrap of information had been weighed, sifted and analysed. Some reports were off the point but at that stage nothing could be disregarded. Miss Pelham delayed the bringing in of a final verdict, preferring to await developments.

One thing was certain, nonetheless: when her decision was reached it would emerge from the most reliable premisses that skilled investigation could make available.

Yet how strange life is, how intriguingly unpredictable! Within the hour something happened that swept aside all the existing ferment about Frances Bromley and instilled in almost every heart a feeling for her so profound it was well beyond affection and bordering on love.

Here is what happened: shortly after her own arrival that morning Frances was returning from the stores where she had collected her clean overall from Florence Birks. She was passing the sliphouse when a chilling sound pierced the great rumbling of its machinery - it was a child screaming.

Fearful as well as horrified she rushed into the sliphouse. What she saw was beyond her worst imaginings. Syd Brammer, a massive man, was about to thrust a wriggling, shrieking little boy into the mouth of a roaring blunger. Within seconds its whirling paddles would pulp the child's body into so much slurry.

Frances launched herself at the man, clawing at his hands and wrists:

"You madman! What are you doing?!"

Completely surprised, Brammer released the child, who fell into a thin pool of slip and scraps. She immediately threw her arms around the boy, lifting him up, cooing to him, stroking his hair and kissing his forehead.

"Well?!"

Brammer's face was a mask of misery. Then his explanations tumbled out:

"Miss - he's in 'ere all the time! He's goin' ter get killed! He sneaks in under the lodge winder so's Ernie Biddulph can't see him! I was trying to frighten him!"

His voice breaking with emotion, the big man went on: "I'd never hurt 'im, Miss. I've got little uns of me own." Frances touched him on the arm - even if she did not approve, she understood. Cradling the boy she took him out of the sliphouse.

Potters crossing the bank stopped in wonder as she carried the child past them. In the lodge a gallery of open mouths watched her take him over the weighbridge and into the streets beyond. Thanks to the soothing murmurs of Frances, the boy had stopped crying though from time to time a great shuddering sob shook his tiny frame.

As she carried him, clearing the dirt and mucus from his face, she suddenly said in pleasant surprise:

"Oh.....I know you, don't I shy-boy?___you're Tyrone!" This was the little boy who had narrowly escaped injury from her father's car on her first morning at the pottery.

"Now, because you've been such a brave boy I think we should find something nice for you. Would you like that?"

They made for a small grocery shop nearby. The shopkeeper and his wife did not respond to Frances' "good morning". They could only gape at the beautiful woman carrying the filthy child.

"Which sweeties would you like, Tyrone?"

His darting eyes had already taken in everything, from expensive, boxed chocolates to penny chews. But he had not been distracted by the vast colourful display. He thrust a forefinger towards his choice. It was a glass jar amongst the many glass jars above the shopkeeper's head. Still stupefied the shopkeeper showed the jar to the child for confirmation. Tyrone's ecstatic face left no doubt and Frances said:

"May we have a quarter-pound, please?"

Despite his trance the shopkeeper managed to carry the jar to his scales and weigh out the ordered quantity of Old Betty Plant's Mint Humbugs. Then he transferred it from brass pan to paper bag.

"How much, please?", asked Frances.

The man's stupor had not dispersed but his wife rallied sufficiently to advise her. She put the coins on the counter, thanked them both and carried Tyrone from the premises. Even then, all the shopkeeper could do was gaze after them.

With some contrivance Frances took a humbug from the bag and gave it to the boy:

"If I remember, you live in Pleasant Street. Will you show me the way?"

By now Tyrone had a unique knowledge of all streets in the area. He pointed her out of Edward Street, into Pleasant Street, past its junction with Wood Street and up to the house where he lived. Frances knocked on the door. In the meantime, some mystical force seemed to have sucked the neighbours to their front doors.

The woman who answered her knock was the one who had chased Tyrone on that September morning when he had almost fallen under the Bromley Humber. Now she looked pale, unkempt and undernourished. In her arms she cradled a new-born child. Aghast and fearful her eyes questioned Frances, who only moved Tyrone from her left arm to her right in order to relieve the strain and laughed:

"Mrs Carroll? It seems we've both got our hands full!"

The mother's attention switched now to Tyrone. He seemed content. His mastication of a humbug was advanced enough to have fused its black and white stripes into a grey fluid. Some of it was emerging from his mouth in two rivulets making for a rendezvous at the point of his chin.

"May I come in for a moment?"

Veronica Carroll answered the question by stepping aside so that Frances could carry Tyrone over the doorstep. Then she shut the door rapidly so as to occlude the neighbours from further knowledge of the event. As Frances stepped into a dark passage the smell was unmistakable - the place reeked of damp. She entered the living room. There was further evidence of it: wallpaper was peeling away in places and the exposed plaster was riddled with black spores and crusty efflorescence. One of the bare patches featured a child's drawing of an aeroplane, another a wigwam being vacated by a group of figures she took to be Red Indians.

Suddenly, from a pile of old coats beneath the tottery dining table a mongrel, tail-wagging dog came yelping its delight. This brought Tyrone into immediate action:

"Stay, Paddy! Stay!", he gurgled as a fresh surge of grey fluid made for his chin.

"Sh....sh...sh...sh!", hissed the careworn mother, turning to explain to her beautiful visitor:

"Only Mester Carroll's just gone to bed. He's on nights."

The mother motioned Frances, still holding Tyrone, to a fireside chair. For a moment she had to set him down, for she was sinking into a lop-sided position because the springs had gone through the bottom of the chair. Having squirmed her way to tolerable comfort she took back the little boy onto her lap.

Though she was aghast at the squalid, poverty stricken surroundings she tried not to look about. However, she had already noted the naked light bulb dangling from the ceiling, the "tablecloth" which consisted of several pages of the "Sentinel" newspaper and the cheap, cracked crockery. Now another child, perhaps two years older than Tyrone, sidled up to her. The child's eyes never left the toffee bag her brother clutched proudly.

"Hallo... what's your name?" Frances asked.

"Angela"

"Would you like a toffee, Angela?"

The little girl reached out but Tyrone twisted his body away from her so as to protect his prize. Finally he was persuaded to let his sister take a humbug from the bag. It may have been the minty constituent of the humbug which was the cause but Angela began to cough - a rasping, unhealthy cough that shook her body. Despite having to hold her infant, Veronica Carroll reached over and buttoned Angela's worn, undersized cardigan as if this might affect a cure.

Angela's rasping continued and caused Frances to notice how cold the room was. She looked at the low fire in the grate, lifeless, for it contained as much "bass" as coal. "Bass" being the local name for slate, Frances concluded that what the Carrolls were trying to burn were pickings, taken in spite of the colliery security, from some waste tip. As slate often does, some of it suddenly exploded and shot out smoking embers into the room. Veronica tightened the shawl around her tiny one and said defensively:

"The coal we're getting' now isn't a bit o' good."

The woman was racked with tension. Frances felt that she must explain her visit quickly:

"Mrs Carroll, I'm Frances Bromley from the Grange Pottery."

"Yes, I know who you are, Miss Frances. I used to work there."

"Oh, really. Doing what?'

"I cleaned the offices. But I had to give up because my mother's very ill and she can't see to the kids anymore."

Frances followed her eyes and now saw for the first time a small shrine to the Virgin Mary fixed to the wall in the distant, dark corner of the room. A votive light in a little blue container guttered before a picture of Our Lady. It obviously burned there for Veronica's mother, affirming the woman's illness was hardly temporary.

"I'm very sorry, Mrs Carroll."

The woman was trying hard not to break down and nodded, imperceptibly almost. Frances decided it was best to move on:

"Actually, I'm here about Tyrone. You see, he's giving us a bit of a problem but I thought that, together, we might be able to solve it. Unfortunately, he's been wandering into the firm. As you know, there is a lot of dangerous machinery in there. I was wondering how we might curb his curiosity before there is a serious accident."

Veronica began to cry. Frances leaned towards her and touched her arm tenderly:

"Please don't be upset, Mrs Carroll. I'm sure there's nothing here we can't deal with."

"But I don't know what to do with him, Miss! He's one body's work....into everything an' he's always having to be brought back from somewhere. The Police 'ave been here two or three times. I've got the others ter see to an' I can't put up with it any more."

"It must be very difficult for you. I can see your problem - but we must try to keep him away from danger. Do you have other children besides these two and baby?"

"Two more - boys - Michael and Luke."

"And how old are they?"

"Michael is six and Luke's seven."

"Ah. So they're both at school(?)"

"Yes."

"I was just thinking - perhaps they could be told to keep an eye on him in case he gets hurt. If they've started school, I suppose they could at least be asked to do it in the holidays and at weekends."

Veronica nodded uncertainly.

"Well, I'd better be going.I do have to get back...."

She turned Tyrone on her knee so that he faced her:

"But before I do young man, I want you to listen to me... no more running away and getting into danger. Mummy must always know where you are. Do you understand, Tyrone?"

Wide eyed but silent, the boy looked at her.

His mother called "Answer the lady!" with that end-of-tether belligerence towards him Frances remembered from the day he was almost run down by her father's car.

Tyrone nodded and Frances gave him a hug. Then she turned to Veronica:

"May I hold, baby - just for a second, Mrs Carroll?" She snuggled the infant to her and looked wonderingly into its eyes:

"It's a...."

"A little boy.....Joseph."

"Oh, he's gorgeous....look at those eyes. And a wonderful name.....Joseph's a much neglected saint."

Mrs Carroll was weeping again as Frances reluctantly handed back the baby.

"Mrs Carroll... .are you... .all right after the baby?"

"Oh yes...it isn't that....I was just touched by you, Miss. I think you're an angel from Heaven."

At the door, the pale, tired woman tumbled out her thanks while Tyrone and Angela, each fortified with a new humbug, waved their confident goodbyes. The little dog had followed all of them to the door and added his own high-noted farewell.

At the Grange Pottery, expectant, they awaited her return. They watched her pass the lodge window. They had always felt respect and affection for her but now this verged on wonder. To their wonderment at her beauty was added a wonder at her character. They had observed and assessed her and found her to be "genuine". It was their ultimate badge of honour.

It fell to Cecil Durber, the saggar maker's bottom knocker to sum up the general mood: though allegedly "puddled", his insight surprised his colleagues yet again when he murmured:

"Her really cares about us!"

For her part Frances was still sick at heart about the appalling poverty of the Carrolls. She was also angry - angry because, for greed of gain, some human beings suffered other human beings to live in such squalidly unhealthy conditions. She had now had confirmation at first hand of what she had always suspected: that if "capitalism" and the "free market" were left to themselves, the less fortunate would never be cared for. Her father and others like him were deceiving themselves into thinking that by providing jobs and paying taxes on their profits they were discharging their obligation to the community. Why should the rewards for risk-taking be so disproportionate when the master was risking only money while the potter and the miner were risking their lives? She saw now how capitalism could be, and indeed often was, savage.

This defining experience had filled her with self-hate. She hated herself for the fine clothes she wore, for the car she possessed all to herself, for the pampered and cosseted life she lived at Bradwell Grange. Yet it is of consequence to note that her reaction to the plight of the penniless Carrolls was not grounded in politics, about which she knew little and cared less, but in her religious faith, which was intensely personal and deeply felt.

To amplify this, it is important to establish that Frances Bromley was matroclinous, which is to say that she was more like her mother than her father. She had inherited her tender concern for the poor from the former Alice McLaren who was a devout Christian. Alice's marriage to Ewart Bromley had been a "mixed" affair. Ewart was nominally an Anglican, though in the daylight hours at least he behaved more like an atheist. Even so he had, for the sake of his deep love for Alice been married in the Roman Catholic Church.

In doing this he had given a solemn understaking to allow Alice the freedom to practice her religion and to arrange for any children of the marriage to be reared in the Catholic faith. Though he had remained impervious to the appeal of that faith he had carried out his undertaking with complete integrity. In fact, though he had never entered the church premises himself after his wedding, Frances remembered how she and her brothers never failed to be prompt for Mass, thanks to her father's solicitude and energy.

Because Frances' formation derived from Alice's example her Christianity went far beyond the accidentals of faith, far beyond the candles and incense, hymns and prayers, verses and responses. The core of her faith was the obligation to act as a Christian, in loving God and her neighbour as herself. Christ had been poor. He had always been concerned for the poor. People who were poor and vulnerable had a special place in the teaching of her faith, expressed as a 'preferential option for the poor.'

What she had seen in the Carroll household assaulted her moral instincts. So now she began to feel that as long as life's rewards were so disproportionate every morsel she ate and every penny she spent was at the expense of people such as the Carrolls. It disgusted her to think that, however unwittingly, she had become an agent of the exploitation she despised.

That evening she was driving down Dale Hall to meet Philip, as arranged, in Longport. The memory of the Carrolls would not leave her. Then suddenly she realised how she might help to curb Tyrone's wanderings. If he had toys to play with perhaps they would help satisfy his boundless curiosity. Her friend Gwen Dempster was a teacher. She would advise on what to buy for a boy of four and a girl of six. And she would take advice, perhaps from their housekeeper, Mrs Foley, on where suitable clothing could be purchased for them both, not forgetting baby Joseph. How to present these gifts without offending the Carrolls' dignity was a bridge she would cross in due time.

She parked her car in Bridgewater Street. As she got

out of it she noticed a woman with two children just ahead of her.

"Sally....(?)"

Sally Gratton turned. Her waxen face trembled with tension and embarrassment.

"Oh.....hallo, duck......Miss Frances. I.....it's nice now isn't it?"

The poor woman was plainly put out.

"Yes, it's a fine evening. Are you out for a walk, like me?"

Tears formed in Sally's eyes and, not trusting herself to speak, she merely nodded. Frances looked down at the smaller child:

"And what's your name?"

The girl looked up. She liked the pretty lady whose hand was being held out to her. She put her dimpled fist around Frances' hand, which was cool and slim, and announced her name was "Maureen".

"That's a very pretty name for a very pretty girl."

Maureen was excited. The lady was like the princess in her storybook so she carried the lady's finger and hand and arm for that matter around the back of her head and onto her neck where it rested among the curls.

"My name is Denise," said the other child who, anxious for attention, had thrust herself forward. Little Maureen looked ruefully from behind her sister anxious not to be forgotten. To reassure her, Frances tightened her grip on the toddler while her other arm went around Denise. She failed to see that by now Sally Gratton was incredibly nervous.

"You're both very good, Denise, to bring Mummy out for a walk tonight."

"We're not goin' for a walk, we're going' to Auntie Florrie's."

As if to deter further conversation Sally put her arm across the girl's chest:

"Ssh. Denise."

Further explanations had to be stifled.

"Denise, what about some chocolate for Maureen and yourself?"

The girl began to jump up and down at Frances' suggestion. Not to be overlooked the little one began to jump too. When she had the silver coins Denise skipped away to a nearby shop dragging a stumbling Maureen with her.

"Be careful!", called the pale, worried Sally, but they were gone.

It was obvious that she hadn't the slightest idea what more to say. Frances, however, was anxious to take up the conversation:

"How old are they?"

"Denise is six and Maureen's almost three."

"Well they're a credit to you, but how do you manage to mother them so well on top of all you do at the 'Grange'?" The tower's face twisted with emotion. Frances watched her tenderly:

"Sally, what's the matter? Are you feeling run down?" Silent at first, Sally suddenly spoke quickly to ward off the tears:

"It's nothing really, Miss Frances. Probably just a bit tired. I was coming down here to see Auntie Florrie, my mother's sister. The girls call her 'Auntie' as well. You know who I mean......Mrs Birks from the greenhouse."

"Mrs Birks! Imagine that. I'd no idea she was your aunt," Frances laughed.

"Well, if you're feeling under the weather, she'll be just the cure." Again, she explored Sally's eyes:

"Tell me, truthfully, is there anything I can do to help you?"

"It's nothing, Miss - please don't think about it."

Her moist, grateful eyes belied the assurance.

The women looked along the street. At its far end a bent, pinafored woman was waiting expectantly. It was Florence Birks, scourge of bad potters, queen of clay-state quality. At this point the children were returning from the shop showing off their purchases.

The old woman was making her way along the street. When she recognised Frances Bromley she stopped suddenly:

"Well! I just don't believe it!"

"Hallo, Mrs Birks. I was just talking to Sally and meeting these lovely children."

By now Sally was clearly on edge:

"We mustn't keep you any longer, Miss Frances."

Florence Birks intervened:

"No, an' she won't think much of me either, standing 'ere in me pinner."

The garment was a bright, flowered thing.

"I'll go home and get my pinny if it means I'll be accepted," smiled Frances. Florence was still overcome:

"I've just made a pot of tea. Would you like to come and join us?"

"I'd love to, Mrs Birks but I'd arranged to meet someone. I think I'm overdue now. Thanks anyway....perhaps the next time I'm down here...."

"It's alright, Miss....but you're welcome at any time. Well, we'd better get on I suppose."

"Yes....goodnight then, Mrs Birks. Goodnight, Sally... take care. Goodnight you two.. .look after Mummy."

Sally was relieved but trying not to show it. Then the women and children chorused their goodbyes as Frances turned away. At the end of Bridgewater Street she looked back and waved. When she was out of sight the woman looked knowingly at each other and shepherded the children towards Florence's cottage.

Frances had turned right out of Bridgewater Street and

continued up to Trubshawe Cross. Then she crossed the road, which was always busy even in those far off times. As Philip had advised she walked past the old warehouse building and made for the humpbacked bridge over the Trent and Mersey canal. Reaching it she looked along the canal to the west. At a quay a few yards distant a barge of the Mersey Weaver company was discharging china clay - the men worked like beavers. Rush, rush, such was life in the busy Potteries these days, she thought. The bottle oven of a teapot manufacturer about a hundred yards behind her was sending off its stinging, early smoke.

It had been a tremendous rush. Before Number Three biscuit oven was set in they had wanted an extra sixty dozen of eight inch "soups". He had worked over so that they would dry on their moulds overnight and be ready for Sally Gratton to tow them the next day.

After his meal he had washed in cold water at the slopstone in the back-kitchen. That particular small space served for everything from food preparation to the boiling and "mangling" of the clothes. Patchy affair though it was he had managed a second shave. His mother, Elizabeth Hughes, had watched him thoughtfully. While he was completing his preparations she had gone to buy the "Evening Sentinel", He always read the "Sentinel" at his evening meal, but tonight he said:

"Not now, Ma......thanks"

This had launched her on a number of questions. Where was he off to?....."oh, just out" (that hadn't got her very far). Was Vin Hogan going along?...... "No."

Supposing Vin Hogan called, what time must she say he'd be back?....he didn't know and, in any case, Vin Hogan wouldn't call. Then, quite gratuitously, he gave her a vital clue....could he have another clean shirt?! To put the matter beyond doubt he was reaching for his new sports jacket .... on a weekday!

He must have seen her gaping still as he said "so long." Heavily, she sat down to consider. The situation made her breathing even more difficult. Thanks to the silicosis and her curiosity-fuelled tension each breath raised the muscles in her neck. The new sports jacket and flannels! On a Monday night! It couldn't be Emma Foskett's girl. Vera never rated the sports jacket of a weekday. Come to think of it, he'd only worn it once before of a weekday - the night of the "Gilbert and Sullivan". She'd wondered about that. He didn't *like* wearing it of a weekday. He had said himself how Hanover Street gawped at him.

Oh.....she'd be so glad if he found himself a nice girl! Since he'd come back from the war his life was all work and books. He was forever reading books! When he'd done a day's work it didn't seem right. He ought to be having a "bit o' pleasure" 'stead of "books". Perhaps things were looking up. She'd tidy herself up a bit and slip next door -to see if the Hogans knew anything.

By now Philip was well up the slope of Hanover Street. Suddenly a door banged on the opposite side of the street. "Ludo" Dunning was coming over to him:

"Hallo, Phil - how come you're dressed up like a dog's dinner?"

He decided to evade the fireman's question for the man's sly smile denoted he knew the answer already.

"Hallo, Mr Dunning - back to the 'Grange'?"

"Aye-Number One's finishin' ternight"

At that point they saw Fred Knapper hurrying down the street with intense preoccupation. Knowing the reason for this the two smiled at each other. The portly boilerman had seen them by now and was crossing over in order to avoid them. It put their surmise beyond doubt.

"'ow do, Phil," he called, while putting out a deterrent arm to the fireman:

"Dunner stop us, Lewdo."

"No fear, lad.....wheert off to?"

"Lyndhurst Street"

He must certainly not be delayed. Lyndhurst Street was some distance away and first he had to go to his home in Enoch Street to collect his bucket and shovel before doubling back to Lyndhurst. Any delay and the deposit of horse manure reported to be lying there would certainly be scooped up by some other allotment holder.

Over the years Fred had put into place an intelligence service. It comprised boys and girls from all parts of Burslem. The task of the service was to report any deposits of manure and for this the alert member would be rewarded with a small bag of Mint Imperials. At the peak of the intelligence service's performance it is said that the Mint Imperials manufacturer had moved to double-shift working so as to cope with the demand from Fred. It is a nice story but probably exaggerated.

Before World War Two horse manure was not hard to come by. Bread, milk, fish and vegetables were delivered door to door by horse drawn vehicles. The breweries had magnificent teams of animals and the police service was not found wanting either. Horses still took away a significant volume of output from the potbank to railhead and canal quay.

Since the War motor traction had made tremendous inroads into the distribution of goods. Consequently, horse manure acquired a scarcity value. No opportunity must be missed. Hence Fred's hurry on this evening, rooted in his tendency to become most exercised over any new find thanks to his strategy in constructing his intelligence network.

Fred, as may be gathered, was a dedicated horticulturist. He was devoted to a small allotment termed his "gardeen". A significant feature of the "gardeen" was his "hut". The "hut" was no more than a cupboard door with sides and a back hammered on to it. The truth was his landlord, Mr Claude Roebuck, had no idea that the cupboard door had ever left Enoch Street for Fred was always careful to pay his rent in the parlour. The walls of the "hut" had been fashioned from wooden boxes supplied by the obliging retailers in exchange for produce from the allotment. So the logotypes of internationally known brands such as "Lux Soap" and "Jeyes Fluid" gave its side and rear elevations a distinctive identity.

To sit in the "hut" was one of Fred's great pleasures. To do this he had first to empty it of its contents for the "hut" would not contain fleshy Fred in addition to the spade, the fork, the hoe, the rake, the riddle, the seed potatoes and the many pots he used for cuttings. Accordingly it had become one of the sights of Burslem to see Fred open the cupboard door take out all of its contents and sit on an upturned bucket in the "hut". In the fullness of time he would emerge from the "hut" and return all its treasures, which explains why a sharp downpour always guaranteed a sizeable audience.

The other distinguishing characteristic of Fred's blessed plot was the manure heap. Even in those times of increasing scarcity it was always of formidable dimensions for his inalienable rule was never to use manure that was not "well rotteed". Clearly this imposed collateral stockholding pressure.

He had a philosophical turn of mind and stood in awe of Nature. It was the miracle worker. Keep with it and you were all right. Go against it and you courted calamity. Didn't the colliery owners and the master potters tip their slag, slate, broken saggars, worn-out moulds and rejected pots all over Burslem's once-green acres disfiguring them, all but destroying them? And didn't Nature struggle to heal the land by sending up blades of covering grass whenever there was opportunity, so as to blot out the eyesores?

It was the same in the allotment. The reason why, year by year, Fred produced potatoes, carrots, parsnips, cabbage, lettuce, rhubarb, antirrhinums and sweet peas which confounded the Allotment Holders' Association was, quite simply, because he stayed close to Nature.

Years of sitting in the hut formulating his theories marked Fred out as an environmentalist well ahead of his time. You could get from the good earth no more than you put into it. It would not be rushed with "chemeecs", as he described the liquids, powders and granules inorganic chemistry had produced for lesser gardeners. The answer was natural products - things known to man throughout the ages. Animal manure was at the head of the list of miracle materials and the noble horse headed the list of its providers. It was when North Stafforshire's newly mechanising farmers had found difficulty in meeting Fred's demands that he had been forced to create his intelligence network.

Now obviously, residents in the streets adjacent to his allotment had not accepted its atmosphere without dissent. The reeking phenomenon had produced arguments, pleas and threats. There had been talk of "petitions". Terms like "police" and "medical officer of health" had permeated the universe of discourse. None of this had any effect, for Fred's unchanging advice to complainants was:

"If you take big sniffs it 'll go quicker!"

No doubt memories of these interchanges emerged as Philip Hughes and "Ludo" Dunning watched Fred waddle away. Then suddenly Ludo turned to Philip with great seriousness:

"Yer know, when yer think about eet, Phil - life's

complicated. But one thing's certain - yer've got ter think about what yer goeen ter do. Think 'ard - aye - eet stands ter sense - but once yer've decided yer mustner 'esitate - do eet!"

So there it was, levity to gravity in a trice with every phrase emphasised by a matey dig in the ribs.

The pair nodded to each other and went their separate ways. In minutes Philip was hurrying through Dale Hall. He knew exactly what Ludo's words had meant and to what problem they had been directed. He found himself in complete agreement. Nothing would stop him trying to win Frances Bromley. When the word about news of her visit to the Carrolls had surged through the potbank he knew he would never be daunted by the difficulties. Even if he failed to win her it would have been an honour to have tried. She was the most remarkable, wonderful creature on God's earth and right now he hoped, desperately, she was still waiting for him in Longport.

Chapter Twelve
A Walk to the Little Wood

She was standing by the bridge. He hurried towards her. By now they had worked together for a number of months. On three or four occasions he had seen her socially. Therefore, her impact on him should have lessened somewhat – he should have adjusted to it. Not so: even now the sight of her made him catch his breath.

"Good evening, Philip."

"Hallo, I hope you haven't been waiting long."

"No, just a few minutes. As a matter of fact, one or two boys were swimming in the canal, but they seem to have disappeared."

He feigned surprise, deciding not to explain. When the

local boys took to the "cut" they were not normally to be looked on by the opposite sex. Bathing trunks were a sign of wealth.

"I don't think this is much of an evening to offer you, Frances."

"How do you mean?"

"Well, just walking."

"Of course it is. On a warm evening, what could be better? I asked to see Westport Lake and that's where we're going – aren't we?"

"See the woods over there?"

She followed his pointing finger, beyond Longport's gasometers, towards the skyline, looking up to the wooded rim of the hollow.

"You see Bradwell Wood?......I believe you live on the other side of it."

She nodded.

"We're going to walk along this towpath here, away from Longport, keeping parallel to that ridge. Within a couple of hundred yards we'll have come to Westport Lake, over to the left.

When you've seen the Lake I thought we'd continue along the towpath for half a mile or so. Turning left again we get to Ravensdale. That's an interesting place – a little village where the bargees live – y'know, the folks who work on the canal.

After Ravensdale we cross the railway line that runs from London to Crewe and Manchester. Eventually, we'll come to the Little Wood. I thought we might take a breather there then you can see how you feel. We can either go on further or return the way we've come. Whatever we do it'll be a good walk if you feel up to it."

"Fine. I thought we were just going to walk around the Lake. Your idea sounds more interesting."

"Well, let's see how it goes."

Westport Lake is one of man's inadvertent creations and they came to it within minutes. As they stood on the grassy slope that flanks the canal and runs down to the Lake, Frances smiled in wonder:

"Oh, Philip – it's really lovely. Fancy something like this being here, among all this smoke and dirt."

"Yes. It's not a natural lake though. I believe it was formed due to subsidence early this century. As you know all this area has been heavily mined. What we're looking at are probably flooded pit shafts dating from the eighteen nineties. Apparently, before the Lake formed, the land was used as a practice pitch by Port Vale Football Club."

She watched people young and old walking around the shores of the lake. Small children played at the water's edge and anglers sat patiently, hoping for some reward.

" A lot of people seem to enjoy it."

"Mm – but it can be dangerous. There are plenty of folk about now but even so those children shouldn't be mucking about down there at the edge of the water. A short way out it's really deep."

He pointed to a spot some seventy yards to the right of where they stood.

"That's where I almost drowned when I was little."

She turned to him:

"How?"

"It was winter. The lake had been frozen over but the ice was starting to break up. I was acting the goat, jumping around on the big chunks of ice when the one I was standing on split in two. I went under the water and felt myself going down into deeper and deeper water. Luckily, a bigger boy, Billy Pemberton, was standing at the edge. He just walked straight into the lake, reached under and yanked me out by the scruff of the neck!"

She curled her arm around his:

"How old were you then?"

"Seven."

He turned and pointed to a canal bridge further to the west:

"See the slope running up from the bridge?"

"Yes."

"On the other side of that slope, next to a big marl hole, there's a tile works. I stood there for two hours at the firemouth of one of the kilns. I daren't go home until I'd dried off."

She shook her head, then came her aggressive concern:

"How could you have been so stupid?"

He laughed:

"You can't grow up around here without getting yourself into a few fixes."

He suggested they might sit for a while and she agreed. They watched in the evening sunshine as the little ones played below them. Older people walking by gave them a friendly nod or smiled "hallo". The pair looked happy with each other so it was natural to assume they were "cooters" - the local term for all engaged in steady courtship. Potters have an understanding attitude to "cooters".

On an embankment to the left of them a little train puffed down the mineral line towards Longbridge Hayes. He explained that beyond an archway which pierced the embankment was the "Little Lake". He indicated a large vertical baulk of timber near the archway and told her it was one of several still in position around Westport Lake itself. During the war steel cables ran from these timbers to a raft in the middle of the lake. The idea was to deter the Germans from landing there. Now the baulk near the archway was being used for peaceful purposes: it had recently supported a twenty two pound pike. A proud angler had been photographed alongside it by the "Evening Sentinel".

She turned to him:

"What have you been doing since Saturday?"

"Thinking about what we discussed – the ceramics course."

"What did you decide?"

"I'd like to try it."

"I'm glad. The courses start in September, so after the Stoke Wakes holiday you'd better be prepared for long nights of hard work. Does that bother you?"

"No. I've got an instinctive distrust of whatever comes easy – it usually isn't worth much. Now I've made my mind up, I'll see it through."

"I know! – I'll give you Peter's notes! He'd practically finished the First Year before he was called up. They'll help you get to grips with things."

It was an unpleasant surprise. He hoped another round of questions on how her brother died was not about to start. Every day he wrestled with this memory, determined never to utter another word about it. It was far from easy, for he had cared deeply for Peter Bromley – loved him like a brother – and the words, gestures, and the smile especially, of his sister, meant that Peter would never be dead as long as she was alive.

Frances sensed his tension and thought she understood. Affectionately, she tugged at his arm:

"Oh....it'll be really good to see you making progress."

"But....."

"Yes.....go on."

"I'm bothered in case it causes trouble for you."

She didn't answer, but gazed at the smoke from the chemical works tucked into the bottom fold of Bradwell Wood. She remarked again on the insistent pressure of industry even in this idyllic spot, adding finally:

"But it will all change soon"

He was puzzled:

"How?"

"Well, as you learn when you start the course, the bottle ovens will be on the way out. It takes three days to fire up an earthenware biscuit oven. When the new continuous tunnel ovens arrive they'll be doing that firing in twenty nine hours. Some of the really revolutionary glost kilns will be completing their cycles in five."

He was not impressed:

"The bottle ovens will go altogether?"

"Yes. The big firms will replace them first then the others will follow suit. Beresfords are building one now. But think of the benefits it'll bring to Burslem, as well as the manufacturing advantages. There's no smoke with electricity and gas. That means a cleaner atmosphere. Every week will be like Wakes week. Think what that will mean for the women on washdays."

He seemed uncertain:

"I suppose I ought to be enthusiastic but, you know, when I was overseas, thinking about home, I could always see our bottle-oven landscape. The bottle ovens are what make the Potteries different from everywhere else. When they've gone how will you know you're in the Potteries?"

She was smiling at his homely philosophy. He continued:

"You'll probably tell me it's progress and it has to come but will it make us any happier – trying to do things quicker than we did 'em yesterday? Happiness is elusive – unattainable if you like. When you've got to where you want to be you're still not satisfied and you want to push on to somewhere else. I know you speak of the benefits but there's more than one crank like me who'll be upset about losing the bottle-ovens. We're a crossomical lot!"

"A what?", she laughed.

"Crossomical –a good Potteries word – it means we don't always think or do what we're expected to...."

She was still laughing:

"I don't think that's the outlook for someone who'll be a pottery manager one day?"

"But what about jobs?.....think of the skills we'll lose when all we'll do is push buttons."

"Well, these things have a way of sorting themselves out."

"That's a real boss's answer!", he grinned.

She looked across the Lake then said suddenly:

"Sally Gratton, Philip – do you know her very well?"

"Ever since we went to school together. Why do you ask?"

"I met her when I was parking the car tonight. She tried not to show it but seemed upset. I've always liked her. She's so friendly, quiet and hardworking – and she has two lovely children".

He seemed so intense she stopped suddenly –

"Is anything the matter?"

"Was she all right? Did she.........look O.K.?"

"Well no, she was upset and embarrassed."

"I've known her for years, when her family was so poor she took her blind father around the pubs in Burslem to beg. How's that for a start in life? But there wasn't a nicer girl anywhere. She was the sort of girl with - well, something about her if you know what I mean. Blokes aren't always careful what they say – even around girls – but with her it was different – they'd always watch their language, an' no dirty jokes."

Frances watched him closely as he went on:

"When she was small she had rheumatic fever. It left her with a weak heart. That's why she's always as pale as death. To top it all, she lost both parents while we were still schooling. Mrs Birks – her aunt – had no children of her own and she reared her to be one of the nicest girls in the town. Lots of good lads would've married her. Instead, she meets this chap, Gratton. If he does two days' work a week that'll stretch it. He's a sick man – tireditis and blanket fever. To rear the children she has to work herself – and you saw how she dresses them, didn't you?"

Frances was sad and bewildered. He was still intent on his explanation:

"Frankly she's not strong enough to work, but she sticks to it. That's why the placers and the other towers carry out her work for her to the stillage, if she'll let them. She waits on that lout of hers hand and foot – in fact it wouldn't surprise me if she blacks his boots when he's getting ready for the pub. Then, when he comes back from his diversions, as a reward, he'll give her a good hiding."

"I beg your pardon."

"He beats her up. What she could do with now is about three months' rest and somebody to look after her, not the other way 'round."

"Poor Sally, it's unbelievable. I can see now why Mrs Birks was so concerned."

"Was she with Sally?"

"She walked up just before I left them."

"Florrie has a heart of gold. Sally'll be desperate when..... if anything happens to her. She scares the wits out of that Joe Gratton I can tell you."

It was reassuring to Frances to hear Florence Birks' name in this context but now Philip's words were so low she could barely hear them:

"I've known her come to work with the bruises he's given her and say something stupid about walking into a door."

"Why does she stay with him?"

He shrugged:

"Why does any woman stay with a man like that? You tell me. I suppose it's for the children's sake and so she won't be a burden to anybody else."

When she asked what she could do to help Sally, Philip

was animated:

"Nothing. And I mean that Frances. You can't put the world right. People appreciate what you did about the "Miscellaneous" bus and the way you visited the Carrolls, but there comes a time when the kissing's got to stop."

She was surprised and hurt:

"What do you mean? I don't do things for effect!"

"I know that. We all know that. In fact, folks think you're so special they wonder where you've sprung from. But Burslem's full of sad cases and if you start getting involved – really involved – you'll wear yourself out. You've got a job to do. That means 'carrying your cup level' as we say around here. If a doctor got emotional about the state some of his patients are in, he'd never do his job."

"I'm not being emotional. I just care about people. It's the way I'm made. You're beginning to sound like my father."

"I hope not!"

To soften the comment, Philip began to laugh but now they were awkward with each other so he said:

"It's getting nippy, perhaps we ought to be stirring."

They walked along the canal for a quarter of a mile or so, passing moored barges which had been discharging china clay into open arks on the wharves. He pointed:

"We move left here."

They climbed a small bank which brought them onto a metalled road. She gazed at the Boat House Inn, and he explained its apt name, for this was where the bargees replaced the sweat of their heavy labours. The couple turned away from it and were soon walking past the twin rows of houses to their right. The rows faced each other across an intervening space of more than a hundred yards. This was mostly taken up by a football pitch which seemed to be the dominant element in the scene, with the houses incidental to it. The goal posts were among the most significant in the

Potteries for there were nets attached to them and even on this June evening the pitch was as assiduously marked as if an F.A. Cup Final were to be played on it the very next day.

"Every time I come down here my inferiority complex starts niggling me."

"Why, what place is it?"

He looked, unbelieving:

"This is Ravensdale!"

She was no wiser then remembered his recent words:

"Did you say the barge people live here?"

"Yes, plus a few colliers and potters. They're a tough lot and sport's a religion with them. They usually win a fair few of the competitions they enter and scouts from the professional clubs are always sniffing around. They've got a half-back Crewe Alex are interested in right now."

"But why is it so quiet?"

"It's the Knock-Out!"

She was still puzzled.

"They've got a cricket team too, you see. Tonight they've gone up to Leek to play in the Knock-Out competition."

"Does everyone go?"

"Men, women and children, the aged and the dying. Remember, this is one of the few places where people still make their own amusement. There isn't a cinema here and very few wireless sets I would think. Tunstall's just up the lane there. It's got three cinemas but to these people it's a foreign land. But they're happy and they look after one another so nobody ever goes short. The only thing that upsets them is if the footballers lose a match. Then the whole place goes into mourning.

They're a tough lot as I say. I'm told that one Saturday afternoon during the War Jerry visited the place. He was after either the chemical works over there, or the railway line, perhaps both. He dropped a land-mine and it landed right here, between the houses. You could have got three

P.M.T. double-decker buses in the hole apparently. On the Sunday morning people trekked down here from all over to see the devastation. The locals were getting on with things as if nothing had happened.

You were talking about change earlier on. If change is coming I suppose this'll be one of the last industrial villages."

Frances looked across to Bradwell Wood. On the ridge, just beyond where the trees ended was her own home. Here, in Ravensdale, more of the district's proud poor scratched a living. Such a short distance – but it separated entirely different worlds.

They walked on, past the houses and over the railway bridge. Entering the Little Wood she was pleasantly surprised. The rich variety of its trees and wild flowers, and its mellifluous bird song, provided a completely different ambience to the one they had just left.

"If you're tired we can rest a little if you like."
He pointed to a grassy clearing among the trees. It rose from the side of the path taking them through the Wood.

She nodded and they sat but she frowned as she saw, just beyond the fringes of this sylvan setting, a sprawling colliery slag-heap. It stood like a big angry boil on the tender, charming face of the land. The headstocks and winding gear of the pit seemed utterly alien to its blue-sky backdrop. She sighed:

"Goodness –look at that!"

"Mm. That's Parkhouse. I remember it from the early thirties. Dad and I used to come up here to pick coal from that slag heap. We've been chased through this wood by the bobbies many a time."

"How old were you then?"

"Eleven. I remember I was just sitting my scholarship for the grammar school. They were terrible times. Dad was out of work. He went down to Cannock on the South Staffs coalfield then to Kent - wherever it was rumoured there were jobs. In the end, he got next to nothing so he came back – and like thousands of others he did what he could to keep us fed, so I had to help him."

She was saddened:

"When I hear you talk like this I just don't know what to say to you."

He laughed:

"You don't have to say anything. We survived didn't we? We're here to tell the tale. Some of the things we got up to were funny. We used to scour these colliery tips and derelict buildings for any waste wood we could find. Then we'd haul it home, chop it up and sell it in bundles for lighting fires. We had our regular customers – they'd tell us what good value we gave in our bundles of sticks!"

He was laughing again and warming to his theme:

"D'you know we even picked blackberries out of these woods and tried to make jam to sell! That was an ill-starred venture. The stuff tasted horrible. Anyway, things started picking up a bit but my Dad was killed soon after they'd started setting on again at the pit. Then the War came."

They were quiet together then and she felt close to him. Presently he said:

"It's funny isn't it – the last time we stopped for a chat we were looking at the sands and the sea. Now it's the Parkhouse muck-heap. Still, in six weeks' time it'll be Stoke Wakes and I'll be off again to the wide open spaces."

"Oh. Are you going back there for your holiday?"

"No. I'm doing some walking in the Lake District."

"Really?"

Immediately she regretted her reaction not so much for the utterance but for the tone of it. She could see he was hurt.

"Yes. I'm sorry if it seems strange. Because I work in the top flat shop some might think my holidays ought to consist of ozone avec fish and chips and "Kiss Me Quick" hats. But

Wordsworth's on my side – he once wrote that the Lakes shouldn't be just for the moneyed few. He was the first one to speak of the Lake District as a national park.....a park for the nation. Perhaps before long that'll become official."

She put her hand onto his arm:

"Philip, don't be mad with me. I didn't mean any harm." His anger passed off and he smiled at her:

"I'm sorry Frances, it's just my thin skin. But you see... ...I have to justify my choices to my own people as well as the toffs who'll gawp at me and wonder what I'm doing there. I feel like a pig in the middle. It's the same when I go to a classical concert or eat in a decent restaurant. But, as I say, I'm sorry."

Her hand was still on his arm. He covered it with his own hand and squeezed gently then whispered:

"I know it isn't in your nature to sneer at anybody."

They looked tenderly at each other. He wanted to say more and she wanted him to say more but he drew back from this. For a while neither of them spoke, then he smiled:

"Where are you off to for your holiday?"

"I haven't arranged anything. You see, I think my father will want me to be at the firm when we've closed down – to watch over all the "whys" and the "wherefores" of the big maintenance jobs that get done then. If need be I can fix a holiday in September."

"Frances, you must see to it that you have a break. Soon you'll have worked twelve months 'round so you must be feeling tired. Did you put your feet up yesterday, by the way, or were you down at the firm?"

"I popped down for an hour or two after Mass......about a big, 'rush' order from Canada – the packers were in, seeing to it, because it had to leave today. Gwen Dempster called on me at home in the afternoon. I don't suppose you know Mr Dempster's daughter. We're good friends. She had tea with us."

"All the same, it's no fun for you is it?" Some people think that bosses have soft jobs but look at you – at Cleveleys worrying about a speech you didn't make, going down to the potbank on a Sunday, going to work in Stoke Wakes Week to see to factory repairs. When you are away from it do you ever manage to get it out of your head?"

"Not really – but that's because management has particular obligations. When you're a manager you'll find that out. You know the cliché – noblesse oblige. So prepare yourself."

She sighed, then went on:

"My father has had the burden to carry on his own. Now it's up to me to help. If I can deal with the day-to-day worries he'll find more time to plan ahead. Right now we've got full order books but that won't last. And all the technical changes I mentioned mean extensive capital investment. Some people say the days of the family firm are numbered, but Dadder will never accept that. If the "Grange" passed out of the family's hands it'd break his heart."

He watched her. She seemed sad and vulnerable. It reinforced her beauty. He wanted to reach out and hold her. Suddenly she looked up:

"Philip, why do you want to go to the packing house to see your work before it's despatched?"

It was on the tip of his tongue to say: "your father's stopped that now" but he managed to stifle it. With difficulty, he tried to explain:

"When I see the marvellous things the paintresses and the other decorators do to the ware it makes me want to send them good stuff to work on. And I like to look at the labels on the crates as well – Jelmoli of Zurich; Ahlens of Stockholm; A l'Innovation of Brussels; Hertie of Cologne; Galeries Lafayette of Paris; La Rinascente, Milan; The Hudson Bay Company of Canada, Macy's of New York; Nieman Marcus of Dallas; Katzenellenbogen, Cape Town; Heath of Sydney and

Mclbourne......"

She was astounded and cut in quickly:

"That's incredible! How do you know all that?.....they're all customers of ours.....!"

"I've always known them. Y'see when I was a boy if mother sent me for stamps or a postal order I always went up to the main Post Office in town. I used to stand in the shadows, waiting for the clerks to arrive from the potbanks. About half past four was the best time to see them, sliding their leather pouches across the polished counters. After a bit I found out that these were the shipping documents. The clerks would call out the names of the consignees on their lists while the folk behind the counters checked the bundles of documents. All rush and bustle to catch the evening post."

She waited, expectantly:

"Well......go on."

He shrugged:

"Anyway all those far away places and names'd ring in my head. Some were even more exotic - the Sultanate of Oman, the Hashemite Kingdom of Jordan, Lourenco Marques. I memorised them all and on the way to school I used to repeat them over and over."

Appraisingly she took in every detail of his words and facial expressions then said softly:

"You're a funny lad, Philip Hughes."

She had made no attempt to disguise the warmth in her words and it gladdened him.

"Anyway, it struck me then that in all these glamorous places there were customers for the beautiful things we made here in Burslem....our town. From our town and the rest of the Potteries we were sending treasures for the rich man's table. Like Josiah Wedgwood made the dinner service for Catherine the Great. We were carrying on the tradition, with treasures produced by the skills of our people. And.....

don't be sneeped about this – I used to think what a pitiful recompense they got for their skills."

His voice trailed off, but she was persistent:

"Well, go on.....tell me more....."

He studied her, considering:

"When Dad died, I had to leave the grammar school. Funnily enough I didn't mind at the time because I didn't want my mother to have to work like a carthorse just to keep me there. You know, if ever she was waiting for the clay carrier she used to go down to the Sliphouse to fetch the clay herself because time was money. I've seen her struggling up steps with a wad of clay that hung down her front, looped over her shoulder and dangled well down her back. She'd fang hold of a massive wad like that so she wouldn't have to go back again for a while. The way she worked would've killed horses. And at night when I was lying in bed I could hear her fighting for her breath.

I hated that but when I began my apprenticeship I begrudged the way life had robbed me of an education. Probably that's why I do so much reading these days – making up for lost time. Then, funnily enough, I learned to love the work: making something beautiful out of a gob of clay's very satisfying. I know it sounds a bit 'away to the woods', but your work tells you who you are, doesn't it?..... it gives you your status in life."

His simple words were sending her a clear message, for this was the instant she realised how fondly she loved him. Yet it was a clarity that brought confusion with it for she knew that her love would make life complex and difficult. Enthused by his own thoughts he was speaking again:

"Of course if I were a thrower, working at the wheel, that would give me even more satisfaction, perhaps as much as I get from books. Watch a thrower building up beautiful objects from the slurried clay – bowls, vases, jardinières. It's as if the clay already contains the object and the thrower is releasing it. Then it goes over to the turner's lathe. He shapes the ornamental foot of the article. Then he adds the beading, or the claw motifs or the Greek keys – as like as not with the tools he's made and shaped himself. Whenever I see a potter at his wheel, or listen to the soft sound of the lathe as the turner's foot nurses the treadle I know another elegant object is about to escape from the clay into an admiring world."

"I have to say, I've never looked at it as you do, Philip. You're certainly one with the words. I'm only a poor scientist – I take a more instrumental view of things."

He was still animated by what he wanted to convey to her:

"Oh I know many people – skilled people even, think of it as just a job. But for me, potting's not like that. I mean, don't you love potting for itself? You have to understand the clay so it doesn't resist the dwell of your hands and tools on its texture. I think it's a great calling. Of course, I don't know why they say we work on a 'potbank' Is it a bank from which you draw pots instead of money? My favourite teacher, old James Clare, used to say the word came from 'banc' or bench. I prefer to think that because 'bench' suggests an individual potter at work. And what matters in the end, even in the biggest potbank, is what happens at the bench of every individual potter."

While Frances was touched by his eloquence she couldn't help but feel that with the coming of highly geared, automatic ways of production, many of the processes he talked about would become extinct and much of the romance of potting would die. Sad though that was, it didn't matter so much right now, caught up as she was in the pleasure of witnessing his exhilaration as he talked of his trade, the town and its people. His love for all of it was one of her reasons for loving him.

For a while the birdsong was the only sound then

suddenly a cold wind bustled through the wood, searching for them. She shivered and he stood up:

"We'd better be getting a move on, Frances.....we've a lot to see yet."

"Oh, I think not Philip if you don't mind. It's getting late....we ought to be getting back."

She couldn't tell him but the later she returned to Bradwell Grange the less likely it was that she could avoid her father and his questions.

He seemed crestfallen:

"Oh......O.K."

She tried to assuage his disappointment:

"What was it that you wanted me to see?"

"Well, we would carry on through the wood to the Talke Road – the A.34. We'd turn right there, go as far as the crossroads, turn right again, down Peacock's Hay, around by Harecastle Tunnel and back along the canal."

"And how long would that take?"

"About an hour and a half, perhaps a bit more."

"Oh no, Philip, I'd love to –but we ought to be getting back."

"Right – let's make a move then."

As they walked through Ravensdale she was still trying to soften the news that they must return. She put her arm in his:

"I really would like to do the whole walk. Perhaps on another night soon – we could start out earlier."

He was buoyed up by this:

"Fine."

"I think I have read about Harecastle Tunnel."

"Yes....what a job that was! James Brindley was a genius. When he said he was taking the tunnel through Harecastle Hill, they ridiculed him. But he was proved right......what a man!"

"I've seen pictures of it. Tell me, how could the barges

go through when there was no room for the horses? By the look of it there was no towpath."

"It was a legging tunnel."

"What's that?"

"Men had to lie on the barge, on their backs, and walk along the walls of the tunnel so as to move the barge forward."

"That's incredible – people really had to do that for a living?"

"That's right. The tunnel's very nearly a mile and three quarters long and do you know what they got for legging a boat through it?......one shilling and sixpence."

They went back along the canal, making for Packhorse bridge near Trubshawe Cross and talking very little. They were preoccupied, for each was thinking about the other. What is more, their thoughts were identical because a friendship already prized was now becoming precious to them.

For a moment or two they stopped on the bridge. She looked at him:

"You said earlier that I can't put the world right. I think it's important to try. It matters to me. You see it's part of my faith. And my beliefs aren't hot house piety, stained-glass attitudes, all of that. They're about loving your neighbour. I live my life by a few principles that seem to me to be important. 'Loving my neighbour' is one of them. Which means that wherever I see want and unhappiness I've got to try to help. That's all."

"I'm worried because it's an enormous job you seem determined to take on. How far do your responsibilities go, Frances? And it's going to cost you....."

"I'm aware of that, but it doesn't matter – and in any case 'The Lord loves a cheerful giver'", she laughed.

She touched his arm again and looked up at him:

"One of our saints – Lawrence – once said: 'the poor are

the Church's true riches, her true treasure.' If I put it like this, it'll probably sound goody-goody but all true love is sacrificial, Philip. So I must do what I think is right."

"I understand, Frances – perhaps better than you realise. You mustn't wear yourself out, that's all. You've a lot of work to do and plenty of years to do it in. So take it easy, and I'm sorry if I bored you tonight with all my waffle about potting...."

Looking at him even more intently she whispered:

"It wasn't waffle. I could listen to you for hours; you're so genuine about what you think and feel."

Her eyes signalled that she wanted him to kiss her but in case he misunderstood the sign he held back from this. Now both of them were flustered by the moment that had passed and, rushing with embarrassment, they arranged to see each other on the following Thursday for the film of Dicken's "Oliver Twist". Then he took her to her car in Bridgewater Street and before striding out for Dale Hall and home he guided her carefully into the stream of traffic making for Porthill Bank.

What they now held in their hearts for each other can be expressed in two words – it was *ineffable* for it was too powerful to be described and it was *ineluctable* for there was no escape from it for either of them.

It was there. She sensed it as she closed the great door. An intimidating tension had made its way into every nook and cranny of the hall.

She had barely moved towards the staircase when Ewart Bromley bellowed:

"Frances! Come in here!"

As she moved into the library/drawing room he was slipping his watch into his waistcoat pocket. His face was working with fury though as she looked at him she could also see anguish there.

For all that she expected another tirade, she was not afraid. His first words were brief and to the point:

"Did you see that potter again tonight?"

"Yes, Dadder."

"And did I make myself clear about that?"

"You did, and while I fully understood your wishes I think that when you appreciate why I saw him you won't be so upset about it."

He looked at her for a second. Then his tone was menacing for all that it was quiet:

"Please understand this – I am not going to discuss the rights and wrongs of the thing with you. I am not interested in any of his patter if that's what you'd like to convey to me. And I forbid you, if that's the word you force me to use, I forbid you ever to see him or speak to him again. Is that clear?"

"No."

"'No'? 'No'? What the hell do you mean, 'No'?"

He seemed stupefied and was moving towards her. She felt afraid but steadily she said:

"I understand you well enough but I want you to understand that I feel in the right about meeting him and though it hurts me to displease you I can't promise not to see him again."

Amazingly he seemed to take the rebuff in his stride and for a moment was almost conciliatory:

"I'm not stupid. I realise you are only human. Some fly-by-night has paid you attention and you've been young enough and foolish enough to lose your head."

Then his voice rose again, after its familiar pattern:

"But that doesn't mean you're not going to be made

aware of your responsibilities!"

Frances was infuriated –

"Someone's 'paid me attention'! I've 'lost my head'! Is that all you think of me? Do you imagine my friendship with Philip Hughes is some capricious whim?"

She had now sketched in the boundaries of the relationship and because they matched his fears and conceptions he was livid:

"Tell me – if he's so marvellous, who are you comparing him with? What other young men have you known, Frances?"

"None, and I don't intend to know any."

Shaking with anger he thrust out a finger towards her:

"Tomorrow you'll be moved to the Decorating Departments. Let's see if Frank Hollinshead and Connie Mellor can keep a closer eye on you than Dempster did. And that fellow Hughes will be warned that if he ever sees you or speaks to you again he'll be drummed out of the firm. If you ever set yourself up in opposition to me again, you'll regret it as long as you live.!"

Frances began to weep and she called out:

"This is preposterous! I'm not your slave."

Her tears had no effect and to emphasise his next words he smacked his right fist into the open palm of his left hand:

"You will be brought to recognise how important your life's work is and when you're seeing things straight again, you'll thank me for bringing you to your senses."

At that point, he lost control totally and thundered:

"But thank me or not – **things are not going on as they are!**"

He marched out. As the rush of air caused by the slamming door was subsiding she sank down into a fireside chair.

What was to be done?

On the terrace at the rear of the house a tall, broad man was looking through the darkness towards Bradwell Wood. There was just enough light for him to see the treetops outlined against the sky. He stood rigidly opening and closing his fists as though that might give him some relief from his tension.

He had heard the quarrel and had left the house unable to stand its sound and fury. There had been family "spats" before, down the years, but nothing like those of the past few weeks. The sounds that pervaded his memories, by and large, had been the boisterousness and laughter of happy children. But now a man and his daughter, both of whom he cared for deeply, seemed continually in bitter conflict. He sighed deeply. Jack Foley, chauffeur–handyman, was sad and bewildered.

Chapter Thirteen

Storm and Solitude

The following day, Frances was handed into the care of Mr Frank Hollinshead, Sales Director of the Grange Pottery and a distant cousin of Ewart Bromley. It seemed curious that Hollinshead appeared to be subordinate to Jack Dempster who, though General Manager, was not a director. It was also noticeable that when Dempster arrived with Frances at Hollinshead's office he was quite curt and quickly on his way. The reasons for both the organisational anomaly and Dempster's coldness will become clear presently.

When young, Frank Hollinshead had worked at the coal-face in a nearby colliery. He had sustained an injury to his right hip rendering him unfit for further heavy work.

At last the colliery owners settled compensation and Frank decided – no rent-collecting for him and no insurance book: he would invest the sum, by no means princely, in a small car.

He approached Messrs Greatbach and Podmore, Pottery Factors, and they considered. There were no tell-tale blue divots on his skin. In fact, there was little of the collier about him. He seemed well turned out, with a genial, likeable personality and a liking for society generally. (In fact, he had two or three good suits, two or three good stories and a pretty good thirst, so "why not have a go at this selling lark?" he conjectured.)

Like most people, Greatbach and Podmore took to Frank. So they tried him out in Lancashire and Cheshire. In spite of the grim times he deluged them with business. They extended his domain to the whole of the North of England. He overwhelmed them with more business. By then Frank wanted a partnership. They were not enthusiastic and Frank left them to weep at their shrinking turnover.

Ewart Bromley had heard of his cousin's legendary ability. A fellow manufacturer told him Frank could "sell you the shirt off your back and leave you feeling you'd got the better end of the bargain." It was 1929 and orders were as elusive at Bromleys as anywhere. Ewart hired Frank who changed all that, so that when the war loomed only Beresfords were bigger than Bromleys in the whole of Burslem. Hungry potters struggled to join Bromleys who, by now, took only the very best. Ewart Bromley respected a "doer", particularly one with links to the family, however attenuated. So Frank Hollinshead became a director, to the grievous discomfort of loyal, long-serving Jack Dempster.

With the war, however, everything changed for Frank. Now it was H.M. Government and not he who told the "Grange" what to produce. He sat at a desk they found for him trying to fathom the forms. The tension rose between him and the bureaucrats as they returned form after form marked "incomplete" or "unclear" Slowly Frank became bitter and fitful. He was losing the will to work and his dazzling smiles were less in evidence.

When peace came had he gone "on the road" again he might have been saved but, without effort, the firm suddenly found itself with an order book which bulged its covers. The assessment was that the wondrous situation would last for at least three years and possibly five. What is more, HM Government decreed that all decorated ware must be sent overseas. The "Grange" made little that was not decorated and the trickle of white ware issuing from its ovens was borne away in triumph by the traders who had queued for it so patiently in the potbank yard.

So this was how the tide of fortune had retreated from Frank's cause leaving him high and dry on the shingle with his self-confidence in jeopardy. Moreover, while it was bad enough to have nothing to sell there was Lucy Pelham to contend with. He lived in fear of doing her physical injury for she stalked him daily with eyes of squinting vindictiveness. It all stemmed from his artlessness. Some with nothing to do contrive to look hemmed in with work and worry. Frank found this impossible to achieve. In moments of his worst anxiety he would print fat capitals on to the labels the packers fixed to the crates and teachests of Bromley ware. By and large though he looked very much out of touch with work and so fair game for Pelham the avenging snooper.

Firstly, he could not hide his colliery background from her - she had known him since childhood. She had disliked him then, thanks to his popularity with teachers and pupils. She also despised Hilda Elsby, Frank's good friend, for no scholastic problem ever seemed to confound her. When the pair were married and Lucy learned that Frank's salesmanship had taken them to the elegance of Hassam Parade, Wolstanton, her animosity reached new peaks.

Frank Hollinshead then, was another "nobody". Pelham handed this finding down to everyone. Even the newest juniors were instructed to watch his activity, rather his inactivity, and report on it. With whispered confidence she explained to her narks that "in the interests of the firm the matter will be taken further". The more imaginative of them saw Mr Ewart Bromley personally authorising a salary increase "for services rendered" and the gaunt figure of Frank Hollinshead peering through the bars of the Burslem Labour Exchange.

It was little Millicent Dean who had entered Frank's office that day to find him cutting his toenails. Oh happy chance – oh joy – Lucy was so bewildered she had difficulty controlling her bladder. Of course, she must act – and without delay. So the very next time she was in Ewart's presence by the most delicately structured and exquisitely nuanced periphrasis she had described the incident, laughing synthetically at this mild joke being shared between equals. He had knifed her with a look and moved Hollinshead to the safety of the Decorating Departments. Which explains why Frank, a director of the firm, became nominally responsible to Dempster, the General Manager.

"Bloody woman," thought Ewart, "people like Frank build firms and people like her live off them. When business gets tight again we'll need Hollinshead – I'll never let him go, but she can leave tomorrow and take her motley crew with her."

When Jack Dempster had brought Frances to Frank Hollinshead's office he had smiled a warm welcome which she had returned:

"Hallo, Uncle Frank."

His response was:

"If I could bottle that smile of yours Frances, I'd make myself a fortune."

She liked him. He had always behaved impeccably

towards her and she knew him for a thoroughly decent man. Now though it was sad that he had become something of a poseur. His insecurity led him to affect the bearing and presence of some of the industry's artists and designers. His beautifully pressed and tailored suits had given way to flannel trousers and sports jackets with leather elbow patches. He had swopped his shining footwear for comfortable brogues. He sported a bow tie and though his eyes were not known to be defective a pair of half-moon spectacles hung from his neck on a beautiful chain. To complete the illusion he carried a folding, pocket-sized magnifying glass. From time to time he used it to examine pieces of decorated ware though what his peering disclosed was never made apparent. Frances felt that a beard was imminent.

Today though he was proud and enthusiastic:

"Let's get Connie in to have a look at you."

Connie Mellor was a pleasant, motherly woman in her mid-forties. As had earlier generations of her family, she had been with the firm all her working life. Originally a freehand paintress, the quality of her output had been such for Ewart Bromley to decide no-one was better qualified to monitor the experienced workers and develop the trainees. Kind and supportive, she was comfortable in her job as manageress and her charges were comfortable with her.

This morning though she was so overcome by Frances' stunning beauty she actually swallowed in awe:

"Please come with me, Miss Bromley."

Frank saw an opportunity to assuage his own vulnerability:

"Before long, you'll know as much about the job as we do."

If the remark sparked any cynicism in Connie Mellor she kept it concealed.

And so a period began in which, professionally, Frances was fulfilled and happy. The Bromley name had been based on a brilliant array of under-glaze and on-glaze decorations. It was fashioned by a rich variety of skilled people: copper –plate printers, lithographers, free-hand paintresses, banders and liners, aerographers, mottlers and so on and so on. The company offered everything from the venerable willow pattern to contemporary floral patterns, chintzes and art-deco interpretations. As a chemist her knowledge of the effects of kiln temperature and "atmosphere" on the various ceramic colouring oxides – of cobalt, manganese, chrome, iron, vanadium, titanium et cetera made her a valuable addition to the department. From the beginning she was able to play a valuable part in ensuring that the blues, browns, greens, reds, golds and yellows that left the "Grange" were fully in keeping with the firm's institutional "image" for quality. She now began to understand her father's pride in the "Bromley" backstamp. Notwithstanding its modest beginnings the traders of the world scrambled to obtain every piece of Bromley ware leaving Burslem.

However, one other thing of significance was happening on that Thursday in June. When Jack Dempster left Hollinshead's office he went to the top "flat" shop. Stopping at Philip Hughes's jigger he whispered:

"Can you come over to see me at lunchtime?"

When Philip entered The Office he was spotted by Lucy Pelham. She recognised him and thrilled with expectation – he was knocking on Jack Dempster's door! It was no good- she had to know what was going on. Grabbing her pencil and notebook she set off. Dempster would raise no objection to her plan, he was as weak as water. Virtually behind Philip she entered his office. For once, he showed his irritation:

"Miss Pelham?"

"Oh – I understood you had some letters, sir."

"No."

"Oh, I see....that Millicent Dean's a stupid girl!", she lied.... "so there is nothing you need?...."

"No. And would you shut the door behind you please?"

She hovered on the other side of the door for an instant then walked back disconsolate. You couldn't hear a thing.

"Sorry about that, Phil. Sit down for a minute."

In the dark office, Dempster went to his own high stool. As he tidied the papers on his sloping desk he looked like a clerk in a Dickensian counting house. Though there was now no-one to overhear, his tone was confidential:

"Mr Ewart sent for me this morning. It seems he knows you've been seeing Miss Frances. Now I don't say there's anything wrong in that, Phil – she's a beautiful woman and she'd take any man's fancy. But she is the boss's daughter and he doesn't want you to see her anymore."

"What?!"

"Phil – it's none of my business what you do when you're off the firm. But still – if you're seeing his daughter in your off-time and the boss objects, I've got to let you know where you stand."

As Philip struggled to keep his temper, Dempster leaned forward:

"If you do try to see her, your job here's finished. You'd be on a minute's notice."

Philip Hughes was bewildered as well as angry:

"What does Miss Frances think?"

Dempster was alarmed:

"Oh, I haven't asked her about that, lad. It's not my place to ask her."

"Look, doesn't he know we're meeting so's she can help me with some examinations – pottery examinations? I'll see him myself. We're not ashamed of anything....."

"Phil, you've got to let it drop. Mr Ewart says there must be an end to it and that's that. Try to understand."

Knowingly, Philip nodded his head:

"Oh, I think I understand."

He went over to the door. As he was lifting the latch Dempster approached him:

"I'd hate to see you get the sack. If everybody knew their job like you do my own job'd be tea-drinking. Don't feel badly about it."

Then came an unmirthful smile:

"You know, perhaps I shouldn't say this but he may think your relationship could develop beyond examinations but anyway, best forget it. If you want to find yourself a nice young woman any number on this potbank'd be interested, Phil."

The potter gave him a withering look and left. As he walked down the slope between the bottle ovens he was in turmoil:

"Bromley's face'd stand clogging! Who does he think he is? The gall of the man. If he thinks I'll forget Frances - on his orders – he can go and take a bath. I'll be in St. John's Square on Thursday night and we'll see what she's got to say. There are plenty of firms in Burslem where I can make plates. Bromley's isn't the only firm around here. Somebody – probably me - 'll soon be telling him his fortune."

As he was passing the boiler-hole, his thoughts were interrupted by the fog of thick twist in front of him. On the other side of it Fred Knapper was outlined.

"Phil, ast sane Billee 'ogan?"

"I haven't seen him all morning, Mr Knapper."

The boilerman brandished a betting slip:

"Ah'm givin' 'im one last chance."

The days went by very slowly. Would Thursday never come? Philip hoped to catch sight of her at work, maybe exchange a word or two but he was disappointed. According to Billy Hogan's daughter, Teresa, who was by all accounts a proficient freehand paintress, Frances had now been moved to the Decorating Departments. That was logical, he supposed, for she was to learn about all aspects of manufacture before being given a specific role.

As for Ewart Bromley's "warning", well that was totally without impact. The man had grand illusions. Every evening the "Sentinel" carried a mass of advertisements for every trade on a potbank. Even if he was given the "shove" by Bromleys at a minute's notice he could choose to join any firm in Burslem. All its master potters were fiercely busy and equally desperate for skilled folk.

When Thursday did arrive he was pressed, as usual, to produce as much as possible for "urgent orders". By the end of the day, poor Winnie Hood was exhausted. With barely a break she had run back and forth to the dobbin store with the heavy moulds for "big flat". He apologised for his relentless pace but she was not too tired to smile at him. He promised himself he would "look after her" on pay day.

That evening, despite his mother's protestations he skimped his meal then washed, changed and hurried from the house with her long, defeated sigh trailing after him. As he tackled the slope of Hanover Street with long strides he felt exhilarated. How fortunate he was to have found a girl whose looks and ideals were all of a piece. In spite of her father and whether he worked at Bromleys or not he was very much in love with her and would do all he could to get her. In fact, in fairness to Frances perhaps he ought to leave the firm anyway.....and the labour situation was such he could probably take Winnie with him if she chose to come. He smiled as he thought of the extra bonus such a move would bring – to be out of reach of Ewart's klaxon horn diplomacy. What a character!.....crying doom whenever he was crossed. You never knew when you'd got him. Was he really Frances' father? It was a funny world.

Within minutes, breathing heavily, he stood by the lamp-post at the junction of St. John's Square and Queen Street. He had made it – seven o'clock exactly. He looked back in the direction from which he had come – Hanover Street, Bath Street, Furlong Lane. Of course she might choose to walk up Church Street, practically opposite to where he stood. He moved to the left a little and looked down the length of it. There was no sign of her yet.

A bobby on the beat (still in evidence then, an extinct species now) nodded amicably as he passed by. He seemed confident Philip was about his lawful occasions. After ten minutes or so, with no sign of her still, the youth felt awkward. To assuage his discomfort he began to think positively. What were those lines of John Clare that were so fitting:

.... "I never saw so sweet a face
As that I stood before;
My heart has left its dwelling place
And can return no more."

While it summarised his situation perfectly no poet would ever find words suited to the depth of his longing for her. It was so profound, so elemental as to be beyond the reach of words. As for now, he knew Frances wouldn't let him down. There was some reason she was fifteen minutes late. Given her responsibilities – small wonder.

When it was half an hour past the appointed time he imagined passers-by were wondering about him. But that was stupid – how would they know how long he had been there? Even so, he decided to move. He turned, walked past the shops on the nearest side of the Square, pretending to be interested in the window displays. At the top of the Square he crossed over to the far pavement, passing the ornate fountain. Now he had reached the mock-Tudor frontage of the Duke William public house. Feigning interest in the shop windows on that side of the Square he took care to keep the lamp-post in sight. To raise his spirits he repeated John Clare's lines

"I never saw so sweet a face ...."

There was no sign of Frances.

When he had completed two more turns of the Square it was 7.45pm. Never mind, she would come, these things happen. Perhaps if he walked along Queen Street, towards Swan Bank , he could look back from time to time. Soon he was passing the magnificent façade of the Wedgwood Institute. It was held by many to be the architectural pride of Burslem. He looked up at the splendid statue of Josiah on its pedestal above the doorway. It had been fashioned in ceramic and flanked by ten large panels, five on each side of the statue. These depicted the key processes of the pottery industry. The whole terra cotta frontage was a statement in Victorian Gothic of the intriguing possibilities that clay offered to a skilled, imaginative architect. It also paid homage to a poor boy of the town who had found world wide fame and in doing so raised Staffordshire pottery to its undoubted eminence.

He crossed to the opposite pavement and walked back towards the lamp-post. She was nowhere to be seen. Then he thought – perhaps she had misunderstood the arrangement and was waiting in the Market Place! He turned back, crossed Queen Street, ran up Brickhouse Street and through Cocks' Entry, arriving breathless in the Market Place. Apart from the occasional double-decker bus making for Longport it was deserted.

To cover every possibility he walked around the great girth of the Old Town Hall in case she was parked behind it. All the spaces were empty. Disconsolate, with some stirrings of anger he walked back into Queen Street, gazed at the imposing entrance of the School of Art and returned to the corner of St. John's Square.

Throughout his searching, Clare's lines had insinuated themselves into his thoughts so that he was repeating them like a mantra ..... "I never saw so sweet a face".... "I never saw....". Standing by the lamp-post again he realised that she was not coming and wondered why. There must be a good reason. She had been delayed at the firm or worse, her father had learned of the arrangement and had intervened. If so, the sooner they confronted him the better. It would have to be faced - confrontation. Yet there was another possibility – one which he tried to suppress – supposing she had finally realised she would learn no more from him about her brother's death and had given in to her father's ultimatum?

The bobby on the beat had now returned. He smiled knowingly:

"Been stood up?"

A handy retort wouldn't come, Philip could only smile weakly. The policeman hadn't finished:

"You should get yourself somebody reliable, then you won't risk being run in for loiterin'."

Philip chose to walk away along Queen Street. If he returned home he would be deluged with questions so he decided to go to the cinema alone.

"Hurry up!", said the cashier at the Coliseum, "...big picture's just started!"

"Oliver Twist" was obviously an excellent film. It held the packed audience's attention throughout but little of it impinged on him. Why hadn't she kept the appointment? And if she wasn't able to see him why couldn't she have sent word to him? It all seemed so out of character.

In the weeks that followed Philip neither saw nor heard anything of Frances Bromley. She had vanished from his life so completely one might almost have said: "was their friendship a tangible thing or an invention of his wishful imaginings?" Via Teresa Hogan he did then hear that she had settled in her new role in the decorating shops where the workers were full of respect and admiration for her. While he was pleased about this the news only exacerbated his sense of loss and longing.

However while things seemed all smooth and easy gliding on the surface, Lucy Pelham could not rest. She had seen Frances Bromley in the company of the platemaker in Blackpool and Millicent Dean's evidence had affirmed that the liaison had started well before that.

Obviously it was beneath her dignity to speak to the potters themselves but further probing was necessary. Why, for instance, had the platemaker been called to Jack Dempster's office? It was mortifying not to have the full story especially since, in its own deluded way, the whole potbank was giddy about the liaison. For instance, she was appalled to hear that Phyllis Eardley, the jug caster, had described the sordid affair as "a lovely romance".

Then Lucy's ferrets returned one day with an absolute gem of information. The potter seen with Frances at Blackpool had been instructing her for several weeks in he techniques of plate making. So that was it! Miss High and Mighty Bromley had taken up with the first man she had come into contact with and a common potter at that! Hadn't she always said it? Hadn't she always declared that the girl's apparent charm might be a mask for something surprising? And when Millicent Dean reported that a cup sponger felt the friendship was "lovely enough to make you cry", Lucy had almost gagged on a Swinnerton's de luxe vanilla slice.

Now had come this latest move - Frances Bromley to the decorating departments. Had Ewart Bromley taken a hand? It was rumoured so. Pelham was frantic. She simply must *know*! This was when she decided the whole matter was of such scope she must dispense with half-measures or hesitancy. Even personal likes and dislikes had to be forgotten – for the time being anyway. Sometimes it was necessary to do unpalatable things but if one was strong and unerring incredible results could be achieved. One person alone could help her now and though the prospect sickened her there had to be some temporary alliance. Frank Hollinshead must be approached.

The Sales Director *was* approached and when the objective of her conversation became clear to him, all the misery he had endured at her hands seized his heart and mind. When she returned to her own office her head was wringing with his words – a torrent of words that had come direct from the coal-face. He had given her a wealth of information but it was all about herself. A printable phrase she remembered with certainty was "two-faced bitch".

With all the resilience of the skilled trouble-maker she countered that her enquiries were "all for the good of the firm".

"How d'you reckon that up?!", snapped Hollinshead.

"Well – what about when that filthy child wandered on to the firm? Giving it sweets was a guarantee it'd keep coming back!"

A long, exasperated sigh marginally reduced Frank's temperature and pressure:

"You know your trouble, Lucy?.....you're such a serpent you couldn't see a girl that was genuine if she was standing right next to you."

Her hate campaign against him would be intensified in due time – that was certain. For now though she must stay occupied with the Frances Bromley issue. But what was her next move?

Three more weeks and no word from her. Yet Philip was proud and resisted the impulse to make contact. He knew she was fit and well and seemingly enjoying her new role. He began to conclude the friendship was at an end. Her apparent lack of manners was out of character and very hurtful. Surely he deserved some sort of explanation.

His irritation and his longing were bound up together. Nothing eased his anguish. In popular music, for example, there were the "blues" songs. Previously he had no difficulty in damming the river of their banalities. Now they suddenly made sense.

He went for long walks, visited the cinema frequently, read voraciously but nothing would dim his memory of her. Perhaps one good thing came from all this – he would no longer have to lie about her brother's death. For the truth was he had known Peter Bromley well and come to care for him like a brother. Alone in Hanover Street one night he had reached up to his bookshelf and taken down a copy of "The Woodlanders" by Thomas Hardy. It had been loaned to him by Lieutenant Bromley, who had directed him to Marty South's words over the grave of Giles Winterborne at the end of the novel. He had avowed it as one of the most powerful pieces of writing in the language. Shortly after this Peter was dead.

No doubt it was his duty to return the book to Peter's family. After all, it was part of his personal effects. Yet Philip knew he could never do this because it would reopen the whole question of the manner of his death. He would never, ever disclose the nature of that to anyone. Peter Bromley was a sensitive man and a courageous one - a man of ideas and a man of action. A special man. When first he had perceived Philip's interest in higher learning he had grinned affectionately and called him "the solitary autodidact". From that point he had fanned a flame kindled by Philip's schoolmaster, James Clare.

This new time of solitude was, for the young potter, a watershed period in which he reviewed the past and tried to imagine the future. Thoughts of schooldays inevitably brought back memories of Mr Clare. This teacher had opened his eyes to the world of learning and the treasures it contained. He had always stressed that "life's too short for anything but the best": and had been overjoyed when Philip had been successful in the scholarship examination. The scholarship had gained him a place at a leading grammar school which boasted a number of distinguished former pupils.

When Philip's mother was widowed Clare had been heartbroken that Philip was unable to stay at the school. He never forgot his young proselyte and whenever they met his greeting inevitably was: "Hallo, scholarship boy. I hope you've remembered – life's too short for anything but the best." This man's pride in him had nurtured the resolve that he would never let his intellectual curiosity decay. He would attend his own university. He would be his own professor. And until he found the cognate area which offered him special satisfaction he would feast on everything. Moreover it was strange that though his appetite for knowledge seemingly exasperated his mother, he sensed her sorrow that things could not have been different for him.

As he fingered again Peter's copy of "The Woodlanders" he recalled his advice that he would appreciate Hardy the more if he walked his "Wessex" – the author's country, with its old tracks, old trees and churches built in the warm Ham stone. He promised himself he would one day, hoping still that she would be with him, for his desire for Frances Bromley was so unbearable he did not know where to put himself for a minute's ease. Further, in body and soul, she was an analogue of Peter so that whenever he came to literature he found them both there among the phrases and philosophies of the great writers.

So, very slowly, mid-July arrived and he booked a ticket for the fiftieth anniversary concert of a local choral society. The programme included many of the works performed since its inception in 1898. Bach, Handel, Mozart, Beethoven, Haydn, Elgar, and Holst were the composers to be featured. On that Summer evening he waited in the Victoria Hall, Hanley for the concert to commence. His eyes devoured the architectural splendours of the building and he remembered schooldays when he had found the Hall as uplifting as the music.

At the interval he filed into the room where refreshments were being served. He was idly matching his teacup for its "nesting" qualities with its saucer when he felt a brisk tap on his shoulder. He turned – it was Lieutenant Colonel Forster – Roehurst, his former commanding officer.

"Ha – Hughes – thought it was you. Listen, Sergeant – you can do me a great favour. Over there is a young woman – entirely alone. Right now I'm tied up with dignitaries and before long I have to make a presentation to a founder member – I'm the President, y'see. Now that girl's father's been a great supporter of this society so she needs looking after – see what I mean? You go over there and keep her company. Here's the coffee – go on – the interval'll be over soon."

Philip craned his neck to see over a press of people. At the far side of the room, inimitably beautiful, was Frances Bromley. Though Forster-Roehurst had left him he could feel the man's eyes boring into the back of his neck. There was nothing for it but to walk towards her.

As he shielded the coffee from countless elbows she saw him and was clearly delighted:

"Oh Philip – what a wonderful surprise! Is this for me? Thank you."

She took the coffee and talked animatedly about the concert, the choral society and her family's long acquaintance with it. In view of her obvious pleasure in seeing him again it would have been decidedly churlish to mention he had brought her the drink at someone else's bidding. She talked as though there had been no gap in their seeing each other and he thought: is this the girl who left me high and dry in St. John's Square? Even so he decided to give no indication he accepted being "stood up" and when the bell rang to signal the end of the interval he said, with a touch of acidity:

"Well, we'd better be getting back to our seats. Nice seeing you again. Bye, Frances."

Seeing her had been a joy. Weeks of misery had been wiped away, but his pride reasserted itself and he was determined not to show this. He was not to be picked up and dropped at anybody's whim.

The concert over, he waited until most of the audience were through the exits until he moved. As the cool air from the square met him pleasantly on the pavement he found her waiting for him. He sensed she had been patrolling the exits so as not to miss him.

'Philip, how are you getting home?"

"On the 'bus –down in Tontine Street..."

"Can we give you a lift? My car's being serviced but Mr Foley is waiting by the Bethesda Chapel with the Humber." He baulked at the prospect:

"No, really - it'll only take a minute for....."

"Oh do come!"

Patiently but firmly she was pulling on his arm.

Though it was dark he could sense Jack Foley's coldness as he entered the Humber. The chauffeur closed the door a little too firmly. Obviously, Frances' arrangements found no favour with him. Frances asked Philip what he had thought of the concert and which pieces he had especially enjoyed. When he said the society was at its sublime best in the excerpts from Handel's "Messiah" she readily agreed. By now the Humber was making its way towards Cobridge Bank and though the man had his back to them Philip could still feel Foley's hostility.

Despite Frances' presence, the potter felt ill at ease so he decided the best way to negotiate the rest of the embarrassing journey was to steer the conversation on to neutral ground. Accordingly, and apropos of the entirely unexpected, he began to talk of his love for Handel's music. He told her of how Handel's father had been bent on a career in law for his son; of how young Handel had smuggled in a clavichord and played it in the attic to escape his father's attention; of how he turned to oratorio after his comparative failure with opera; of how the "Messiah" had raised more money for charity than any other musical composition; of how it was still being performed throughout the world by large choirs, small choirs and large and small ensembles; of how the masterwork was composed in three weeks with Handel barely stopping for sleep and with his meals untouched; of how George II had stood up at the Hallelujah chorus establishing a tradition; of how, on hearing the work, the composer Haydn had declared: "He is the master of us all"; of how Handel, a devout Christian was able to feel the Saviour's torment as he composed and of how Handel's tears mixed with his ink as "I know that my Redeemer liveth" and "He was despised" flew from his pen; and of how, returning to London after the Dublin premiere of his work, he had found the church hierarchy enraged because "the Bible has been used for musical entertainment."

Only the Humber's arrival alongside the fountain in St. John's Square brought the tour de force to a halt for Philip suddenly asked Jack Foley to stop the car. Despite Frances' remonstrations he refused to let them take him to Hanover Street. She looked at him fondly as he moved:

"Philip, how do you know all that? It's astounding?"

This was his opportunity to get back at her and he was human enough to take it:

"Frances, I've told you before, human identity can't be forced into uniform moulds – "the workers", "the plebs", "the great unwashed" let's lump them all together. You have to make room for the occasional eccentric – like me!"

He deterred Foley from leaving his seat to open the door for him. Before he closed it himself and walked away, his feelings for her forced him to say:

"I did appreciate the lift, Frances. Thank you very much. Goodnight. Thank you, Mr Foley."

Walking down the slope of the square he felt a great sense of release. He loved her with all his heart but she had better know that never again, in all his life, would he be at anyone's beck and call.

Not being with her was grinding him to dust. The latest item on the "Hit Parade" was making its way from the Hogan's wireless next door:

"You smile the song begins
You speak and I hear violins
It's magic.
How else can I explain
That rainbow when there is no rain,
It's magic."
....

While he had never experienced any of the specific

phenomena alluded to, in terms of the general impact she made on him, the song was right on cue.

Then, when he doubted it would ever happen, the Saturday preceding Stoke Wakes Week actually arrived. He picked up his belongings, bid his mother goodbye and made for Longport station. Never missing an opportunity to counsel caution she called after him:

"Don't do anything daft. I've heard it's dangerous up there in them lakes."

At Crewe he joined the Glasgow train, feeling reassured when the announcer called "change at Oxenholme for Windermere."

Oxenholme Station was small, bleak and windswept, hardly the ideal gateway to a corner of the country that enthralled him. However, the little local train puffed ponderously out of it but a short distance before the fells appeared and his heart soared.

Mary Ormond's "B&B" was only a tiny way from Windermere Station – down the slope and around the corner. Mary was tall with strong features. A fine complexion saved her from being plain. With the same belligerent benevolence she sounded like a regional edition of his mother, though she did not struggle to breathe. She set out her guidelines for good conduct:

"I'm a Dales-bred Yorkshire lass an' I keep a good table so I don't expect to see owt left on your plate, Mr Hughes."

Mary had been recently widowed and Philip asked her about her husband. This was a mistake: she treated him with such a torrent of adulation for Alex Ormond, lowland Scot, he felt it might extend to the end of his holiday:

"He were a wood turner, y'know. Worked in yon place down by Troutbeck Bridge. These are some o' the things he made for us. An' he addled good brass – enough to set me up i' this place. By, he were a man were Alex. Not many men can wear the kilt, y'know. But Alex were handsome.....knees as fat as butter!"......and so on.

Presently Philip discovered that listening to Mary's extended eulogies was a small price to pay for her crisp bed linen and copious meals. The latter made a mockery of post-war shortages. Notwithstanding the attention she paid to her other guests she was especially on the lookout for Philip's welfare. On the Sunday morning after his arrival she wanted to know his plans for the day. He said he hoped to take the ferry from Bowness and proceed via Far Sawrey to Hawkshead.

"You're walking?"

"Yes."

She pointed to his Oxford style low shoes:

"In them?"

Less certainly, Philip said "Yes".

"They'll be off your feet in no time, m'lad. Wait here!"

She produced a pair of boots seemingly with strength enough to traverse five Continents.

"Try them!", she commanded.

When he expressed his approval she found a pair of suitable socks for them and wished him on his way with a proud declaration:

"My Alex has tramped over many a pass, up many a fell and through many a beck wi' them on his feet. See you look after 'em!"

On this the first day of his holiday he enjoyed Hawkshead, made the more memorable by his fleet-of-foot journey to it.

Monday was also an interesting day. He journeyed to Ambleside and took an excursion 'bus from there. Its outward itinerary included the Kirkstone Pass, Patterdale and Glenridding with a diversion to AiraForce. It returned by way of Ullswater, Keswick and Thirlmere.

At breakfast on the Tuesday Mary Ormond could scarcely let him sit down before she handed him a letter.

Having an observation for every circumstance she muttered uneasily:

"I don't get many letters for weekly boarders. I hope it's not bad news."

Then she stayed conveniently near.

His heart thumped when he saw the handwriting. He had often seen it in his settle-book. The letter ran:

"My dear Philip,

Forgive me for butting into your holiday but I am coming to Windermere on Wednesday morning and I wonder if you could meet me at 11 o'clock? I shall be parked outside the Railway Station.

If this cuts across plans already made I shall understand, of course, if you can't be there.

I hope you are enjoying your break – you deserve it!

Yours affectionately,

Frances Bromley"

"Are you all right, lad?"

It was some time before he heard Mary's question. Still preoccupied he smiled at her and said:

"Oh yes.'

"Well I'm glad its not bad news. You look like Death warmed up."

She glanced at him again then clattered her way to the kitchen.

He had intended to spend the Tuesday at Grasmere but the letter threw him into such confusion he wandered aimlessly both in Windermere town, then Bowness, turning over in his mind her possible motives for contacting him and the possible ways he might react on seeing her.

When Frances stepped from her car the following morning, caught sight of him, smiled and waved he was so awestruck, he almost walked in front of a delivery van. He was somewhat silent at first, Frances less so. She was clearly delighted to see him. Recognising this, he gradually relaxed.

"Right – I'm here for the day, where shall we go?", she grinned.

Seeing he was perplexed she asked him if he had originally planned anything for the day. What was he going to do?

"Well, in Wordsworth's 'Guide to the Lakes' he recommends walking around the Langdale Valley, seeing the Langdale Pikes. I thought I might do that then see if I can get towards Borrowdale and the Scafells."

"I'm sure we can do that and perhaps more. We've got the car."

"No. No thanks. He says the best way to explore it is on foot. That's what I'd like to do, perhaps later in the week. We could go to Grasmere to day. How about that? We could look around the village then walk over to Dove Cottage. He lived there for quite a few years."

"Fine."

Within the hour they were in Grasmere seated in a café by the side of the River Rothay which at that point looked little more than a stream. He pointed across it to the graveyard of the 13th Century Church of St. Oswald explaining that many of the Wordsworth family were buried there, including the poet himself.

She looked at him admiringly:

"You have quite a soft spot for Wordsworth."

"I like to think he was a man after my own heart. He wrote the Lyrical Ballads with Coleridge because he wanted to show that 'men who do not wear fine clothes can feel deeply.' And he always insisted that this area was for the people and not just for the land grabbers. But I admire him as a craftsman as well, for his skill and imagination in using words. If I am a craftsman I should be able to take a lump of clay and turn it into something worthwhile, beautiful perhaps. Words were his clay. So he could take a word like "hills" and turn it into "woody steeps", which is better. Does that sound cock-eyed?"

"It sounds sensitive and impressive."

When their coffee and biscuits were served they were immediately besieged by birds of various sizes, types and colours. The contingent was hoping to feed from the crumbs of the biscuits. Frances was thrilled by the invasion:

"Philip!....look....there's a Dipper! It's fantastic! Those are Sand Martins and there's even a Sedge Warbler! Oh, and look......a Yellow Wagtail!"

Philip, unable to identify anything other than a House Sparrow, was mildly embarrassed by her enthusiasm and searched for some laconic phrase. He could only say:

"Is that good?"

"Well yes – the Yellow Wagtail isn't resident you see, just a Summer visitor. The Grey Wagtail is the most common one but that's the Yellow all right. Isn't it gorgeous?!"

"I'm more impressed with these little acrobats up here. What are they?"

"Oh, Philip – surely you know – they're Blue Tits! I think if we wait long enough we may see a Kingfisher. That bank is perfect for a nesting hole."

"In the bank.....not in a tree?"

"No, you clot....in a sandy river back.....with a nesting chamber at the end of a tunnel and eggs laid on dry fish bones."

"How come you know all this?"

"Don't forget we live next to Bradwell Wood. The types we see in our gardens are very varied. I used to list them in a book then draw them from memory. I've still got the drawings."

Before long the biscuits were gone and, though still around, the birds transferred their interest to other patrons in the hope of further sustenance. So the tumult died down, people on adjacent tables returned to their own conservations and the couple looked at each other. He must now deal with what was plaguing him:

"May I ask you a question?"

She was puzzled:

"Of course."

"Why didn't you come to St. John's Square on that Thursday evening as we arranged?"

She was staggered as was a patron on the nearest table.

"You mean you went there and waited for me?"

Now the conversations were dying on other tables......

"Yes – as we arranged."

She looked at him and lowered her voice putting fellow diners at some disadvantage.....

"Weren't you told about father's attitude and the fact that he didn't want us to meet again?"

At this all other conversations stopped......

"I was, but frankly it didn't make much difference to me. My only worry was whether things would be difficult between you and your father. So I turned up to see what your reaction was. I thought we might discuss it."

She looked at him anxiously, apologetically:

"You thought I'd be frightened off, didn't you?"

He searched her eyes and dismissed the idea she had been underhand, uncaring. Here was a girl of great virtue who, apparently, was now visiting the Carrolls regularly. It would be unjust to think she had been devious and unconcerned.

"Frances, we've always been honest with each other so I have to say I was disappointed. Then, thinking about it, I realised you're so ready to give a helping hand it's liable to land you into awkward situations. You had considered the whole thing and thought it better we stopped seeing each other."

As the diners in the café became increasingly absorbed, Frances looked serious:

"But that's wrong and unfair – to yourself especially.

I've never seen you out of charity, I've seen you because I enjoy being with you. Whether father realises it or not I've never taken my responsibilities to the firm lightly. And I've tried to make him see reason about our friendship but he refuses. Sorry to tell you that. Without being disloyal to him I still felt right about seeing you. He has forbidden it.

Philip – that doesn't mean I accept it – that I'm docile – but do realise that apart from me he's completely alone shouldering all the burdens of the firm. He's planned sweeping changes for the next few years. They're necessary if we're to survive. The financial implications are enormous, especially if the firm is to stay in the family. He sees me having a major part to play in its future and I know how much it means to him but I can't agree with him that I shouldn't see you."

Now she looked at him even more earnestly:

"It wasn't solely because of father's opposition I didn't keep the appointment, though. I hate to displease him. There was another reason....."

"What?"

"Well, I didn't think that, in your presence circumstances – you know, with your mother's reliance on you – you could afford to lose your job. I honestly didn't think you would be there either......but I never wanted not seeing you to be a permanent thing."

With some exasperation, he sighed:

"Then you underrated me. Frances, you'd better understand something. I've been pushed about from pillar to post, shouted at, sneered at and shot at, all the way from Burslem to Burma and back again. And when I put my civvy clothes on I decided all that was over. I'm no longer going to jump when the man says jump. I'm my own man now. Your father doesn't frighten me. I'm sorry if this offends you but he acts like a dictator when he hasn't got that power anymore. As for him sacking me - how long do you think

I'd be out of a job? Have you seen the advertisements in the "Sentinel" ......for every trade on a potbank?"

For the first time Philip became aware that people on other tables were listening. Quietly he said:

"Anyway, whether or not we see each other socially – I'll go ahead with the course at Stoke Tech. Don't feel if you have to end our relationship you'll be doing me out of that opportunity."

Shyly, she put her hand on his:

"Philip - if you want me to help you, father's attitude won't make any difference but beyond that – I want to see you."

As they left the café a matronly soul dabbed at her eyes and said:

"Ooh, Sam –weren't they a lovely couple? I think they'll have one another!"

Sam might well have been keeping his options open on that for from behind his copy of the "Racing and Football Outlook" he only grunted.

With her arm in Philip's Frances accompanied him to the hamlet of Town End. There they spent a great deal of time at Dove Cottage, sometime home of the Wordsworths.

They were overjoyed to be together again. Their feelings were intensified by their period away from each other. When evening came, wishing to prolong her stay, Philip suggested that as he was "booked in" for dinner at Mary Ormond's she might accompany him.

When they reached the B&B for perhaps the only time in her life Mary was reduced to silence. All she could do was gaze at Frances. Yet her hypnosis did not prevent her from producing a sumptuous meal for the two of them – again, completely out of keeping with those austere times.

Before leaving for Garstang Frances arranged to meet him at St. John's Square on the following Monday evening though she explained it could not be before 8pm because of a company meeting at the firm.

"That's all right, Philip said, "just see that you turn up this time because if you don't I'll come and get you!"

She seemed thrilled by the admonition.

When he returned Mary Drummond had found her voice:

"Wherever did you find that lass?"

"Why?"

Brandishing an egg-whisk for emphasis Mary snapped:

"Now don't start actin' half-soaked. You know what I mean."

"She's just a girl I know."

"Are you gettin' wed?"

"Oh.....it's nothing like that."

"Well, you'd better grab her, afore somebody else does. Because I'll tell thee this lad - she's the gradeliest lass I've ever seen. If there were a contest tomorrow, the 'Beauty of Buttermere' wouldn't get a look-in!"

Chapter Fourteen
The Reckoning

The following Monday was even busier than usual. For the whole of the morning and most of the afternoon Frances was bent over the settle books of the decorating department. The piece work earnings for every paintress, printer, bander, lithographer and so on were calculated and agreed with each individual on the basis of output (in dozens) x price (per dozen). So the door of Frank Hollinshead's office rattled open and shut, open and shut, as a constant stream of decorators came to "settle".

On the management side of the table, Frances was flanked by Frank Hollinshead and Connie Mellor. Today, as always, the other two were agog at the length and breadth of Connie's knowledge. She knew every process, pattern and price like the back of her hand. She knew the previous week's output figure for every worker and the extent of any adjustments to be made to a settle count because of poor quality. On this last point, the workers knew their manageress to be firm but fair.

"You guard the firm's money like your own, Connie," Frances laughed.

"I think it is my own, Miss Frances. I've always felt that if they rob the firm they're robbing me."

The "real" work of the settle was done by Mrs Mellor with Frances now playing an increasingly knowledgeable part as the complexities of the job yielded to her intelligence. Frank Hollinshead, as in most matters administrative, had a peripheral role, noting each sum settled on his long list, divided into decorating processes. The process totals and the grand total were then submitted, by custom, to Mr Ewart Bromley who, for a second or so, feigned interest in them.

Frances could hardly help glancing unobtrusively at her uncle from time to time. He laboured over his list so as to infuse it with importance. He was like some animal struggling to survive in a strange environment. She felt very sorry for him and it crossed her mind she ought, in some way, to help him safeguard his self-esteem.

At the end of the settle came the other ceremony – tea and Connie's home-made cake. Shortages could bite as hard as they might Connie always had some new delight to offer them. This day, when she left, Frank nodded agreeably towards the door:

"Isn't she a wonder? You know if, God forbid, she was hit by a bus crossing the Market Place, we'd need about three people to replace her."

Frances had the opening she was seeking:

"Yes...we're blessed having Connie with us, and Florence Birks and Frank Eardley....people steeped in the firm, who've become living catalogues of what we do and how much we should pay for having it done....but that can be a weakness, Uncle Frank."

"Whatever do you mean?"

"Well suppose Connie was knocked down, how would we cope? Could either of us do her job? I certainly couldn't. And the problem doesn't stop at the decorating shops. Mrs Birks isn't getting any younger and there are others like her. We depend on them - crucially - and they all keep their office in their hats – very little is written down – and that makes us vulnerable."

He looked at her, thoughtful, silent. Frances smiled at him encouragingly and went over to one of the showcases which lined his office. She slid open its glass door and took out a soup-plate, showing him its decorated face:

"Do you like this, Uncle Frank?"

"Yes....it's the "Indian Tree"...one of our best sellers."

"Do we make any money on it?"

"I should hope so. We sell enough of it."

"That's not the same, is it Uncle Frank?"

"What's on your mind Frances?"

"Well, you set me thinking when you said 'supposing Connie meets with an accident'. I'm really wondering if we know the true cost of producing anything. You see - if you pick up a book on cost accounting it states quite simply that the selling price of a product should equal the fixed and variable costs of production plus the target rate of profit. I don't think we know, for instance, what fixed costs, "overheads" if you prefer, we should charge to this piece of "Indian Tree" and the same goes for all our lines. Do you know, when I was settling wages in the clay department for Marlborough shape saucers I was told the settle price was the base price plus a string of percentages. When I asked about the "base price" I was told it was the price before the war – not the recent war, the First World War!, and the percentages were the national wage awards since then! In other words, the "base price" hasn't been altered since grandfather's time!

Now that may be a grisly exception – I certainly hope it was, but I'm sure that all over the firm we have no clear, accurate idea of our current costs –so how can we set valid prices?"

"Yes – but don't forget Frances, the customer has a lot to say on what his buying price should be – 'specially our big customers. Now nobody is a tougher negotiator than your father – nobody – and there've been times when he's had to bite his lip and settle for a low price just to keep the firm going."

"I know that – but if the range of what we offer is unbalanced – with too much break-even business then we've got to have some high-yield products in the range so the profit comes right over the total turnover. And if we don't make sufficient profit, how do we replace machinery or develop new lines or pay bank interest?"

"It sounds like an enormous job – re-costing everything.... doesn't it?"

"I think we have to start somewhere – say here, or in the clay end, and look at everything we make. We need a bright young lad, say somebody who's working his way through the Cost and Works Accountants' exams. If I'm right, Uncle, he'll save us his salary ten times over."

He smiled at her in undisguised admiration, but she hadn't finished yet:

"Obviously our pricing strategy is a commercial consideration which is why I raise it with you and there is another point which is just as important...." He watched as she picked up a blank letterhead and held it out to him:

"Did you ever see anything as dreary as that? A plan view of the factory which might have been taken, presumably, from a balloon in the 1850s. Now, a hundred years later, we're still saddled with it. Is this the image we want to convey? Or do we want to say – "Here we are, ready for the second half of the twentieth century". We need a logo type that commands attention – perhaps a "B" for Bromley or "G" for Grange – maybe the whole word "Bromley" or "Grange" and carried out in a particular colour – our livery colour if you like – and that logotype should be repeated in that colour – on letterheads, envelopes, invoices, catalogues, price lists, advertisements, delivery vehicles, workers' clothing - so that the cumulative, repetitive force of it establishes us in the mind of the buyer and the user."

"You really are talking big changes now, Frances"

"Yes – but necessary changes and changes which must come soon. The orders are rolling in now but soon the Germans and the Japanese will be catching up with us and markets will become harder to penetrate. We have to sell what is unique, distinctive – and the logo has a big part in that. I'd like to see it on every carton of ware that leaves us."

"*Carton* of ware?"

"Yes – that's another aspect of updating the image. When I was at University I noticed the leading manufacturers of laboratory glassware made their deliveries in eburite cartons, frequently incorporating strong cardboard cut-outs to make certain even the most fragile, complex pieces of glass travelled safely. Why can't we do that with pottery? Wooden crates, second-hand teachests, disinfected straw – these things are out of the Ark. Think how much cleaner and easier it would be for a department store to be able to place the ware from a carton, straight into the display cabinets. Dispense with the straw certificates and the export documentation's a little bit easier."

"My word Frances – you have been thinking things out. Of course, you'd be putting the crate makers out of work, you know that, don't you?"

"No – not out of work – they'd still be in the packing business – but working with cleaner, lighter materials."

Frank shook his head in wonder:

"Well, talk about turning things upside down......."

"But that's not all Uncle Frank. We need to look at the range we offer. There are too many patterns people can get from anywhere. Everybody does a version of "scattered roses", for instance. When this boom is over, wherever there is duplication we will only be able to compete with one another on price, which means we'll follow each other down as far as our basic costs, never breaking out of being a low-cost, low-priced industry. What we need is to plan a pathway to the markets of the future and we should be doing that now. It isn't sufficient for Dadder to be buying new machinery, we've got to decide on the kind of firm we want to be. I believe it is called strategic planning."

"Frances – you're a Bromley all right, but I don't know that your father will agree with everything you say. Still, I'd like to be there when you tell him, because agree with you or not, he'll be proud of you."

"I'm not going to tell him, Uncle Frank – you are. Rather, I should say, I hope you are."

"Me?! I can't tell him! I can't understand the half of it to begin with!"

"Look – it's no good Dadder talking big technological decisions without understanding that some of the biggest decisions we must take are commercial decisions. You're the commercial director and he respects you. He says without your skill and effort the firm would have gone to the wall years ago. He'll listen to you whereas he'd tell me I'm trying to run before I can walk, I know he would."

"But I'm not an accountant, maths isn't my strong point."

"Accounting isn't about maths Uncle Frank, it's about logic."

"Yes but....."

"I promise you that if we could go through one or two things together, with your powers of persuasion you'll sell them to him."

"Hm. – what was that about fixed prices?"

"No, fixed costs, Uncle – fixed costs – I'll explain another important thing – the 80/20 rule."

And so it went on with Frank Hollinshead gradually recognising where his own pathway to recovered self respect now lay. And when Frances left him she also left a copy of a book on Business Management which she had bought from Webberley's Bookshop and which she had read avidly during her visit to Garstang.

That evening as he reached the top of Hanover Street and walked into St. John's Square he felt the cold wind of Autumn against his face, so he was especially pleased to see the Ford Prefect car of Frances parked alongside the lamp-post, their arranged meeting place.

There was still enough light to see she looked radiant as he slid into the seat beside her.

"Hallo....,meeting went off O.K. then?"

"Yes, Philip and I've got some good news."

"What's that?"

"I've been made a director of the company."

Whereas she had expected smiles and congratulations there was only a puzzled silence:

"I...er...I don't understand."

"What don't you understand?"

"Well...I mean...you're the boss's daughter aren't

you?"

"Yes...but I wasn't a director...now I am."

"But what difference does it make?"

"It's a promotion, if you like to call it that. I was a management trainee now I'm a director. I was a salaried employee, now I have a stake in the future of the company. The better it does, the better I do."

He was smiling, with gladness and sincerity:

"Oh....well in that case....I'm very pleased for you. It's well-deserved, Frances."

"Thank you and thank you for all you've done to help me since I arrived. I hope you see now why I want to help you."

"You want to help me because it's your nature."

She put a hand on his arm and looked at him earnestly:

"Listen, I want to talk to you about something. Can we find somewhere quiet do you think?"

"Well it's too late now to leave the Potteries but there is a little café near the top of Hamil Road....how about that?"

"Fine...you direct me."

In a few minutes the Prefect purred its way down Queen Street, up Swan Square, across Chapel Bank and into Hamil Road while from the crown and the shoulders, the hips and the feet of Burslem town the smoke from the bottle ovens in its grubby undulation made its way skywards.

Luckily the café was open and they were the only customers. Frances looked hungrily at a glass fixture containing pastries:

"Do you think I might have one of those, Philip? I met you direct from the meeting."

"So you haven't eaten? Well in that case maybe we could get something cooked for you...."

"I could poach you an egg," said the proprietress willingly.

"Oh that would be fine, thank you", smiled the grateful

Frances.

She fell on the food with much gratification. Philip said nothing while she ate. As she was finishing he said:

"Thank goodness for that. The smell of that buttered toast was making my mouth water."

"Oh....shall I get some for you?"

"No, no...but I will get another pot of tea for us and then you can tell me the other big secret."

When she had poured cups of fresh tea for them, Frances slid a newspaper cutting across the table:

"When I got back from Garstang, I saw this in Friday's "Evening Sentinel". It's in again tonight."

She had highlighted an advertisement which read:

"A departmental manager is required at the Burslem factory of Beresford Ceramics. The person appointed will have first class practical experience of clayware production and tool filing. The post carries complete responsibility for the output and quality control of clay-state production in this up-to-date and progressive factory. The successful applicant may currently be working at the potter's bench. When ability has been proven there are excellent opportunities for further promotion. The starting salary will reflect the importance of the post. All applications will be acknowledged if addressed for the personal attention of Mr Clive Beresford (address below)."

He passed the cutting back to her and murmured his thanks.

"Is that all you're going to say, 'thank you'?"

"What else is there to say?"

"The advertisement might have been written about you. That's worth saying."

"I know what you're trying to do, Frances and I appreciate it. I'm sorry to say this... to you especially...but bosses are clannish. Supposing Beresfords were seriously considering me, they'd ask your father about me, wouldn't they? And that'd put the tin hat on it."

"Look – I've known Clive Beresford for a long time and I like him. He's got the right ideas and the right outlook. You're just the man he's looking for and you'd be very happy working for him."

"But your father would put the kybosh on it!"

"Clive Beresford is strong enough and fair-minded enough to make his own judgements. If he thinks you're the man he wants, he'd give you your chance."

"It wouldn't work."

"Well I know it *would* work. You're immensely skilled, you have high standards and you're a talented trainer. He'd choose you, Philip and I've got enough faith in you to know you could hold the job down. What's more, you could even build it from there – when you start your studies."

"I'm happy with what I'm doing anyway. I earn good money."

"In that case there's no point putting yourself through five years of study then is there? I think I'm wasting my time with you Philip."

From the café's counter, in the space between a pickle jar and a display box of Rizla cigarette papers, a single eye watched the couple. It was one of a pair of eyes belonging to the proprietress and behind the eyes a brain was ticking like a meter:

"Why are men so bloody stupid?! The lad ought to go down on his knees and thank God this gorgeous girl has even looked at him, let alone try to get him a boss's job. He needs his head examining."

She stopped conversing with herself as Frances reached over and put her hand on Philip's arm. In genuine entreaty she said:

"I wish you shared the faith I have in you."

He was moved by this and looked up at her, then retrieved the cutting:

"O.K. I'll think about it."

When they left the café, Frances thanked the proprietress who smiled:

"You're welcome, duck. Thank you. Look after yourselves."

Then she gave Frances an outrageous wink as if to say "keep at it, duck, they're all a bit slow."

The door closed behind them and the woman went over to clear their table. What a little toff the girl was – she'd left a one shilling tip!

"Jesus, Mary and Joseph, she looked like an angel from heaven. I could eat her", she thought, "an' if she was my wench I'd be the proudest mother in Burslem!"

Despite his protests Frances ran Philip to the front door of his home in Hanover Street. Before she left for Porthill she turned to him:

"Philip Hughes, I want you to understand one thing – I'm not saying the things I say for my good. If you choose to remain a platemaker all your life, that's your decision. It won't make the slightest difference to our friendship. What I'm concerned about is you making use of all your talents and if you don't take up a management job it'll be a shocking waste of a good man."

"O.K. Perhaps I will write. If we could meet on Friday night at the Theatre Royal in Hanley, I'll let you see what I've said."

"That sounds fine and I can make Friday – say about seven. And before I leave there's something else."

She handed him a foolscap envelope.

"What's this?"

"The application forms for the ceramics course at Stoke Tech."

As the exhaust fumes swirled around him and the Prefect moved away he shook his head. He loved her so much he sometimes felt his heart would burst.

When Frances reached Bradwell Grange she was tense, half-expecting the tirade that inevitably followed a meeting with Philip. Tonight, however, her father seemed depressed and his question had a worried tone:

"Couldn't you wait for me after the Board meeting? We could have come home together and Foley needn't have hung around waiting for me. We have a lot to discuss you know, Frances, now you're on the Board."

She was cautious:

"I'm sorry, Dadder. I had an appointment."

Thankfully he seemed not to have heard for, preoccupied, he was gazing into the fire. Sitting with him like this, she in her mother's chair, before the great fireplace, brought back childhood memories. She would be sitting reading her brightly pictured first books while behind her, for as long as they could stay in one spot, her brothers were outdaring each other in sly whispers.

Ewart Bromley must have been thinking such thoughts too. His eyes were saddened with remembrance as he looked at her:

"You're very much like your mother, sitting in that chair."

He was struggling for more words:

"Frances, what's happened?" These days you won't even wait until I get home so that we can have a meal together and talk about the day's doings. You're always racing in, asking Mrs Foley to manage something quickly and racing out again."

"That's hardly true, Dadder. I'm here with you most nights."

".....but you don't enjoy it, do you?"

"Of course I do."

"Frances – remembering Denzil and Peter at the firm and the way your mother worked hard with me to build it up, I'd have thought you'd be proud to come back from University and give it your all. Yet you only seem to be on the fringe of things – you don't put your heart into it. I'm not saying you haven't done well at the "Grange" but you're not as fiercely proud of it as I thought you'd be. Then there's this other thing....", he added quietly.

She didn't answer so he became animated:

"Could I have treated you better? Haven't you been made a director in less than a year? And have you had a tiny interest? You've had the whole of Denzil's and Peter's shares made over to you. Don't you think Frank Hollinshead would have felt due for some, after all he did for the firm when we were close to going out of business? He didn't even get the chance. And what about Esther and her side of the family? They lent us money when times were tight, perhaps they feel entitled to some reward."

He pointed fiercely in the direction of the hollow:

"Jack Dempster has been with the firm for over thirty years. He isn't a director. Don't you think he'd like to be and why would anyone want the shares? Because the "Grange" has got a great future. I've told you what's being planned – all the bottle ovens to be scrapped – continuous firing, biscuit and glost; the dipping-house mangles to come down – new glazing machines. No more rope driven jiggers in the making shops – semi-automatic plate making machines. Same in the cup shops. But have you thought of the expense? How's it going to be covered? Basically we're sound, because we've always been prudent – we've redeemed all our loan notes – we can look anybody in the eye. But now – we've got to borrow. I'm not just talking about increasing the overdraft to finance stocks now. I'm talking big ticket investment. I've been sweating it out for days. It's beyond the local bank's resources but obviously they'd want a charge on our assets anyway. If we go to a merchant bank they'll secure their loans against our assets as tight as a drum – they'll have no feeling for the industry and we won't be able to call our soul our own. Then as far as going public and raising the money through a share issue – not while I'm alive. This firm is staying in the family. D'you see the problems I'm wrestling with – I've enough on my plate for three men."

Ewart paused for breath but Frances decided to say nothing.

"I'm planning the best general earthenware factory anywhere –with a name that means something and who is it for but for you, Frances? And the improvements won't be just on the works side, oh no – I've been talking with Frank Hollinshead. He's brimful of ideas on the commercial side – how we should revamp the literature, how we should work out a new logo and put it on everything. People think he's up at your end on a quiet loaf. Oh yes, I'm not daft – I go about with my eyes open. That Pelham woman and her crew. Frank's been telling me about something called the 80/20 rule – how we might be spreading ourselves too thinly over too many lines and how the last ten per cent of any production run is where the net profit is and how the warehouse is full of those ten per cents. He's been explaining something called "product planning". I wish you could have heard him but you'd gone."

Frances smiled and said:

"I'm glad you're listening to Uncle Frank's ideas. He's a good man."

"Of course he's good. He's one of the family isn't he? Your grandfather started from nothing – nothing! And you're going to have the "Grange" as it's going to be, built on everything the people before you have made it. But you must give it your heart and soul, Frances. Don't ever let me think this directorship of yours is an ill-starred venture. Forget that guttersnipe in the flat shop. You've no time for larking around. If you do I could be the mug who took the firm from clogs to clogs in three generations."

Frances' head was bowed – her silence masked her anger – anger for his lack of faith in her and for his disparaging description of the man she loved. When Ewart next spoke he tried to be placatory:

"Don't think I'm stupid. I've always realised that as a young woman you'd want a family of your own some day. But there's time for that when you've seen to your duty. That's why I asked Esther to have you at Garstang for the week."

Frances looked up at him with dread:

"You asked her!"

"Of course I asked her! Because it was for your own good and because if you saw more of Gordon, you'd not be filling your head with this tripehound at the "Grange"."

Gordon Bromley, a junior in the firm of Henshaw and Bromley, Solicitors, was despite his youth a second cousin of Ewart, who knew that Frances and Gordon had always been fond of each other. What he did not know, or perhaps wish to know, was that from Frances' standpoint, and even perhaps from Gordon's, it was a family fondness and nothing more.

The master potter was talking again:

"Gordon's a grand lad. Hughes couldn't black his boots. In a few years' time you'll see that, if only you're saved from yourself. What's more he's a Bromley and the two of you'll make sure the "Grange" stays with the family."

Her blood boiled with rage. She tried to control herself but failed:

"That's all that matters really isn't it, Dadder? I'm a parcel to be passed around so that I can see Gordon. Then a marriage has to be arranged so that we can save the firm.

You're becoming obsessed."

"What the hell are you talking about?"

This was when Mary Ellen Foley, surreptitiously and fearfully, came to the drawing room door and tactfully pulled it shut. She was the only other person at Bradwell Grange but knew her duty. Frances was now beginning to shout:

"I mean, Dadder, that I don't intend to marry Gordon Bromley or any other man you care to arrange for me. And your treatment of Philip Hughes has been grossly unjust."

"Unjust? Unjust? Enoch or Isaiah would have thrown him out neck and crop!"

"I don't happen to believe that. You were unjust. You can't bear him because he stood up to you in the biscuit warehouse that day. You thought you were entitled to make him look incompetent in front of everybody and he wasn't entitled to defend himself. He carried me to the lodge when I fell and you ordered him out! If I'd broken my neck on those rickety steps would that have been his fault too? You say we've been 'larking about'. Why don't you use the words you have in mind, such as 'wanton depravity'?"

Before her next words, her hands became fists. She rose from her chair and beat the space in front of him:

"He hasn't even held my hand!"

She began to speak quietly again:

"You've done the most to make our friendship the common property of everyone by the way you've treated him – which is why I have to put up with laughter and giggling and constant stares."

This gave Ewart a fresh opportunity. He thumped the side of his chair for emphasis then stood up quickly:

"It's your own fault! It's your own fault! You've cheapened yourself running after him and you don't seem to know how to behave. I've even seen you laughing and joking with that troglodyte of a clay carrier, Hogan. The man's a bloody criminal! He owes money to people all over the bank. Now I believe you've started to visit these people in their houses. You didn't think I knew about that did you?"

"No...but it doesn't surprise me. You seem to know everything else I do."

"Not quite. Mention of Garstang reminds me of something. I'm told you disappeared for the whole of one day and wouldn't be drawn on where you'd been. Would you like to tell me?"

Frances looked at him squarely but said nothing. Sneeringly, Ewart smiled:

"I see. Now that silence worries me and leads me to one conclusion. You've seen him again tonight, haven't you?"

"Yes....and what's more I'll continue to see him because you're making a much bigger issue of this than you need to and because he's the finest man I know or am ever likely to know. As for visiting "those people", as you put it, I visit one family, the Carrolls, who need help right now. I like to think they're my friends and their friendship is important to me. In fact the only difference between them and us is the accident of money. They've got nothing – like so many others in Burslem – but that doesn't make them the offal of the world."

She shook her head despairingly:

"I don't know how you can speak of those who make your fortune for you with such contempt."

Bromley was so enraged, every vestige of colour had drained from his face. Instead of shouting he now spoke with measured menace.

"Well, now the truth is out. Little Miss Innocent is really a scheming liar...."

"How dare you speak to me like that?!"

He held up his hand to silence her:

"Now let me tell you a couple of home truths. One – he was told not to see you again or his job was at risk. He's ignored that, so he's sacked. Tomorrow morning, within the hour, he'll be seen off the firm. Two – you say you'll continue to see him. I would think about that because if you do, you will also be leaving the firm. What is more, you'll be leaving this house."

To emphasise his resolution in these matters, as he left the room he closed the door loudly. Frances gazed into the fire and continued gazing until its smouldering remains turned to ashes.

Philip's face was tightly drawn and white with anger:

"I'd like to see him myself, Mr Dempster."

The works manager's discomfort bordered on fear:

"It won't do any good, Phil. He's in a micky about it and just told me to pay you up and see you off the bank."

"You can but ask him."

Dempster was unsure; then he sighed:

"All right. I'll ask him."

"I'd like to come with you."

"Suit yourself – but it won't be the slightest use."

They walked into "The Office". The first one to see them was Lucy Pelham. As the aproned potter walked past her, despite her facial control as a practised intriguer, she could not hide her expectant delight. And yes, her wild surmise had been unerring, they were heading for Ewart Bromley's door! Her thrill had intensified, leaving her quite light-headed. In the next few minutes she took her thick body and bladdered feet to every room in the building. With her comings and goings the entire building eased itself into riveted calm, a calm so perfect the tap of a single typewriter key would have been barbarity.

Jack Dempster emerged from Bromley's office closing

the door very quietly. He whispered:

"I'm afraid not. He says if you're not off the firm in half an hour I'm to send for the police."

Philip did not waver:

"Mr Dempster – tell him I just want two minutes of his time. After that I'll go."

Dempster was clearly afraid:

"I can't go in again, Phil....I..."

To put out some stiffening into the man Philip pointed menacingly towards Ewart's door:

"Look....just do that for me, will you?....because if you don't, I'm going to push past you and see him without his agreement."

With a face that would make a fortune for an undertaker, Dempster knocked. In a minute or so he returned:

"All right," he muttered.

From the desk by the far wall Ewart Bromley looked at his watch, then at Philip hatefully. The young man stood in a shaft of light from the window.

"If you've come to be set on again, you're wasting your time."

"I haven't come to beg for anything. I just want to ask you something."

"Well ask it and then clear off."

"Why have I been given a minute's notice?"

"Don't come the old soldier with me, Hughes. I think you're as deep as a draw–well, but you don't suck me in. You know damn' well why you've been sacked. You asked your question, now leave!"

The potter stood firm:

"I still don't know why I've been sacked."

As his anger rose, Bromley pushed back his chair and stood up:

"Have you, or have you not, been seeing my daughter?"

"Yes."

"And were you told not to - if you valued your job?"

"Yes."

"Then you know why you've been sacked, don't you?"

"Do you think that's sufficient reason to fire me?"

The master potter scowling, walked towards Hughes, and pointed a finger towards his eyes:

"Listen to me, lad. There isn't a living soul who's worked here can say they haven't had a straight deal from the family but my daughter means a lot to me and she means a lot to this firm. She's got a brilliant future and it's not going to be spoiled by foolish mistakes. And I'll see to that, even if I have to be ruthless. You've had two weeks' wages in lieu of notice and I don't want you near this place or near her again. Now you'd better understand that – fully and finally. You can bring all the Unions in creation into this if you like – it won't make a ha'porth of difference."

"But...I don't see why all this is an issue. Frances is going to help me with my studies and..."

Bromley cut in, at the top of his voice:

" 'Studies'! 'Studies'! D'you think I was born yesterday? D'you think I'm blind? D'you think I haven't looked at my own daughter?....and you talk about studies. Incidentally m'lad, she's 'Miss Frances' to you and she always will be."

Now he stood immediately in front of Philip. They looked at each other:

"Can you tell me that apart from 'studies' you're not interested in my daughter?"

"No. I can't."

There'd been no hesitation in the reply. Ewart was incensed though this came as no surprise:

"Then that's why you're leaving! And you come in here with the gall to talk about studies! Was it about studies when you got her to see you at Blackpool? I've met your kind before and you want to sup all the broth. Now get out!"

It flashed through Philip's mind that he had promised Frances he would apply for the management job at Beresfords.....but what notice would they take if he was sacked at a minute's notice from Bromleys? Nevertheless he regretted his next words immediatcly they were spoken. Leaning forward he said:

"Mr Bromley – I have responsibilities."

He hated Bromley then when he saw his reaction. His look of triumph conveyed it all – he had Philip on the rack and was enjoying it. The sacking had been no more that a cold, calculated act of revenge. Sneering, the master replied:

"Oh yes – responsibilities. Well so have I and I'm thinking about them right now. You should have thought of yours before this."

Ewart was so full of scorn that Philip had to purge himself of his self-disgust at having seemed servile before this man. So finally, he lost control, for as Bromley was saying:

"You've a fortnight's money, Hughes....'

Philip stepped closer to him:

"Money! Money!...do you think I'm worried about money? Do you think it means as much to me as it does to you? You listen to me – I've given value for every minute I've been here. And I've never in my life eaten idle bread! I don't want your two weeks' conscience money. If it comes to that I don't want to settle this week's work either. What bothers me is who'll set me on when all I've got to show for my time here is one minute's notice! You have no right to destroy my character when I've done nothing wrong!"

He walked towards the door then turned:

"I'll go from here and gladly, especially if that means you'll give Frances a bit of peace. You're nothing but a little tyrant – you run this place like a dictatorship but that isn't enough is it? You want to control all its life forms, right down to the cockroaches. Well you don't control me, Mr Ewart – bloody – Bromley!"

Now it was Bromley's turn to lose all control. He rushed after the young potter and bawled at him from his doorway:

"Hughes!....I'll ruin you! Don't you ever dare see her again!"

The main door to "The Office" slammed behind the platemaker. Ewart Bromley's door slammed in reply. There were, perhaps, fifteen seconds of absolute quiet then, tentatively doors began to open. Lucy Pelham's office lay in the middle of the building. Its door had never been shut. It was the other doors that were now opening...the doors of U.K. Sales, Export Sales, Export Invoicing, Wages and all the rest. Then the process accelerated, for the minions were flying to the centre in order to tear at the tit-bits.

The minions were fleet of foot. Throughout the rest of the day they ran from Pelham's office to every nook and corner of the "Grange" bearing the news. Then they ran back with the reactions, Lucy could never remember when life was so full. Never, ever, had she imagined that one day she would preside over so magnificent a post-mortem. Oh dear, there was that light-headedness again.

In the Decorating Departments they had glanced at Frances furtively and then at each other sharing their sorrow and understanding. Only the younger ones were excited for they felt it was just like being at "the pictures" and they wagered with one another as to whether she would "'ave him". They were not the only ones who wondered. Soon all Burslem would wonder for the town had more than its due share of incurable romantics.

It was Frank Hollinshead who told Frances what had occurred. He put it with as much loving care as he could and when he saw her sorrow, he squeezed her arm:

"Never mind sweetheart, it'll all come right."

He was undoubtedly sincere.

At the close of the day when the decorators were approaching Connie Mellor's little box of an office to hand in their individual counts of work done, Frances looked at Teresa Hogan. When the girl's settle book had been checked, Frances whispered:

"Teresa – please do something for me. See that Philip Hughes gets this as soon as you can, will you?"

Tense and pale, Teresa nodded. It was a small envelope.

Chapter Fifteen
Vale of Tears

When he left the potbank Philip decided not to go home until the end of the day. An earlier arrival would have precipitated a barrage of questions from his mother and in his present state of mind he had no heart for providing complex, interrupted explanations. Nor was he minded to search immediately for new employment. His self-respect urged him to do so but there was the complication of the job at Beresfords – was this a chimera or a prospect still? He didn't know and, without Frances to talk to, he was at a standstill.

So his first call was at the reading room of the public library where he studied the news of the day in the "tabloids", which told him what to think in sledgehammer prose ("Turn it in, Attlee"; "You've had it folks") and the "qualities" which were somewhat subtler, but still hell-bent on keeping their prejudices warm. Mid-morning found him wandering aimlessly up Moorland Road. On an impulse he turned into Burslem Park where, after receiving some doubtful looks and his subsequent declaration that he was between jobs and not just "an idle bugger" he was invited to join an old men's "parliament" for the rest of its morning session. Two items, nationalisation and racing pigeons, did not delay that assembly for very long. The main item for discussion concerned the joy and despair of supporting one or other of the local football teams (Stoke City and Port Vale). Through this debate Philip realised that the mutual disregard the respective supporters of these teams had for each other went back down the years to the clubs' inceptions.

He walked back on to Moorland Road, chilling somewhat as he passed the Miners' Hall for it brought back the memory of the Union official telling his mother that her right to concessionary coal was extinguished by the death of his father. He continued to climb the hill: the walk had no object other than to "kill" time until he could safely return to Hanover Street for his evening meal. He thought of Frances throughout his journey and of his regrets that their friendship had resulted in his sacking, of his concern that she should not be made unhappy by her father's abusive reproaches but most of all he thought about how much he loved her, though whether their friendship was now over he had no idea.

Reaching the top of Moorland Road he turned along High Lane, out of the smoke. By now it was lunch-time and he remembered the little café in Hamil Road. Before long he was eating and enjoying a snack meal there, the long walk having given his appetite a keen edge. The proprietress hovered around his table. At last her curiosity won through:

"Your girlfriend isn't with you today then?"

"No....she's not my girlfriend actually. We just...sort of...know each other."

The woman was not put out, seeing only opportunity in the news:

"Well, that's a start lad but I tell yer...if I was a young fellow and I knew somebody like her, I wouldn't let the grass grow under my feet!"

Philip then said more than he meant to, for he added, with a forced unmirthful laugh:

"I'm afraid she's way out of my league!"

The woman was about to return to the argument when the arrival of a bunch of hungry, hurried customers took her away from his table.

As he was leaving she fixed him with a resolute stare and whispered:

"You speak up for yourself and don't be so bloody soft!"

He returned to High Lane and turned left again, passing before long the Haywood Hospital then reaching the Riley Arms at the top of Greenbank Road. Now he was able to look down into the valley below. Tunstall, the most northerly of the six Potteries Towns was spread out before him. At the foot of Greenbank lay the town's greatest landmark, the Church of the Sacred Heart. He marvelled that in the Depression years Tunstall's Roman Catholics had scraped together enough money to build this cathedral-like structure. It was a testament to their fervour and energy.

A few yards beyond the church, at the junction with King William Street and Victoria Road, Station Road began. It derived its name from Tunstall Station, on the North Staffordshire Railway Loop Line. The Station itself was quite close. He passed it and arrived at Barber's Picture Palace. On an impulse he paid for a seat and went in. After a "B" category "Western" and the latest edition of the British Movietone News the main film began. This was "Abbott and Costello meet Frankenstein". Though he was not without a sense of the comic, Philip soon lost his grip on the tortuous plotting, for all he could think of was Frances Bromley.

It was a little after five p.m. when he caught the P.M.T. bus in Tunstall Market Square reaching Swan Bank, Burslem a little later. He decided to go home and his heart sank when he saw the rebuke in his mother's eyes. She obviously knew about the sacking. However, she did not open the subject but satisfied herself, rather stiffly, with handing him an envelope:

"Teresa, from next door's called with this!"

He settled himself in his chair and opened the envelope.

"My dear Philip,
        I am desperately sorry for what has happened. Please believe me.
        It is important that we meet – quickly. I'll go down to the Bridge at Longport tonight and wait for you there at seven.
        Please try to make it.
        Yours ever,

        Frances."

Elizabeth Hughes now moved into the second phase of the confrontation by adopting what Philip always remarked to himself was her "full-back stance". She was a tallish, solidly built woman with powerful forearms. When she settled herself, rock-like on her feet and folded her arms she looked very much like a beefy defender in one of the "Evening Sentinel's" contemporary photographs of football teams. The stance was usually the signal of her gathering belligerence.

She watched him for an instant then could contain herself no longer:

"Well?"

"Oh. I'll be going out. So I'll need my meal fairly soon."

She sighed:

"Don't start acting the goat with me, our Philip. What have you got to say for yourself?"

"About what?"

"About you 'avin done at Bromley's, that's what!"

"That's neither here nor there. If I want another job at the jigger I can get one in half an hour."

"But why did they sack you?"

"I suppose my face doesn't fit any more."

'Oh no – it isn't that. You've been going out with Bromley's daughter."

"Well if you know so much, what are you asking me for?"

"It's no wonder I know so much, the whole street knows. People have told me in the corner shop, people have told me in the butcher's. Even old Mrs Simister has knocked at the door and told me. But it's your place to tell me, then I wouldn't have to find out from strangers. I've wondered for weeks why I'm being gawped at, then I get to know you've been seeing his daughter and the next thing I hear is – you're sacked! Don't you think I have a right to know?"

"It's true I'm friends with Frances Bromley. And it's also true that he's got the najjers about it, because he looks down on me. That's what it's about, at bottom – though that doesn't justify him sacking me. Still, I haven't got the patience to argue with him about it."

She looked triumphant:

"I thought so! Ewart Bromley's against it, is he? Well, he might be like a running bull when his blood's up but I'm with him this time!"

"Good. It's nice to have your vote of confidence."

This remark released the safety catch on a higher gear of her agitation:

"You listen to me, our Phil – I'm older than you an' I know what I'm on about – oil and water don't mix. Don't let her put any fancy ideas into your head. If your sacking hasn't already put the tin hat on it, stop seeing her altogether – now! If you don't, you'll sup sorrow in bucketfuls, I'm telling you."

"I'll never come to any harm through knowing Frances Bromley. I wasn't born yesterday. How can you talk like that about a girl you've never met?"

"It isn't my fault I've never met her!"

It flashed through his mind that if the conversation went on any longer, the subject of studies at Stoke Tech would emerge and even, possibly, his application for a post at Beresfords. At this stage, this could only generate more heat than light. So he decided to bring this interchange to a close. He put his hands on her shoulders:

"Mother I didn't deserve the sack and I'm not about to be disagreeable with you or anyone else but I'd better tell you this – nothing that you or Ewart Bromley or the whole of Burslem might say will stop me seeing her as long as she wants to see me."

For a moment Elizabeth quietened but then she rallied:

"Well, why couldn't you bring her here to see me instead of sneaking off after her all the time? Can't you let your own mother have a look at her? Are you ashamed to bring her here?"

"I don't go sneaking about and I will be bringing her to see you – perhaps very soon. I know what you're thinking, but you're wrong. She's not a stuck-up piece and I'm not getting out of my depth. You'll understand when you meet her."

He looked at the clock on the mantelpiece:

"I'll have to leave at twenty minutes to seven. I'll go for the "Sentinel". It was his way of requesting his meal. She seemed to be somewhat happier but on her way to the back-kitchen she fired another salvo:

"I want plenty o' notice when she's coming! Never mind your 'very soon'. This place'll want turnin' out from top to bottom!"

After the meal she accompanied him to the door where he kissed her on the cheek and smiled:

"Stop worrying, mother. It'll sort itself out, including the job – you'll see."

Then he strode out towards Newcastle Street.

When he got to the bridge she was already waiting. Despite her heavy coat she looked cold and certainly anxious. She reached for his arm:

"Oh, Philip....I'm sure you realise how sorry I am."

He smiled reassuringly:

"Don't blame yourself. It's really my own fault. I think I've imposed on you....something I never meant to do. It's got you into trouble with your father and probably made you a boke-finger for everybody on the bank."

"Philip, what we have is a good, wholesome friendship. If it's anyone's fault it's my father's. I'm not excusing what he's done to you but...well all I can tell you is...he has a lot on his mind at the moment."

"It's over and done with now, so don't worry. I'll get a job within a day or so. What I'm more concerned about is you. I don't want him making you unhappy. So if you think it best that we don't meet again, don't struggle to find the words, Frances – I'll understand."

Frances was dumbfounded and drew away from him:

"Is that....what you want?"

"No, of course not – but I'd rather sacrifice seeing you if it's going to make things rotten for you at home."

Now she was floundering:

"....But I'm going to help you with your studies...and there's·the application for the job at Beresford's..."

"Frances...we've got to be realistic....they're not going to give the job to somebody who's just been sacked. And I can't hang around...I've got to get work...I need money coming in again..."

"Well, I can help you with that..."

Philip was angry:

"No you can't...that's never going to happen. I lost my temper with your father when he implied I was after your money!"

"We can't talk here....can we go..."

She was interrupted by the sound of rushing feet and a babble of what sounded, at first, like high-pitched conversation. They looked over the bridge: coming along the towpath towards them was Cecil Durber, the saggar maker's assistant, accompanied by two or three small children. All of them were very distressed.

As Cecil came over the bridge, Philip went to halt him. He tried to brush Philip aside, not recognising him at first, and babbling furiously:

"I've got ter tell Aggie!"....

Beyond that he was incomprehensible. Frances bent towards a little girl in the group of children, trying to discover what had happened. The girl began to cry, very loudly.

Philip grabbed Cecil by the shoulders:

"Cecil...tell me what's the matter!"

The poor, frightened man again babbled forth his terrors but Philip understood none of it except, suddenly for two words. One of these was "lake", the other was... "Tyrone".

Immediately Philip turned to Frances:

"Frances! Frances! Follow me! I'm going to the lake!"
As she stumbled along the towpath after him he was already disappearing.

When she reached the top of the grassy slope adjacent to Westport Lake she was astonished to see all the activity. Two or three police cars were parked quite close to the water as was an ambulance. She could hear the 'phut-phut" of a generator and saw, at that instant, two arc lamps mounted on steel frames come alight. They had been synchronised to illumine, in the gathering gloom, a particular spot at the edge of the lake.

Now Philip was coming towards her. He took her arm tenderly:

"Frances...I'm sorry to have rushed off...Tyrone Carroll has fallen into the lake."

She was rigid with shock but managed to ask him when it had happened. He swallowed and whispered:

"About four o'clock."

She was about to cry out in despair when a group of police and others standing slightly back from the margin of the lake parted and she could see Veronica Carroll being supported by a neighbour. Frances ran towards her. Perhaps it was because of her immaculate appearance or perhaps because she obviously knew the mother, at all events when she reached the police cordon they let her pass.

Veronica saw her and reached out to her:

"Oh, Miss Frances!....it's Tyrone!...he's in there."
Frances followed her pointing fingers to the surface of the Lake where the heads of police frogmen appeared and disappeared. A miserable, penetrating Autumn wind flicked the surface of the water into little dishes which, caught by the arc lamps, gleamed malovently over their prize. Frances shuddered and said soothingly:

"I know. I know, Veronica...but they'll find him, you'll see."

It sounded so futile but what else could she say?

For the first time she now saw Veronica's cracked plimsolls and thin pinafore. Drawn and tired, her face grey with the cold she seemed about to collapse. Frances slipped off her own warm coat and quietly insisted Veronica put it on. For ever after, Philip would remember that scene as he watched from beyond the cordon, Veronica Carroll in Frances' coat, held by Frances and the neighbour and Frances herself with the wind streaming her hair and rippling the folds of her white silk blouse. What he did not see was that, after bending to her handbag, while one hand was around Veronica the other was around her rosary beads. Whenever she rested from comforting the mother, Frances Bromley was offering her intense supplication for a little boy she had helped to learn his letters and to play with his toys, a little boy she had come to love.

The vigil went on for two hours, during which time the crowd added steadily to its numbers. Only three policemen were holding back the crowd from swamping the rescuers but they did it unobtrusively and effectively – which said something both for the police and the crowd. And as he heard their whispered conversations the crowd were voicing Philip's own thoughts: "only four?"; "poor little soul"; "but if he lives in Pleasant Street, Burslem, how's he got all the way down here?"

From time to time Philip saw a Police Inspector, obviously in charge of the operation, return from the lake to the car and its radio link. As a result of this, soon the police were asking the crowd to make way for the arrival of a doctor. As the doctor made his way through the cordon Philip saw his chance and moved forward. One of the police spotted him but had also seen his earlier arrival with Frances and nodded him through. When he reached her reassuringly he put his hand on her arm. It was like ice.

Philip could hear the Inspector talking to the doctor in

low tones.

"Doctor, I'd prefer it if we can get Mrs Carroll away from this place. She's in really poor shape and has been here for hours, but she won't budge."

"O.K. I'll have a look at her. If you can open up the ambulance we can get her in there, perhaps. She won't then have to move away and maybe I can sedate her. It's worth a try."

While the doctor talked earnestly to the distraught Veronica, Philip sidled up to Frances. As, after much protest, Tyrone's mother was shepherded to the ambulance, Philip took off his jacket and wrapped Frances into it. She seemed not to notice and when he suggested she might come away from the scene she was alarmed:

"I can't! Veronica needs me! I've got to stay here."

Calmly, he replied:

"The medical people are seeing to her now. I think she needs the sort of help we can't give her. You're frozen through. That won't help find Tyrone any quicker."

The neighbour edged forward and also remonstrated with Frances:

"You can't keep a limb still. Mrs Carroll'll be all right. I'll stay with her."

Philip nodded to the woman, put his arm around Frances and began to shepherd her away from the scene. When she realised what was happening she pulled away from him suddenly:

"No! Where are we going?"

He could see she was in shock and had to think quickly:

"Just over here...away from all these people...out of the wind."

"Why?"

"Because you need to get warm and I want to talk to you."

"What about?"

"You'll understand when we get there."

As Veronica Carroll was at last being helped into the ambulance Frances looked back anxiously then let herself be slowly guided away.

In the next few minutes they tried, in the gloom, to search each other's features, for they were now standing together under another of the canal's many bridges. There, in the stillness and the comparative warmth, reaction set in and Frances sobbed from her soul. She was thinking of that day when she had gathered Tyrone up from the sliphouse floor. All the misery, dejection, pain and lack of future in his world of "doing without" had been encapsulated in the tearful face of that little boy and its impact had pierced her heart. She had played with him in the freezing dampness of his faith-filled home and he had progressed but ultimately she had failed him because all her love and all her stratagems had been unable to cope with his curiosity, his need to know the world.

Philip held her tenderly until her grief abated. Then he slipped a hand into his jacket, took out a handkerchief and lightly dabbed at her eyes and cheeks. She looked up at him through the gloom:

"I hate this place," she murmured.

"We'll move out of here when you're a bit warmer."

"No...it's not just this place...it's the whole area."

"Why?"

"For what it is, for its ghastly appearance, for what it has done to Tyrone, for what it has done to you...."

"Then you're a mystery to me, Frances Bromley, because I don't understand how you can hate the place yet love its people the way you do."

She put a hand upon his shoulder:

"Oh, Philip."

And that's how it was that in that squalid place, next to

that contaminated canal, near to the scene of that appalling death, they reached for each other and held each other and kissed each other and spoke of their love.

Fortuitously, Ewart Bromley was away from Bradwell Grange at this time negotiating with financiers and machinery suppliers. So he did not know that it was in the early hours of the morning following Tyrone's drowning that Philip finally persuaded Frances to leave Westport Lake and return home. She was traumatised and dispirited but, as they stood by her car in Bridgewater Street she was still taken up enough with his concerns to plead with him to apply for the post at Beresford's and agree to attend the Ceramics course at Stoke Technical College.

"O.K., Sweetheart," he sighed at last and kissed her goodnight.

At her home both Foleys were still awake, waiting for her return. She refused refreshment of any kind and explained about Tyrone. Mary Ellen's hands went up to her mouth and stayed there as she whispered:

"God help him. And God help his family."

Jack Foley, who had survived Armageddon and seen death arrive in the most bizarre and horrifying guises, was even more affected, remembering the child he had swerved to avoid one year before.

Because Philip decided he would make an application to Beresford's he had time on his hands. Sensing that something was in the wind, and grievously upset by the drowning, his mother did not question this. He toyed with the idea of looking for casual labour on the canal wharves, but Tyrone was still missing and the Lake drew him towards her desperate scene.

On the day after the disappearance, the police presence seemed to have doubled. Philip learned that many members of the force, their shift at an end, had elected to stay voluntarily. They had been joined by miners off the night-shift who should now be sleeping. Longport, Burslem and Tunstall were enveloped in a pall of pain. It seemed that Tyrone Carroll was everybody's child. He could not be found.

By the second day the waiting and the tension were almost unendurable. In the impossible hope that he might not be in the lake some of the crowd searched and re-searched the undergrowth on its far side. Others wandered around aimlessly and were shepherded by the police away from the tragic spot. Others yet stood like statues awaiting events, many praying no doubt. Throughout the Potteries, people flocked to the Masses and other services and hundreds of candles burned for an exasperating, loveable child. The frogmen submerged again and again but without result.

It was about ten o'clock on the morning of the third day. Philip had already twice circled the lake merely to subdue his anxiety and once more had come abreast of where Tyrone had disappeared. He could hear the Police Inspector, the same man who had been there on that first night, saying that Tyrone was very well known to them. He heard him tell an ambulance man that the members of his Division now knew Pleasant Street as well as they knew their own Station.

Philip had walked on, commencing on a third tour of the lake and was fifty yards or so past the Inspector when he became conscious of a buzz of activity behind him. Instinctively he knew what was happening and returned to see what looked like a balloon being brought ashore by frogmen. He got close enough to see one of the medical staff take the object and invert it. Water gushed from its base which quickly took the form of a small human head and Philip could see as the water had completely drained from the "balloon" that it was a tiny body which was being suspended from its feet. They had found Tyrone.

"Tell Terry! ", "Fetch Terry!" "Terry!!" some of the crowd were shouting and a youth ran at speed to the far side of the lake where Terry Carroll, the child's father had been trampling, with fellow miners, through a large patch of tough, broad-bladed weeds. He came running to the spot like a man possessed.

As he arrived, Philip, through the huddled rescuers, could see quite plainly the state of Tyrone's remains. The grey body had been lacerated and Philip swallowed as he recalled there were pike in the Lake. The right eye socket was just a black mass and the left ear was missing. A sprig of chickweed, on which Tyrone had initially choked, lay over his lips and down his chin.

By now his father had arrived. Without speaking he clutched the body and seemingly oblivious to its condition he gathered it to him, sat down and began to rock it to and fro. The Police Inspector advised his colleagues to move back and not disturb the blue-scarred miner.

"Well, well - my little babbee..." they heard him begin. "Yer've come back. I knew you'd come back. I told yer Mammer you'd come back. I knew you'd come back. We're goin' up 'ome an' we'll see little Joe an' the others. And your Mam. My little babbee......, I said you'd come back."

The crowd was transfixed by what was happening. Many of its women were weeping. The Inspector knelt by Terry and said in low tones:

"Mr Carroll, there's no need to walk home. We can give you a lift."

Terry seemed not to have heard and continued to coo at the

corpse. Nevertheless he let himself be shepherded onto the rear seat of the Inspector's car where the willing hands of the rescuers swathed him and his son in heavy rugs. Before getting into the car, so no one could hear, the Inspector whispered to his driver:

"Haywood Hospital – and go Tunstall way."

The crowd stood as the car negotiated the lake shore, turned through the arch below the railway line, went past the Little Lake and over Packhorse bridge to Trubshawe Cross. Soon it was purring at quite a speed up the Brownhills Road to Tunstall.

Now Philip began to react to what he had seen. He became very cold yet, incredibly, he began to perspire. But it was a cold, frightening sweat, cold enough to be a harbinger of death. He was well acquainted with death and mutilation. He had seen headless corpses with thrashing limbs. He had seen comrades pleading for help as they tried to stuff back their own entrails into their lacerated bodies. Yet who could have forecast that the mask of this proud, hard man would have been sundered by the death of a roguish little boy?

He stumbled away from the Lake towards the bridge where he had stood with Frances. He reached it just in time to vomit into the canal. What he had just witnessed was even worse than the horrors he had experienced in the gripping undergrowth and sucking swamps of Burma. He leaned back against the curving brickwork of the bridge and covered his face with his hands. Yet what did it avail him to hide his tears when the dispersing crowds could plainly see his body shaking with grief?

When he went back along the towpath he was seized with only one thought – "thank God Frances wasn't there when they took him from the water."

Clive Beresford smiled and leaned forward over his desk:

"You wrote a very good letter, Mr Hughes - and told us almost everything we want to know."

"To be honest, Mr Beresford, I didn't write that letter without help. I'm happier around jigger boxes than I am writing letters. But I've told you the truth anyway."

"I appreciate your frankness but, after all, we're not looking for a letter-writer are we? We need someone who knows all the 'ins and outs' of clayware production – preferably someone who's been bench-trained, like yourself. We'd like to appoint a bright, energetic man who can take complete responsibility for the volume and quality from our flat shops and cup shops."

Philip nodded. He felt completely at ease with this mannerly, amicable man.

"We have two factories at Beresford Ceramics – this one, Whitfield Pottery, produces earthenware. Our other works – Grosvenor Pottery, in Longton, produces bone china. The post available at the moment is here, at Whitfield. It's a new one because of the continued expansion of the business. Our Works Manager, Mr Chidlow, is able to devote less and less time to the potting shops."

Beresford stopped:

"I noticed you smiled when I mentioned Mr Chidlow. Have you heard of him?"

"Who hasn't? If you had another Dick Chidlow working for you, there'd be no need to advertise this job."

"That's true. Much of our reputation for quality stems from his knowledge and his approach. Now - to fill in a few more details for you – the man we choose will be directly responsible to Mr Chidlow and we hope he'll show he's capable of doing a bigger job. You see, Dick is over sixty now and while we hope he'll be with us for years to come we have to groom his successor."

"You won't be short of men in Burslem who'd want to be *his* understudy."

"Yes....I'm sure that's right, but when the qualifications are set out you'd be surprised at how quickly the field narrows itself down. Of course, it's easy to extend the qualifications until the man chosen is expected to be a paragon of all the virtues. Yet it's not a perfect world so if an applicant approaches eighty percent of the ideal, we must consider him – seriously - I think you could boil down the *decisive* criteria for success in this job down to just two or three. I wonder if you could have a try at telling me what they might be?"

Philip considered:

"Well the bed-rock requirement is for knowledge and ability in clayware production. If you don't have that the potters will see through you in about five minutes. If there is a fault to be corrected, you've got to be able to see to it, otherwise the sham will show. Respect goes to the root of things. The next quality is honesty. Really that should come at the top of the list. Workers don't mind a man being firm as long as he's fair, and doesn't play favourites. I think honesty ensures you won't have too much friction on settle day."

"O.K. Anything else?"

The man must be able to *manage*, which means more than getting the best out of people and sorting out problems, it means showing people *how* they can improve their standards and helping them *want* to improve. And of course there's the planning side to that – planning for a smooth work flow – no waiting for clay or boards – no log jams with carrying–out to the ovens – making sure the fitters are on hand for machine repairs, making sure the tools turnaround is up to stratch."

Clive Beresford was secretly pleased that Philip had not dealt in safe generalities but had explained the management tasks in relation to clayware production. He seemed to have the alertness and awareness and, of course, the practical knowledge to succeed in the job. Beresford smiled:

"Well, that's a fair summary, I think. Perhaps another thing I might add has to do with *intelligence* which is bound up with the ability to take the long view, ...most important now that the industry is becoming much more sophisticated. So I was particularly interested to see you've enrolled at the Technical College for the ceramics courses."

"Yes. If I get a start in factory management I'll want to know all about the technical side of potting and how it's developing."

"You're keen to make progress then....(?)"

"Yes.

Beresford was no theorist in human relations, being more reliant on his instincts and natural courtesy. Nonetheless he decided to test Philip's temperament for management by ruffling his composure a little:

"I think ambition is commendable...but I see you finished school at 14...."

The observation had been expected and Philip also smiled:

"A plodder can achieve things, if he puts his mind to it, Mr Beresford."

The managing director considered. He had learned a great deal about the young man's background from Frances Bromley. Hughes had not pleaded his family circumstances in defence of his lack of more than a basic education. He had given a neutral answer.

At this point Philip was noticing how organised and well-appointed Clive Beresford's office was. It was fresh-flowered, light and welcoming. He contrasted it with the office of another managing director he knew, which seemed so dark and forbidding.

Beresford eased his dictating machine a little to one side so that he could lean further forward over the gleaming top of his desk.

"Mr Hughes, how far do you want to go in this industry?"

"Well, perhaps one day I might make Works Manager."

Clive leaned back and laughed:

"Actually, I was hoping you'd say you'd like to end up in this chair. In case that surprises you I must explain that at Beresford's we like everyone to feel that the sky's the limit. That is quite genuine, I assure you. I'm afraid that British management isn't all it should be at the moment. There's a vacuum at the top and I think our overseas rivals sense that. We ask for honesty, loyalty and willingness to learn and we are more than ready to give loyalty in return.

You may feel this is a strange interview because I've done most of the talking but you know, often too much time is spent telling the applicant what is expected and not enough about what the employer is like, what the job entails and what opportunities could be available for someone who does the job well. Answering an advertisement doesn't mean a person will take the job even if it's offered. A man wants reassurance he's making the right move, wouldn't you think so, Mr Hughes?"

"Yes sir, but I wouldn't want too much reassurance. There's your standing as a firm for one thing and having met you and talked to you, I'm sure it's a worthwhile job and one with prospects."

Philip laughed then:

"And not overlooking the fact that I don't have any sort of job at present."

Beresford decided that the boy's open features did not belie him. He had integrity and was self-possessed. He also seemed committed to make a success of whatever he undertook. Frances had been right about him.

"Yes....I noticed in your letter that you were unemployed at present. I don't want to dwell on your departure from Grange Pottery unless it was connected with the way you did your job."

"It was a personal matter, Mr Beresford."

"In that case I don't think it's really relevant to your application for this post."

Philip's heart thundered thankfully and for a second the men smiled their understanding at each other.

"Just be patient with me for a little longer, Mr Hughes. We have an important point to clear up. Then I'll take you into the shops and I want you to meet Mr Chidlow, of course."

He paused:

"Now....if you were engaged, what starting salary would you expect?"

"Well, at the bench I've always earned good money - about £11 or £12 a week. If I go back to the bench I would expect to earn the same again. So if you offered me this job I'd like that sort of income to be covered. I realise, of course, that I'm inexperienced and untried as a manager so for a trial period I'd work for less provided it could be reviewed when I make progress."

"You've made that clear. I'd just add that the position is a staff appointment – salaried, with staff holiday entitlement and automatic eligibility for the superannuation scheme."

"I see."

"Right Mr Hughes – will you come on to the factory with me please?"

As they approached one of the cup shops Philip noticed the cleanliness of the factory. There was not a scrap of clay on any of the floors. In fact, he noted an operative with an industrial vacuum cleaner busy in the area. He contrasted this with the "wet method" still employed at the Grange consisting of a water sprinkler and a sweeping brush – virtually guaranteeing some level of silicosis for the night sweeper.

The women in the cup-shop nodded respectfully as Clive Beresford passed them. He took Philip to the only empty machine in the shop.

"Could I trouble you to make me a cup? Put this coat overall on but don't get it dirty. It belongs to Mr Chidlow. He's been tinkering here today."

As Beresford laughed, Philip was momentarily taken out of his stride. He was a platemaker with no experience of holloware production but did not protest. His competence was obviously being tested. He saw two or three cup moulds, for the production of London Tall tulip shaped 7oz teacups. A small wad of clay had been left next to them. It lay beneath a piece of damp press-cloth.

The jolley was motorised, as was every other machine in the shop. He had heard Jack Dempster say that the "Grange" would also be making this change. Dempster had added that the whole process might take five years.

Philip clicked on the electric current, threw a ball of clay into the bucket shaped mould and brought down the steel profile into the centre of the spinning clay. The tool shaped the inside of the cup, its external shape being fashioned by the mould. Then he brought a steel needle to the edge of the mould in order to scrape off the excess clay which had risen as the tool was driving the clay into shape. Clive Berseford noted with satisfaction there was very little excess clay. This signified Philip had judged the amount of clay required for the production of the cup with exactitude. He was certainly not a wasteful worker thought the Chief Executive as he watched Philip rounding the top of the spinning cup with a wet middle finger.

He handed the mould to Beresford who looked at the gleaming newly-made cup it contained.

"Mr Hughes, what's this?"

At the bottom of the cup, in its exact centre, was a tiny lump of clay.

"It's a pap."

"I don't know very much about this but doesn't the tool setting have to be altered to clear it? In other words, if the tool is moved further over centre, won't the pap disappear?"

The youth took back the mould. He drew from his pocket a small, slim pen-knife, put this into the mould and sliced the cup into two halves. He pulled out one of these and discarded it, showing the other half clearly outlined in the mould to Clive:

"Not in this case. You see the side setting – it's just thick enough for a London Tall teacup. We can check its weight if you like but I think moving the tool further over centre will make the cups too heavy in the side. This tool is short in the nose. It needs grinding down, scribing against the correct template and filing through to the correct profile."

"I see. Shall we go to find Mr Chidlow?"

This encounter was short and sweet. They entered the Work's Manager's office. A round-shouldered, hook nosed figure was peering into a jug mould. This was Dick Chidlow, renowned as the best potter in Burslem. His hair was absent from the crown of his head but grew luxuriantly at its sides, long and straight over the ears. His toga-like coat overall gave him the appearance of some old world philosopher. He looked at them over his half-moon spectacles and Philip noted the eyes that fixed him were blue and young. He sensed the mind was young too.

"Good morning, Mr Chidlow."

"....mornin', Mr Clive."

"This is Mr Hughes, who's applied for the position of clay manager."

"Hughes? Hughes? Where d'yer come from?"

"Hanover Street, here in Burslem."

"You any relation to Jack Hughes?"

"He was my father."

He looked levelly at Philip for a second or so.

"Hm. I was sorry to hear about his accident. It was a bad job by all accounts. We started together in the pit, as lads. I don't know how he stuck it all them years. I was up an' out of that place within a week!"

His eyes pierced Philip:
'An' are you as good a worker as your father?"
"I try to be."
"What are you doing now?"
Clive Beresford came in quickly:
"Mr Hughes is a platemaker – of some experience."
The old potter considered.
"Mm. Do you set your own tools?"
"Yes."
"Can you file tools?"
"Yes."
"I mean can you file 'em properly – everybody says 'yes'."

Philip had to laugh:
"Yes, I can file them properly Mr Chidlow."

"I think I've just heard some evidence for that in the cup shop," Beresford said, indicating that Philip had come through the "test piece" Chidlow had set up for him.

"What do you think's the biggest fault in tool filing?"

"Well, the profile has to be in register with the template but I think after that the biggest fault is when the rake is wrong."

"How d'yer mean 'wrong'?"

"Not steep enough. If a potter files a tool with too soft a rake – half round in the worst cases – he'll find it easier to work with but that tool will have to keep going back for re-filing. So what he gains in output he loses by trips to the fitting shop."

"I see. So you reckon you know all there is to know about pottin', eh young man?"

"No – but when I've had your experience I should be getting warm."

It was time for Clive to laugh again. Even Dick gave a small smile.

The Works Manager picked up the jug mould. Within

was a jug in its clay state. It had been "cast" which is to say it had been made by pouring a clay slip, to which certain chemicals had been added, into the mould.

"Well let's see how much you do know. What's wrong with this?"

He passed the mould to Philip. Clive Beresford was somewhat concerned:

"I don't think he's had any experience of casting."

"If a young man wants to get on Mr Clive he generally learns more about the trade than he's presently being paid to know."

The two men waited as Philip turned the interior of the mould towards the light. He saw that within the jug casting were a number of small lumps.

"It's wreathed, Mr Chidlow."

"Why?"

"There could be too much silicate in the slip."

Dick began to walk towards the door:

"That's right, lad – an' I'm just off to stick my foot up somebody's fat end."

He was gone.

A few minutes later Philip Hughes and Clive Beresford were standing at the gates of the Whitfield Pottery.

"Thank you very much for seeing me. It's all been very interesting," smiled Philip.

"It's been a pleasure to see you, Mr Hughes. You were the last applicant to be seen so we should be able to let you know something very soon. I take it that if we offered you the job you'd be prepared to come to us....(?)"

"I would....yes, Mr Beresford."

They shook hands.

Soon after, Beresford was sitting in his office thinking and smiling to himself. He flicked down the key to his communication panel and heard his secretary respond briskly.

"Mrs Webster, will you ask Mr Chidlow to come over as soon as he can?"

Philip walked back to the Market Place. He felt elated. Whether or not he got the job he had enjoyed the experience – it had been more like a discussion between professionals than a job interview. And if his mother had had to work "in the pots" he was glad she had trained to be a caster. Otherwise how would he have known what would happen when there was an excess of sodium silicate in the casting slip?

Chapter Sixteen
Parting of the Ways

Frances Bromley and Philip Hughes were destined to live significant lives. Naturally their love would not escape difficulties or adversity. Yet, just as it would remain strong in spite of real setbacks so it would persevere through life's merely irritating and drab days. Finally, in the pattern of their progress there were to be some significant occurrences to temper and anneal them indissolubly together. An example here was their attendance at the Requiem Mass and interment of little Tyrone Carroll.

As if it was not already harrowing enough to endure, that day was rendered even more painful by the absence of Terry, Tyrone's father. When the child's body was recovered there had been a double tragedy to announce. The chilling message swiftly carried through Burslem's streets was:

"Young Tyrone's bin drowned an' 'is faether's gone doolally!"

Despite the mother's desperate protestations, medical opinion was that it would be difficult to assess the effect on him of his son's burial and that, therefore, Terry must be kept "under observation" for the time being. So on the day, Veronica Carroll had to look to others for support, not least Frances Bromley, her new and dear friend. When the priest turned and uttered the "Dominicus vobiscum" the congregation's "Et cum spiritu tuo" response was strong and fervent. "How could I have forgotten that the Mass would be in Latin?", thought Philip. It brought to mind the jibe of an Army officer as he watched the Catholics departing for Mass: "There they go. Soon they'll be jabbering away in a dead language and few of them will have the slightest idea what it all means." How baseless the criticism was came home to Philip in the next instant when Frances was offering to share her Mass book with him. He could see that for each Latin verse and response an English translation was next to it so that understanding, as well as reading, was automatic. Now he also realised that a universal church was best served by a universal language.

As the Mass progressed he looked from time to time towards Margaret Gilligan, Tyrone's grandmother. Old now and very sick, he remembered that she had worked as a tower at Bromleys for many years. His own mother had once told him that Margaret was merely twelve when she left school. Yet here she was manipulating the page markers in her battered Roman Missal, totally involved in the liturgy of the Mass.

At the "Credo", the "Sanctus" and the "Agnus Dei" Margaret sang through her tears. At the Preface she responded confidently to the invocation of the priest:

Verse: Dominus vobiscum (The Lord be with you)
response: Et cum spiritu tuo (And with thy spirit)
V: Sursum corda (Lift up your hearts)

r: Habemus ad Dominum (We have lifted them up to the Lord)

V: Gratias agamus Domino Deo nostro (Let us give thanks to the Lord our God)

r: Dignum et justum est (It is meet and just).

When the bell was rung at the most solemn moment of the Mass, as the priest was elevating the newly consecrated Host, Philip noted with a sidelong glance how old Margaret's lips were forming the humble petition prior to her communion:

"Domine, non sum dignus ut intres sub tectum meum sed tantum dic verbo et sanabitur anima mea"

("Lord I am not worthy that thou shouldst come under my roof but only say the word and my soul shall be healed").

There were many things Philip would remember: the reverence and awe at the recitation of De Profundis, the beauty of the entire liturgy, and the simple piety of the congregation – the stricken family itself, and the old and the young, the potters, the miners, the weak and the disabled. The candles, the incense, the reverence of the priest and his many altar servers were part of the dignified ambience within which these obsequies were so respectfully conducted. The hymns soared to the heavens especially the one by Cardinal John Henry Newman, a convert to the Catholic faith:

"Lead kindly light amid the encircling gloom
Lead thou me on;
The night is dark and I am far from home
Lead thou me on ..
.........."

Yet the most stunning recollection Philip Hughes took away from those rites and solemnities was the fervour of

Margaret Gilligan as she joined in the plainchant of the hauntingly beautiful "Dies irae":

"Dies irae, dies illa
Solvet saeclum in favilla
Teste David cum Sibylla
Quantus tremor est futurus
..............."

The dignified old woman was giving all the strength of her sick body and tired mind to pious supplication for the repose of the soul of a mischievous infant whose time on earth had been no more than the darting flight of a tiny bird.

When the cortege formed up Philip was thunderstruck. A large group of men were arranging themselves into two columns in front of the hearse and its tiny coffin. There were at least forty of them and he recognised them all as miners. They were making the silent statement that since Terry Carroll could not be here for his son they would take the child to his rest. Choked with emotion he looked towards Frances who, he knew, had arranged the funeral on the family's behalf. There was love and sadness in the smile she gave him. Then, beyond the final car in the procession, he noticed another large group of men, and women too, forming up for the long walk with Tyrone to Burslem Cemetery.

The funeral made its way out of the Market Place and into Moorland Road. The police, who had come to know Tyrone so well in life and death, marshalled the traffic at that busy junction efficiently and without fuss. The crowds lining the pavements stood in mute witness and respect. Today there was no irritation at the hold-ups and congestion – no-one wanted to hustle away to make another penny or to hurry to the kitchen fire away from the wind.

The mourners went up, out of the hollow, and as they passed the Miners' Hall, the leading men looked over to the right. There was the winding gear of the Sneyd Colliery. On a New Year's Day, just a little while ago, an explosion had killed fifty seven of the men who toiled there. For many of the walkers "Sneyd" was their pit but today their own lives were not at risk...today, for Tyrone and Terry, they had had a "day's play"...their grimly humorous term for absence from work for any reason.

Suddenly, spontaneously, as if he were in the June Procession for the Sacred Heart, one of the miners began to sing:

"Sweet heart of Jesus, fount of love and mercy
Today we come thy blessing to implore
O touch our hearts, so cold and so ungrateful
And make them Lord thine own for ever more
............"

Soon they were all singing and there were other hymns....all the way, yes, all the way, to the graveside.

They laid the little body to rest close to a small tree. Veronica Carroll seemed comforted by this. She whispered to her mother and to Frances:

"I shall know where to find him now."

As they walked away from the grave Philip, searching for a word that would ease his own sadness, murmured:

"The air's lovely up here."

Frances looked back to the little plot:

"Yes, it's a pity he'll never enjoy it."

As they went to the hall, rented by Frances for the gathering of the mourners, Philip was thoughtful. He had been dazed by what he had seen and heard today. It was easy to see how a Church with such a history, such a liturgy had been responsible for the development of so much of Europe's culture – including its education, art and music and architecture. Britain had benefited greatly from its influence. The impulse of its faith had led to the building of many of its cathedrals and yet today, Catholics were treated as outsiders and words such as "alien", "forcign" and "disturbing" were used in relation to them. Yet, in furthering the aims of the British Empire and latterly in two World Wars, thousands of Catholics had perished.

These thoughts reminded him of Peter Bromley and his faith – so devoted it had supervened in the horror and despair where it seemed that God was absent. Then Philip felt that little charge of conscience – about the secret he felt forced to keep, especially from the girl who was so important to him. Speedily and because of its discomfort, he put the thought aside and, on impulse, decided something else – today he would take Frances to meet his mother.

When Frances was taking her leave of Veronica and the other mourners Philip could see respect for her etched on every face and love on many. Before the final goodbye he could hear her, unobtrusively arranging to take Veronica to "Cheddleton" on the following Sunday. "Cheddleton" was shorthand for the mental institution located there. They would be going to see Terry Carroll.

Outside the Grange Pottery Philip kissed her and arranged to return at six o'clock in order to take her to Hanover Street. Going back for her that evening his thoughts returned to the Requiem Mass and how the majestic liturgy of a world-wide Church had been employed to mark the death of a tiny scrap of humanity from one of Burslem's poorest homes. It stirred the memory of something he had learned at "Sunday school" – "for as much as you do this to the least of my brethren, so you do it to me." Frances had been right: in keeping with Christ himself, hers was the Church of the poor.

The instant they met on the doorstep of the Hughes' home the women's eyes searched each other for an instant. What they saw there, reciprocally, was warmth and fellow-feeling. Then Elizabeth Hughes was overcome by the girl's beauty and struggled for words as the mourning clothes she wore signalled Tyrone's importance to her. Frances smiled:

"Hallo, Mrs Hughes – I'm very happy to meet you."

"Thank you, Miss Frances. I'm happy to meet you."

Then Elizabeth Hughes found more words:

"Here, let me take your coat."

Frances slipped out of the coat and eased the silk scarf from her neck. With decorum, though breathing heavily, Mrs Hughes showed her into an immaculately kept parlour room and invited her to sit. Carefully smoothing Frances' coat and scarf she said with a note of triumph:

"I'll put these where they'll be safe!"

It was as if she knew the one spot where the garments would be secure and free from burglary and damage.

Philip followed his mother as she made her way down the narrow hallway. He could hear her difficult breathing. When they reached the light of the kitchen he saw the beads of perspiration at the nape of her neck.

"Ooh....what a kerfuffle!", she sighed.

His hands went to her shoulders:

"Mam, relax...she's not going to eat you! And there's no need to call her Miss Frances."

"What shall I offer her to drink....a sherry?"

"I'm sure she'd love a cup of tea...but that's all by the way. She's really here to meet you and talk to you."

"Talk to me?!.....but she's one of the Bromleys and she looks so stunning!"

"Well....you're one of the Hughes's and you look stunning. Look....I'll just ask her about the tea."

He returned to confirm tea would be welcome and he carried the tray, with its cargo of Brooke Bond "makings" and malted milk biscuits, back to the parlour. He then decided to withdraw so as to let this meeting of the women find its own level. Moreover, when he had returned from the funeral his mother had handed him an envelope. She had watched the procession from the precincts of the church and subsequently had been so full of questions for him there had been no opportunity to open the letter. Now he could do so.

Returning, he was pleased to see his wiliness had worked, for his mother was relaxed and talking animatedly:

"Oh....and I remember your grandfather, Miss Frances..... er, Frances. He was a lovely chap. You see...when I first left school, I went to work at the "Grange", running moulds for Mary Turner, Dick Chidlow's wife...... "Turner" as she was then. And your grandfather used to come and pay all the makers out of his big leather apron and he'd give all us young uns treacle toffee your grannie had made. When I was older I started casting."

Although Frances was smiling encouragement, Elizabeth stopped then, awkwardly. She feared she might be bringing the conversation to a topic better avoided – that of Grange Pottery in its latter-days and the manner of her son's leaving it. It was the hiatus which gave Philip his opportunity. He handed his letter to Frances:

"This came today. I wonder if I know somebody who was behind it all?"

"May I read it?"

"Of course."

Below the address and the date, the text of the letter was comparatively short:

"Dear Mr Hughes,

It was a great pleasure to meet you when you were interviewed in connection with our advertisement.

We are offering you the position of Clay Manager at the Whitfield Pottery, at a starting salary of £12.00.d. per week. This salary will be reviewed within six months.

You will recall I explained it was a staff appointment and as the engagement is dated from today I am enclosing your first week's salary.

Please come to this factory on Monday next at 8 a.m. and ask for Mr Chidlow.

I am sure we will benefit from your skill and experience and I hope you will be very happy with us.

Yours sincerely,
Clive Beresford,
Managing Director"

Frances leapt from her chair. She hugged Philip:

"Oh....this is wonderful. I'm so happy for you."

She waved the letter.

"This is exactly what you deserve!"

Unsure, Elizabeth Hughes looked to Frances:

"What is it?"

"Well, Philip....No....you tell your mother!"

"I'm going to be Clay Manager at Beresfords."

His mother sat down. Her breathing became more laboured and the blood drained from her features. Frances was concerned:

"Mrs Hughes, are you all right?"

The older woman struggled:

"Ooh, dear.....", she managed at last.

Philip laughed loudly:

"Well!..... that's great!....is that all you're going to say, 'Ooh dear'?"

She looked across at him:

"Did you say 'Clay Manager'?"

"Yes! Look.....", cried Frances, passing the letter to her. The mother seemed hardly able to look at it. When she did it was obvious that while everything was seen, nothing was perceived.

She rose quickly:

"What must you think of us? I'd better make some more tea."

And she left, abruptly.

Philip's lip tightened. Sensing his disappointment, Frances touched his arm:

"I think your mother's a bit overcome."

He shook his head:

"No. This is typical. I'm afraid she's always the damp squib."

"I'm sure she doesn't want to be. Let's give her a minute then I'll go in to her."

He put his arm about her:

"I wasn't born yesterday, Frances. You're the one who's responsible for all this. How else would he know a week's salary would be very welcome?"

"I've told you....you've done it yourself. There's no-one more worthy of having the job than you are. And you'll go higher...you'll see."

Feigning exasperation he shook his head then kissed her with great tenderness.

A minute or so later Frances was at the door of the small kitchen:

"May I come in?"

Now that she was back at her "station" and "in control", Elizabeth was calmer:

"'course you can. Philip said you'd be coming here straight from work so I thought I'd better cook you a meal."

She moved to the stove:

"I hope you like this, it's best Scotch halibut."

"It looks lovely. Thank you."

"The potatoes are on. I'm just finishing the vegetables. They won't be long. I'll make some tea and bring it in. You can have it while you're waiting."

"Why can't I make the tea while you carry on with the meal?"

"All right. If you're sure....but mind your lovely clothes."

They worked in silence for a little while then Elizabeth said:

"Do you think he'll be able to manage this new job? It's a big responsibility ......"

" He'll be superb at it, Mrs Hughes. He was respected all over our firm and he deserves much more than platemaking for the rest of his life."

Frances was surprised then for, soundlessly, Mrs Hughes began to weep. Immediately, the younger woman put down the tea things and held her:

"What's the matter?"

When her tears abated she murmured:

"I was just thinking....our Phil's had to make sacrifices for us. Now his chance might be coming after all. It's wonderful to hear you speak so well of him. I wish his Dad'd been here."

Then motherly feelings burst forth:

"'course, he was always a good son. I remember, just after his father died, we were told the rent on this place was going up....by two shillings a week! It was such a lot in them days. I told him we'd have to leave but he said: no we're not....you'll never give this place up. And, unknowings to me, he got a Saturday job in the market.....humpin' sacks o' stuff and big boxes o' fruit. He came in here that first week and gave me four shillings. 'That's for the rent', he said

He was only twelve and he'd had to leave the grammar school because I couldn't keep him there. Every week he went to that market – sometimes it was two shillings, or three, four shillings on a good week. His hands were raw and he'd come in here sometimes blue with cold, but he never flinched. He's as hard as nails.

Then when he started work running moulds he used to turn all his money up and trust to what I could give him for his pocket. He did that right up to when he went in the Army and he's looked after me ever since."

She dabbed her eyes on the corner of her pinafore:

"So you think he'll be all right doing this job, do you Miss?"

Impulsively, Frances kissed her on the forehead:

"He'll be outstanding. You'll see."

The women looked at each other earnestly. Elizabeth said:

"You think a lot of him, don't you?"

The answer was simple and undramatic:

"I love him, Mrs Hughes."

The mother seemed about to weep again so Frances gave her a quick squeeze:

"Listen, why don't you go in there and tell him how proud you are?"

Elizabeth looked tormented and, almost inaudibly, said:

"I can't."

Not for the first time or the last Frances despaired that the brutal culture in which they were forced to live inhibited them from any display of finer feelings.

"Hey! Have I been abandoned?"

It was Philip. Now the opportunity was lost for his mother's congratulations: events were moving on; the three of them left the kitchen for the small sitting room and before long the evening meal was under way.

When it was almost finished they heard the rattle of the latch at the back door:

"Are yer in?"

The voice was unmistakeable. A shade doubtfully, Mrs Hughes called:

"Come in, Mr Hogan."

The elf appeared carrying a mackerel. Its head and tail emerged from a piece of rolled up newspaper.

"I wus wonderin' if you cud do me this in your stove?", he enquired as he appeared. Then his cap came off:

"Ooh, Miss Frances. I didner know you wuz 'ere. How are yer?"

"Fine. How are you, Mr Hogan?"

"Middlin'....unny middlin'," he confided..... "I'm not without me troubles but I keep smilin'."

At this, he paused to glance towards that sector of his own home where he imagined his wife, Margaret, would be at that moment. But then he rallied:

"An' 'ow are you, me ole Phil?"

"Pretty fair, thanks."

"Fixed up with a job yet?"

Frances could not resist answering:

"As a matter of fact, Mr Hogan, you're looking at Beresford's new Clay Manager. He starts on Monday."

"Clay Manager?! At Beresfords?! Bloomin' ummers! That's champion! I'll be 'round there next week, Phil, so's yer kin fix me up with a job.....summat light."

Then he gave Frances a ridiculous wink.

Sensing Billy's visit might be well extended if given a modicum of encouragement, Philip looked towards Frances:

"Well, I suppose we ought to be making a move..."

"Ah thote a bit o' competition ud give thee the wind up, Mester Clay Manager," quipped the elf.

Frances was uncertain:

"Well, I was just going to help your mother with the washing up..."

"No you won't," said the scandalised mother, "you get out for a bit while it's still light."

Then she took the mackerel from Billy Hogan.

Reluctantly Frances rose:

"Well, thank you very much, Mrs Hughes. For the lovely meal and for having me here."

"You're more than welcome.....at any time."

Frances kissed her and Billy said hopefully:

"What about me?"

He had to be content with a delightful smile.

As the door closed behind the couple, Elizabeth knitted a teacloth between her fingers. Her tears were forming again:

"Oh, Mr Hogan – I've never met a more beautiful girl since God put me on earth."

Billy fished out a cigarette from his pocket. He lit it slowly, and with some show, for he felt a weighty pronouncement coming on. Twice then he pointed its wet end symbolically towards the front door for he too was becoming emotional:

"Aye, missus....she's got the face of a film star an' the nature of a saint. Ah slipped off the bank today an' ah seen 'er at the funeral – 'er really loved that babbee. An' ah'll tell thee summat else, missus...."

For emphasis, he put his hand on Elizabeth's shoulder:

"....if your Phil 'as 'er....'e'll never look back!"

As they stepped into Hanover Street Philip asked Frances what she would like to do for the rest of the evening. She thought they might walk for an hour or so before they returned to her car and she made for home. So he took her down to the corner of Enoch Street and turned left, skirting St. John's Church and its grounds. Continuing along Regent Street West they again turned left, into Waterloo Road, and began a slow ascent to the Town Centre. Subsequently, they reached the Market Place and went on to St. John's Square before re-entering Hanover Street.

When the walk began, Frances had asked:

"Why did Mr Hogan want your mother to cook the fish? Don't they have a stove?"

Philip started on a long explanation which might tire any reader were it set out verbatim. So what follows is Philip's story, "condensed into headlines", as it were.

After years of struggle Mrs Margaret Hogan discovered that times were becoming slightly more plentiful. Her children, Vincent and Teresa, had grown up and found work. Finally, work had found her husband, William Liam. Margaret had a "dream"and now, each week, a few shillings went into a cardboard box in the cockloft so that the dream could become a reality. This dream of hers had a front elevation of glass and chrome and its premises contained a frier, fired by gas, no less. In its "dining salon" there would be tables with plastic peppers and salts and teaplates in gay, assorted colours.

"Hogan's High Class Fish and Chip Restaurant" need not necessarily be on the busy Waterloo Road. It could be on any street in Burslem for its resplendence would make the whole of Burslem gape in wonder. All in the hollow would run to its door. There would be battalions of relatives and friends hoarding newspaper. Smilingly, Margaret and her "staff" would scoop up additional chips for anyone they knew. And even in the face of dripping shortages, Government restrictions or even another World War a notice would always be in place, declaiming to the Potteries that the Hogans were "Frying Tonight".

Clearly, when the coins in the cockloft amounted to £63 all told, Margaret felt her dream was taking on both shape and substance. Her son Vincent, however, accidently discovered the treasure chest when he had ascended to the loft searching for a pair of shin pads. Misguidedly he had told his father, adding that the box sounded as if it contained money. Billy's lightning reaction was to swear Vincent to secrecy, explaining that if the "tax man" ever found out about it he might just be low enough to pay them a visit, even to search out the box himself.

Now, Margaret Hogan's dream was no more. She felt the elf had been put up to it by two people she needn't walk a hundred miles to meet. This was unjust, for when Fred Knapper and "Ludo" Dunning had been invited to join him for the trip to the Steeplechase Meeting at Woore (organised by a local hostelry) they had believed his explanation that the trip was being financed thanks to a "long-priced 'oss" which had romped home a winner. Had they been told they were making the trip courtesy of Maggie Hogan's savings they would, at the very least, have had to absorb considerable liquid persuasion before agreeing to go.

In a temporary lull between her tearful episodes, she had asked:

"Why did you do eet, Billy?"

"'cause I wanted to double yer money. Me only mistake was 'cos I dunner know as much abite racin' over the sticks as racin' on the flat!"

"But you never win anything on the flat either!" she protested, "an' why couldn't you have told me at least?"

"Because ah wanted it be a surprise!"

Momentarily, she was silenced by his cunning logic, but then she swung back to the attack:

"Yer went racin' on my savin's and never asked me whether I wanted to go."

He was stupefied:

"There was unny three seats left on the bus, woman!" Whereas previously she wept now she was howling.

When her tears finally abated she reached a decision: she would never speak to him again. To a man of his sunny disposition, the "silent treatment" was particularly difficult to endure. He became seized with the desire to make amends. But how? Ah....she was a house-proud woman so he would win her back through interior decoration. Yes - that was it – he would paint something for her.

First he looked at the kitchen door then dismissed it as a project. Painting a door would necessitate the painting of the other doors and, what was worse, skirting boards. On the other hand, a gas stove was a small, self-contained thing and, where its black, vitreous enamelled surface was worn, their own stove did need a bit of a "touch up".

Billy found a tin of what he took to be black paint. When opened, the viscous fluid was thixotropic enough to thin itself as he stirred it. Though its volatile odours attacked his eyes and lungs, he was heartened:

"....that shows it's good stuff!"

However, the pungent atmosphere persisted and it took a horrified wife to explain that he had renovated the stove with an aged disinfectant. Nor was that the end of it, for the ageing process had produced in the material the concomitant phenomenon of rock-hard setting. Nothing that he or Vincent could do would dislodge the "paint". Lighting even a single burner on the stove produced an uninhabitable atmosphere.

For the time being and due to the stubborn refusal of any of Billy's horses to win, the Hogans were unable to purchase a replacement stove. Which explains why the stove in the Hughes' household was cooking for two families. As Margaret had explained to Elizabeth at the onset:

"It won't clean an' we can't cook in the thing!"

In support, Billy offered a pseudo-scientific addendum:

"No....because yer see, missus....if the gaseous vapers get in the snappin' we shall all snuff eet."

In fairness, he had tried to resolve their problem by a "back to basics" culinary process. This utilised an ancient set of hangers and a tin-bonnet he had retrieved from the coal shed. The "hangers" consisted of a metal platform some ten inches square, with hooks at the front and a handle at the back. The hangers could thus be hooked onto the bars of a coal fire and a plate or a tray of uncooked food then placed on its platform. To keep in the heat of the fire and to speed the cooking process a cowl-shaped tin bonnet was placed on the platform behind the food.

"More natural", Billy smiled as a further flake of rust fell into his spluttering cheese and bacon. Trying to win converts he would look around his family:

"Warm the oatcakes Mag! Ah tell thee what – Fred Knapper knows a bit o'summat. He's never 'ad owt else but 'ingers an' tin-bonnet."

When he had left for "Bromleys" on the following day, Margaret handed down her verdict on the arrangement – both the hangers and tin-bonnet were handed to Eddie Cullen, the rag-and-bone man, in exchange for three coloured balloons. She tied these to the back of Billy's rocking chair.

Philip told the story to Frances for a clear purpose, she was still "on the edge"....choked with grief at the memory of Tyrone's interment, sick at heart that she would never again see his mischievous face. The "gas stove incident" was intended to provide some respite for her. It produced in her the same reaction it did in everyone who listened to Billy's adventures – despair and delight. As they walked through Burslem's streets, sometimes she shook her head sadly at what Margaret Hogan had to endure. At other times Philip slipped an arm about her waist as she rocked with laughter.

When they reached her car in Hanover Street he kissed her goodbye with great tenderness. Watching her drive away he knew how harrowing the day had been for her. It was a day he would remember all his life.

Reaching Bradwell Grange, Frances was surprised to see her father's Humber car parked outside the entrance to the hallway. She knew he was due to return from London but expected him to have done so earlier. In which case, Mr Foley would have garaged the car by now.

She was even more surprised, on opening the hall door, to find her father standing there. He was slipping his watch into his waistcoat pocket and was clearly furious:

"What time d'you call this?!"

"It's about eleven thirty. Why, Dadder?"

"Don't soft soap me lady! Have you seen that tripe-hound again?"

"If you're referring to Philip Hughes...yes, I've seen him again...."

"And did I tell you not to..."

She searched for words. She wanted to save the situation but if she told him he had no right to forbid her to see anyone, this would make things worse. He was impatient for an answer:

"Did I tell you not to?!"

Still cool and self-possessed she answered "Yes", quietly.

"Did you have anything to do with him going to Beresfords?"

This was incredible yet, though feeling awkward and taken aback, she squared her shoulders:

"I did speak to Clive Beresford about him, yes – seeing that he was never given a written reference from us....but he got the job on his own merits."

She had "turned the tables" on him and he seemed about to strike her. His eyes bulged and his fingers tried to impale the closed fists that contained them. She was physically afraid now. If he lost his struggle for self-control he would spring at her. He gasped finally and his fury gave way to heavy sarcasm:

"Of course you spoke to Clive Beresford. I could have answered my own question and d'you know why? Because when I got to Stoke Station I dropped into the Association Chambers. The members there were full of it....sneering and laughing....I'd sacked a platemaker and he'd got a manager's job at Beresfords. That Clive Beresford's a serpent but I've got you to thank in the first place for making me look a bloody idiot!"

"It wouldn't have anything to do with how you handled

the situation originally, would it?"

She immediately regretted the remark for his arms were flailing like windmills. He pointed at her, menacingly:

"You have got us all talked about from one end of the Potteries to the other. When you joined us I thought we'd benefit from it but all you've brought us is worry and chaos. I understand you've been out of the place all day today......"

Frances was incensed:

"No....your spies are wrong for once.....not quite all day, Dadder. I was there this afternoon but this morning I was at the funeral of a little boy. He died a little while ago. And do you know why he died? BECAUSE HE HAD NOWHERE TO PLAY. They didn't mention that at the inquest and do you know why he had nowhere to play?.....because you and people like you take everything out of that place down there and put nothing back! If chaos does reign at the 'Grange', which is a lie, you are more responsible for it than I am"

He gathered himself for a final onslaught:

"You listen to me, lady – I care for those people down there but I don't get hysterical about it. Caring doesn't mean being luvvy-duvvy – it means making sure there are orders and jobs!"

She tried to step past him into the hall:

"Dadder, may I come in please?"

Now he lost control:

" 'Come in'? 'Come in'? Like a sneak-thief come in?"

He raised his hand as if to strike her, his face twisted with rage:

"What d'you want to come in for? To do more damage? For the last three days I've waited hand and foot on three smart lads from Franklins, Canada. Waited cap in hand for a massive order. And d'you know who got the order - Beresfords. I told you not to see your fancy man again. You not only see him you fix him up with a job!.....at Beresfords! And you ask if you can come in? Well the answer's "No" because Bromleys Earthenware and Bradwell Grange can do without you. And I can do without you until you've learned the meaning of loyalty!"

She looked at him, astonished:

"Very well, I'll leave in the morning if....."

Again his arms threshed the air:

"You'll leave now!"

Fiancee turned away from him and placed her keys on the hall table. As the heavy door closed behind her all the strength suddenly seemed to leave Ewart Bromley.

Sobbing, she ran down the broad drive out of Bradwell Grange. She turned left into Bradwell Lane then stopped. Where could she go to? If only for tonight, where could she go to? Instinct drove her towards the 'bus stop at Porthill Church. She began to run for the last few yards and clambered onto the platform of a double-decker 'bus which she thought was waiting at the stop. But the 'bus was merely in a line of traffic which had halted before negotiating the roundabout at the top of Porthill Bank.

"Not this one, Miss – we're out of service now – goin' to the garage," explained the conductor.

"Oh dear, I've got to get into Burslem. When's the next one?"

"Everythin's off the road now, Miss – it's past midnight."

The conductor looked at her. She was a beauty, even dressed in mourning clothes. He took in the unmistakable signs she had been weeping. He shepherded her to one of the long seats just inside the 'bus:

"I tell you what....sit just inside here. Let's hope an inspector doesn't cop us."

During the journey, surreptitiously, he looked at her from time to time.

When she alighted in Burslem's Market Place she stood still, wondering. The conductor stepped off the 'bus:

"Are you all right? Do yer know where yer goin', Miss?"

"Oh yes.....it's just over there."

She began to walk towards the fountain at the top of St. John's Square.

"Well, be sharp. You don't know who's about."

Then the conductor went briskly to the driver's cab:

"Hey!", he called to his colleague "I know 'er. That's the wench from Bromley's potbank – our Kitty works there. The poor kid looks poleaxed. Dust think I ought to go after 'er?"

The driver thought not:

"We're overdue now. If we take much longer we're both in trouble."

As the bus moved towards the traffic lights at Swan Bank, the conductor peered anxiously through its rear window but by now Frances had disappeared.

She walked to the bottom of the Square and was soon in Hanover Street. Philip lived somewhere near but she wasn't quite sure – oh yes!....here it was. However, like every other house, his home was in darkness. Disconsolate she walked past it and continued towards the bottom of the street. As she turned the corner into Enoch Street she bumped into someone:

"Up, duck!"

Fred Knapper was winded. He was accompanied by his nephew, Percy Birchall, so that Frances was now hemmed by two portly figures. Full of apology, she looked up:

"I'm terribly sorry."

Fred peered into the gloom:

"Why...it's Miss Frances!"

She looked down again, not knowing what to say. Fred's mind was working.... "summat was up".

"Er....you look a bit offside, Miss. I live just along 'ere. Would yer like ter come in and sit down for a minute?"

Frances nodded, dumbly, as she fought back the tears.

"Now Percy... you be off 'ome...an' say nothin' to anybody", the boilerman whispered.

Percy Birchall did not think as quickly as his uncle. He gaped at the hand that was waving him away then, resignedly, set off up Hanover Street;

"O.K. Unc. G'night. G'night Miss Frances."

"Oh, aye.....g'night Percy", said Fred on behalf of his intended guest and himself. As he guided her towards his front door he thought some small talk was appropriate·

"Er...that's Percy Birchall....me sister's lad. Yer might a seen 'im on the 'Grange'. He always comes ter 'ave a drop o' lobby with me on Satdee nights. He was just off 'ome and I was goin' to see to summat when we bumped inter you."

What he did not explain was that, following a report from his intelligence network that a deposit of horse manure lay in Velvet Street, he was on his way to survey it in case its size might justify being dealt with before morning when other gardeners were sure to appear.

When they reached his house Fred conducted her through a dark parlour and into his living room. As the light came on Frances saw the black range containing the fireplace. Unlike the gleaming one in the Hughes' house, this had a mat surface. The biggest iron saucepan she had ever seen sat on one of the hobs.

"I'm so sorry to trouble you like this, Mr Knapper, but the fact is – I've had a bit of an upset."

"Of course you 'ave", he replied as though commending her for her powers of observation.

"Come on.....sit yerself down."

He motioned her towards a wooden bench. Lacking either upholstery or cushions it offered the comfort level of a church pew.

Fred stood over her, thinking:

"I know! Would yer like a drop er lobby? That'll put yer right! We put a ham shank in eet ternight."

"No, thank you. I just want to sit for a little while then I'll be going."

At this, he was galvanised:

"Oh no yer won't! Now you jus' sit yer still for a bit. Don't stir! I'll be back in a minute!"

Frances sank back into her own thoughts but it was not long before she heard the front door being opened quickly:

"Frances...whatever is the matter?"

With a raincoat over his pyjamas Philip was looking down at her in tender consternation. Her arms went up to him:

"Oh, Philip....."

He sat beside her and held her tightly while she sobbed.

"That's it," said Fred, "best let 'er 'ave 'er cry out."

Then he withdrew to his parlour.

When she had quietened Philip stroked back her hair from her temples.

"Is this to do with your father, Frances?"

She nodded.

"Can you tell me what happened?"

"I.....I left the house."

He put her hand on her cheek. It was burning.

"The thing is....not to worry anymore tonight. Mr Knapper says you can stay here. He'll make up a bed for you on this bench. I can't bear to see you being put through this misery because of me. I'll go to your father in the morning and if he won't see reason I won't ask to see you anymore."

She was wide-eyed:

"....but I don't want that, Philip!"

He put his hands on her shoulders and looked at her earnestly:

"Well then, we've some deciding to do. Will you let *me* look after you?....I'm talking about for good, Frances!"

She had scarcely said "Yes" when on her lips she felt his own.

It is unlikely that a proposal of marriage and its acceptance were ever made in such unromantic circumstances. Only the depth of love from which they sprang made the circumstances unimportant.

Philip called into the parlour:

"Where are you going to sleep, Mr Knapper?"

Fred reappeared:

"I wuz goin' up to me own bed. Miss Frances is welcome to it but it's a bit....untidy....up there. Still, if you're werrited about Miss Frances you can 'ave eet. I can doss down in the boiler hole at the "Grange'.....I've done it afore."

Just then they heard someone bustling through the parlour. It was Elizabeth Hughes who had come into the house through the door left open by the rushing Philip. She was carrying an enormous amount of bedclothes. She nodded towards Frances:

"I'm sorry to come barging in, Mr Knapper, but I'm so worried about her."

"That's all right, missus," Fred assured her.

"Well I just heard what you said, but you must sleep in your own bed, Mr Knapper. It'd be good of you if you'd have Phil here.....I'll make him comfortable on this couch, if you don't mind."

"But what about Frances?", asked her son.

"She's coming with me. I've stripped your bed and remade it so's she can have a night's proper rest."

It was over an hour later when Elizabeth Hughes tip-toed into her son's room where Frances had now settled off to sleep. She sighed and thought:

"What a terrible day this girl has had – first the funeral, then all this upset.....and no mother to turn to. Oh, but she looks lovely, even in my night things."

She bent and kissed Frances lightly on the cheek. And why not? Wasn't this the daughter she'd always pined for?

Chapter Seventeen

Love is Enough

Well, the hollow was astounded! Not only had Philip Hughes left the "Grange", so had Frances Bromley! In fact it was whispered that she had left that other "Grange" as well. And as if that were not enough for the populace to contend with, the news that the two of them were to marry was apparently more than a rumour!

Many in the Potteries were happy and many were horrified. One thing was certain – there were few people in the hollows without an opinion on the matter. It was talked about on all the potbanks but especially on the "Grange" and at Beresford's Whitfield Pottery where Philip was now taking up his new duties. The situation was appraised everywhere, from the libraries of the "somebodies" to the reading rooms at the Public Libraries where the "nobodies" gathered. Alluding to Frances' "immaturity", the "somebodies" found ways to paraphrase their common feeling that she had dealt a terrible blow to the class structure. The "nobodies" in the reading rooms, impressed by Philip's good fortune studied the "Mid-day" and the "Racing and Football Outlook" with a new avidity for if Lady Luck was abroad to this extent who was to say she might not smile on them at long last?

Most of the female population had the feeling that they had not been so captivated since their cinema visits to "Gone With The Wind" but strangely, Miss Lucy Pelham was affected in the most unhappy way. True, Frances Bromley had indeed "brought her pigs to a nice market" but what did it profit Lucy Pelham? Nothing – because Lucy Pelham could not feel that she had had anything significant to do with the debacle. Oh, she whispered and hinted to her disciples that she had been at the hub of things but she knew in her heart, as did the disciples, this was not so. Facts had to be faced – fate had taken a hand and events had moved without her. Understandably, she was peevish. Then she suddenly rallied –true she had contributed little to the crash of the High and Mighty Frances Bromley but this now enabled her to concentrate on another objective – the downfall of Frank Hollinshead.

Ewart Bromley brooded alone. He had gone much further than he had wished. Now pride forced him to maintain his position. Not that he wasn't given many a chance to retrieve the situation. Within days he received a letter from Frances apologising profoundly for her part in their quarrel but, with respect, making it clear that her return depended on his acceptance of Philip. He ignored it. Because of Philip's concern for Frances' happiness, unknown to her, he visited Bradwell Grange and asked for Ewart Bromley. On Bromley's orders, Jack Foley refused him entry. The whole situation began to have a long-term look about it.

Of course, at that time, it was one thing to agree to marry but another to actually marry, for the big stumbling block was finding somewhere to live. Crippled by shortages of every description, Britain's housing drive was not yet under way so that each Council's "housing list" was as long as the queues at football matches. Our couple's problem had two underlying causes – firstly, and surprisingly, the couple could not yet afford to buy. Frances' cash reserves, gladly given, had gone into Tyrone's funeral. Philip, because of financial commitments to his mother, had mobilised little or nothing. So, until they could accumulate a deposit, they had to "find a place to rent", a synonym for "impossibility".

The alternative for couples not prepared to wait and save, and Frances and Philip came into this category, was to live with in-laws. This was firmly dismissed and by none other than Elizabeth Hughes herself. She had looked Philip firmly in the eye and made it plain that his subsidies to her were at an end. He had "done more than enough", was entitled to a life of his own, and she would "manage". Then she looked Frances firmly in the eye and made it plain that the girl was entitled to "a hearth of her own", that Elizabeth herself had started marriage with in-laws, then "in rooms", then knocked about from pillar to post, so that the marriage itself was endangered. Mother Hughes was not to be moved in her standpoint, to say she was "resolute" is only the half of it. In the meantime Philip would continue to live at home and Frances would go to an old school friend, Mary Meakin, who lived in the once-full Meakin family home near the bottom of Porthill Bank.

Elizabeth assured them that rented accommodation *would* be found for "we know what to do". The couple discovered that the "we" consisted of four females: Elizabeth herself, Mrs Maggie Hogan, Mrs Sally Gratton and Mrs Florence Birks. Assisted by many helpers they constructed another "information network" and laid it over the hollow. While it is not a felicitous comparison it has to be said that this quartet's network was even more fine-meshed than the one Fred Knapper employed in his quest for horse manure.

The mission to locate rented property had to be accomplished. Even if curtains came down to be washed, network members descended to inspect and enquire. Frightened landlords were marched to the scene in some instances. The hollow's sick were afraid to go to hospital. How sad it is to state that every effort came to nothing.

This was when three other people decided that they had waited long enough – it was time to get involved. The first was an oven fireman with the reputation that he could "drink a sea dry", then there was a "little whippeet", an "elf", whom many thought decidedly "slippery" and a boiler fireman who sported a shirt deemed to be "the colour o' the cat's cod". The oven man, Ludo Dunning, was prepared to curtail his drinking time; the elf, Billy Hogan, was prepared to scale down his activities as a bookie's runner and the boilerman, Fred Knapper, was prepared, for some space of time, to forego his belly worship and his manure management activities. The enormous amount of time thus saved would be devoted to finding Frances and Philip a rented home.

They were agreed that no time would be wasted on peripheral figures in the property field. And who in the hollow was a more noteworthy and extensive property owner than Mr Claude Roebuck? So extensive, in fact, was his domain that he was known to collect the rents accruing to it *himself* as a "blind". For he was abundantly astute enough to know that if his tenants realised his star was so clearly in the ascendant they might feel justified in refusing to make further contributions to its progress.

Claude had faced the potters on their doorsteps through the lean years. Ultimately he had realised that the surest way they could be induced to meet their commitments was to plead that they saw in him a man even poorer than they were. He knew they belonged to a gentle culture and would not let him starve. And he was right, for as a result of his dramatics some paid him happily. Some, though not happy, paid him with a smaller degree of misery and the gentlest souls of all paid him willingly and could not, for shame, ask him to do repairs. Though he lived a split life, Claude was happy with himself. Privately he prospered, publicly he could look hungry at will. Yet he did not fool the trio for down the years, winkingly, they had watched him. He lunched each day at the George Hotel, which is Burslem's best and stands at the foot of Swan Bank. It was the elf who had first drawn attention to the anomaly:

"He's as poor as a crow – but the unny poor crow as stuffs his 'odge at the 'George'!"

No record of the district's notables would be complete without some description of Mr Claude Roebuck. He was tall and pale, with a doleful face like an impoverished clerk except that his nose contradicted such a suggestion. For whereas the noses of impoverished clerks are usually long and drooping, and as pale as the cold cheeks they stand upon, Claude's nose, variegated in tone, took up a fair proportion of his face. He wore a three piece suit of thick serge and it was the waistcoat that had first aroused the trio's suspicions for it bore the testimony of too many dinners.

He wore a Homburg hat which had left its makers as black as Burslem's smoke but as part of his plan of deception he had let it go green with age hence his nickname "green 'at".

Throughout *all* the seasons of the year the equipage of this needy magnate was completed by a "mackintosh" raincoat. Its buttons had once been covered with cloth but attrition from the flourish of hundreds of rent books had let the daylight on to them. In support of its master's cause the raincoat had faded satisfactorily and at the back of the collar, because it knew his journeys were long and perpetual, a hump of grease helped to keep out the weather.

It was when the news broke that a property was "for sale" near the junction of Park Road and what is now called Minster Street, that the trio made its first move. A notice in the window of the property declared that all enquiries should be directed to Claude Roebuck who was "acting on behalf of the owners". Now it was "Ludo" Dunning who was the planner, the guiding hand behind many of the moves the trio made. When his preliminary reconnaissance revealed that this 'superior, terraced type lobbied" property was solidly built and overlooked Burslem Park, he concluded it might be a highly suitable first home for Frances and Philip. True, the house was "For Sale" and not "To Let" but that did not deter "Ludo" for the involvement of Mr Claude Roebuck in the matter was enough to kindle suspicion. His next quiet move, since he was a man addicted to quiet moves, was to consult Mr "Drummer" Durber, street bookmaker, and himself a considerable property owner in the area. On the strict understanding of "no names, no pack drills", "Drummer" confirmed that Claude was, in fact, the owner and not just the rent collector of the house in question. "Ludo" rubbed his hands in anticpation.

The very next day Ludo, Fred and Billy watched, from the entrance to the Gents' Conveniences at the bottom of Swan Bank, for Claude to emerge from the George Hotel. They then followed him stealthily and saw him enter other licensed premises in a run-down sector of the town. Here it should be explained that after a substantial lunch at "The George" he invariably visited a less salubrious hostelry – sometimes in one part of Burslem, sometimes in another. There he would plead poverty, for an adequate length of time, while gazing into a half-pint of Parker's Pale Ale. It was a subtle strategy, expressly designed to maintain the aura of destitution he had so carefully constructed around himself.

Roebuck hated Knapper, Dunning and Hogan and they hated him. It all stemmed from a horse called "Swamp Fire", an "absolute certainty" according to Billy Hogan, which was listed in the "Mid-day" starting price guide at 100-1 and, Billy conjectured, would probably be backed down to "80s" by the time it went to the post. 80-1 and as near a racing certainty as ever ran a race! Mr Claude Roebuck would be the entrepreneur on an "equal shares" basis. They asked him for one solitary pound out of his rotting millions. It was a necessary evil and they knew they were supping with the devil. In the event, he refused. Their dislike of him hardened into hatred when, unlike any other "certainty" of Billy's, "Swamp Fire" actually won. Claude had lived in fear of these "dreadful men" ever since.

Which is why Claude quaked that afternoon in late 1949 when they burst into the "Saloon Bar" to find him occupied with the dregs of his half-pint. Barely waiting for him to unwedge his nose from the glazed world he beheld they heaved him almost bodily into the secluded "Smoke Room". When "Ludo" Dunning put a *pint-glass* of Parker's in front of him he trembled. When the three talked excitedly of a "great favour" they wanted to do him, he swooned and tried to fall but they hemmed him in so he had to listen.

They believed that a house near Burslem Park was vacant due to the sad demise of the widow Tunnicliffe and they had found most desirable tenants for it. It was too much for Claude: he had to cut in sharply. First of all, didn't they realise he was not the owner of the property? Also didn't they realise that the "owners" would not countenance the letting of the property which, in those days of desperation, they could sell for very many times its original value? Why he was already "receiving enquiries" on their behalf.

They looked at him steadily – no fuss, no strong arms,

no loud voices. For the sake of friendship, they felt bound to tell him that all his clients in Burslem town were of one mind in wishing for the future Mr and Mrs Philip Hughes to enter into occupation. They were also clear that his clients in the Longport area would feel the same. They intimated that the longer it took for a decision in the couple's favour the longer hundreds of rents in the hollow would remain unpaid. He could call it a "gesture" if he liked, but they went on to explain to him something they found no joy in telling him which was that when the rent-defaulters discovered who the real, and not the apparent owner of property was, the gesture they had made might well become a habit. Roebuck sweated visibly.

Now here we have to bear in mind that Claude's knock on any door would terrify all within. His cry of "Rent please!" would chill the blood. And the "poshness" of his accent was an added fear factor – in fact there is evidence for the story of an old lady in Middleport who, on first hearing his dulcet tones, slammed the door in his face thinking him a German. Now, at the end of his "discussion" with the trio, he seemed no fiercer than a little mouse peeping out of some crevice or other in brickwork. That evening when Philip returned to Hanover Street from the Whitfield Pottery they gave him the key to the late widow Tunnicliffe's house, "just to see what you think".

When Frances and Philip arrived at York Street (now Minster Street) the next evening, they found a small crowd of townsfolk were waiting outside the house. The crowd parted lovingly as the couple made for the front door. They went through a small passageway from the entrance and turned left into a large dining room with a fireplace. This then gave access to a kitchen, a scullery and a small yard. Re-entering the house and turning right from the passageway they entered a drawing room with large windows looking out over the Park. It also had a fireplace. The straight stairway was dark and rather steep. Frances was thrilled to find a modern bathroom at the head of the stairs and three good-sized bedrooms opening off from a landing. The whole building appeared to be solidly built and in good repair.

"What do you think, Frances?", asked Philip, trying to curb his own excitement.

"Oh Philip – it's a perfect place to make a start. Don't you think so?"

When he nodded, she went on:

"We can make it really pretty. Do we know about the rent?"

"Yes – Billy Hogan said Mr Roebuck was asking for ten shillings per week but apparently, after some discussion, he agreed as a gesture of goodwill to reduce this to eight shillings and sixpence."

"Oh, do let's go ahead! It's so near to your work too, at Whitfield."

Again Philip nodded.

When they left the house, Frances spotted the comic trio who were standing at the edge of the crowd which had now grown larger. "God bless you", she said to them. For the first time in their lives the three had nothing to say. Of course, if she had known how they had worked the miracle she might well have prayed for their forgiveness. As the men returned down Moorland Road, en route to lubrication after a long day, Fred Knapper averred that if they did not want the bathroom then, of course, there was no need for them to use it.

Well the date was set for the wedding – it was to be at the end of April and in the meantime they had some months to prepare for it. Frances wrote a long letter to her father. It was a plea for reconciliation and a request that on the day he would be there to "give her away". She received no reply. In spite of the rebuff, in mid-February Frances sent him a pair of silver cufflinks for his fifty sixth birthday. He snorted contemptuously and threw them into the back of a rarely-used drawer.

Shortly after that he received a 'phone call from his nephew Gordon Bromley who proposed to visit him. The visit turned out to be more of a confrontation than an occasion of consanguineous pleasure for when Ewart had confirmed his intention not to attend the wedding, Gordon flew into a rage. First he asked the obvious question:

"How can you treat Frances like this – your own daughter?"

"She's betrayed this family and I'll never forgive her", thundered Ewart.

At this, Gordon lost control:

"'Betrayed?', 'Betrayed?'....Frances wouldn't know how to betray anyone! I have to tell you this, Uncle....your decision causes me almost as much pain as it causes Frances, because I love her....we all do. You should be proud of her, she's certainly given you cause to be proud. And what's all this about family? What is a family uncle? Is it a group of human beings loving and supporting each other? Or is it some creative, mystical force that's only here to blaze a trail for the pottery industry in the second half of the twentieth century? I think you've got your wires sadly crossed on this one, Uncle Ewart. Frances is human enough to want her own home and a family with someone she cares for and who cares for her. Well, I'll be there for her and I'll give her away and you'd better take note that it'll be a long time before you see me again."

With that Gordon Bromley returned to Garstang.

This stormy exchange triggered another thought in Ewart's mind. Next day, at the "Grange" Pottery he sent for Frank Hollinshead and came quickly to the point. Waving the wedding invitation contemptuously he asked:

"Have you had one of these?"

"Yes."

"An' are you going?"

"Of course."

There was a silence, broken by Hollinshead:

"I take it you are Ewart?"

"No", he replied. "I wouldn't be found dead there!"

Frank's mouth was open:

"Am I hearing this right? You're not going? What would Alice think? Frances is your daughter Ewart and a daughter to be proud of."

"I'm not being dragged in to regularise matters because she's got some daft idea in her head about marrying that lout. Don't forget she's a Catholic and that means marriage is for good. And I know my own daughter. Even when she comes to her senses, as she will, she'll stick it out because of her faith."

"You say he's a 'lout', Ewart. How d'you reckon that up? He's a striving lad with a good war record....I know men who've served with him....and from what I hear he's making his number over at Whitfield as a manager. I....."

Bromley cut in:

"I don't want to hear what he's doing! She's throwing herself away!"

"Why?"

"Because he's a nobody!"

"A nobody'?....what does that mean? I'm a 'nobody', a coal-face worker dressed up like a dog's dinner. If it comes down to it Ewart....you're a 'nobody'...because I remember you telling me your grandfather started work running moulds. Apart from his lack of opportunity, Phil Hughes is every bit as good as we are."

"Yes – but it isn't all as simple as the way you put it."

"Listen, man – you ought to be thinking and planning for the day you retire. With Frances and her husband to help you, it wouldn't be long before you'd be able to hand over all the day-to-day work to them."

"That'll never happen. First of all, I'll never retire. When I leave this place it'll be in a pine box. I haven't forgotten what's been bequeathed to me, if Frances has. And secondly, there'll never be a place for Hughes here. By durs – he's got some old buck that one! Within a couple of years he'd be giving me orders. And Frances has got a helluva lot to learn yet when it comes to managing a firm."

"I wonder whether she has, Ewart. Listen – it's not in my own interests to tell you this but whose ideas do you think they were about giving this place a face-lift - with a new letter-head, new packaging? And these ideas about a proper costing system and statistical control on the number of shapes and patterns we produce? That's all down to Frances, Ewart. And she insisted on *me* telling you as though they were my ideas. That's the sort of girl she is. You've got a wonderful asset in her, Ewart, if only you could see it."

At this Bromley became testy:

"I don't need anyone telling me about the sort of girl she is! That's why I don't want her throwing herself away!"

Without waiting for the signal that the discussion was over, Hollinshead walked to the door. Reaching it, he turned:

"Ewart, don't think I don't appreciate what you've done for me. You've kept me on these past years when there was really no job for me. But without wanting to upset you, I've got to tell you this – Hilda and I are going to Frances' wedding even if it means you deciding there's no room for me here anymore."

Then he closed the door firmly behind him.

In the event and despite the disgust of others, Ewart Bromley persisted in his attitude and so did not attend his daughter's wedding. It is difficult, if not impossible, to understand his callous treatment of a daughter he undoubtedly loved. What might be done, as an *explanation* of his behaviour is to sketch in some of the framework to his heartless decision.

He was a martinet, for sure – perhaps the last in a line of factory owners who ruled his work force like some medieval despot – "when I ope my lips let no dog bark". Certainly he was a world away from the best type of manager to come after him – who believed in the "competence of the underdog", who reached decisions by negotiated consensus, who genuinely believed that equality of opportunity should never be mediated by "class" or gender and who recognised that the only method to retain any authority in the workplace was to share it. We must also remember that his strict disciplinary behaviour was honed in the slaughter-house of the First World War where an immediate response to his commands might stave off mutilation or death. Finally his actions were legitimised by a minimally educated, utterly deprived work force who would allow news of his imminent arrival to kindle in them a virtually physical fear because that was a better option than death by slow starvation on the "dole".

The death of his sons, followed by that of a wife he worshipped, coupled with the insistent pressure of technological change and the need for capital investment of hitherto unheard of proportions fuelled in him a transient madness in which hc could only see that "the firm" must be saved at all costs. To venerate the memory of its family members lately dead, it could only be saved by the "family". So perhaps these are some of the reasons why he was so much a victim of his own make-up, why he viewed Philip Hughes' defence of his own craftsmanship on that "drawing day" as unforgivable and why he could only see Frances' wish for a life of her own as a "betrayal".

One other incident prior to the wedding deserves mention here. Soon after arrangements for their tenancy were concluded with a defeated Mr Claude Roebuck, Philip arranged to meet Frances after work at the house in York Street. She brought a brown haired young woman with her. He looked at her grey eyes and was not surprised when she was introduced as Gwen Dempster, daughter of Jack Dempster, the General Manager at the Grange Pottery. She had Jack Dempster's thin mouth which, on her, was not unbecoming for her features were small. Her nose was thin too and its bone curved slightly at the bridge, as did her father's. At the time, since she was small, Philip thought her "well-proportioned" though he owned that later she would have to guard against becoming "dumpy".

She dressed with the same middle-class elegance as Frances and seemed genuinely pleased to meet him. He was pleased to see her and realising that the friendships of young women are usually open and sometimes intense affairs he supposed that to some extent Gwen had taken the place of Frances' mother and he was glad if that was so.

When she said:

"I'm very pleased to meet you Philip – I've heard so much about you," he became thoughtful. The greeting was surely sincere if conventional but he wondered whether Frances had eased some of the strain of their courtship by sharing her anxiety with Gwen in their "girl talk" sessions and whether Gwen, via her father, had become the innocent conduit of information to Ewart Bromley about the couple's meetings. It would certainly explain Bromley's seeming omniscience in such matters.

When the day for the wedding arrived the sun shone as well as it does in the story books. In their eagerness not to miss anything the bottle ovens seemed reluctant to work that weekend, a late Saturday in April, for the air was unusually clear over Durslem. The word had gone through the town that it was meant to be a "quiet do", so folk descended on Hall Street in droves, to satisfy themselves that the secret was being kept. When, in a few minutes, Frances and Philip appeared at the church door they would be astonished to see that crowds lined both sides of Hall Street, spilling over unbelievably into Liverpool Road at its top and Blake Street near its bottom. The hollow waited - young and old, sick and healthy.

Undoubtedly the best view of the couple's exit would be that of a group of well-dressed women standing to the left of the church door. A shrewd observer would have noted that while at the hub of things they had a certain detachment about them. They were there but not committed to the event. They were outside and not inside the church lest, mistakenly, they were thought to be part of the proceedings. At the centre of this fashionable cabal was Miss Lucy Pelham and at that instant she was speaking with feigned astonishment:

"Why, do you know, when he finally ordered her out she went and spent the night at the house of that filthy old boilerman who works at the "Grange"! Really, she's obviously a tile short, unbalanced."

Lucy tried to expand on this but was interrupted and had she not been so intent on sowing malice would have seen the arrival of the interruptor. He had waddled along Riley Street, achieved the near impossible in pressing through the crowds in Hall Street and now stood behind her. Minutes earlier he had clocked his exit from the Grange Pottery on a card marked "312. Knapper, F."

"She's better balanced than you ever be, Lucy duck.... and so much of a lady she wouldna let the remarks of a two-faced, old varmint like you trouble 'er any."

She twisted around as if the words had actually pinched

her. Rivulets ran down Fred's face. They were far more than perspiration for some of the water from the boiler-hole tap has escaped the towel and, supported by the perspiration, was drying reluctantly. Lucy did not recognise him in that first instant for he had camouflaged himself in a serge pin-stripe suit, new boots and a clean shirt with a new tie. Perhaps it was the smudge of coal-dust on his collar that gave him away but then again, it was probably his cap which seemed to have acquired a new coat of oil/dust amalgam for the occasion.

Under her immensely elaborate lace blouse Pelham felt herself go clammy. Terror gripped her to the extent that she could only gasp – "Well!" in reply. It was an exclamation devoid of spirit. None of her acolytes knew what to say and looked at one another for guidance. However, the boilerman was anxious there should be no awkward gap in the conversation:

"Aye, yer might well say 'well' – an' as fer the filthy ole boilerman – he wasn't so filthy when 'e was spendin' 'is pocket brass on yer, was 'e? It was th' Hippodrome one night, then the next day when yer saw 'im comin' from Parkhouse in his pit-dirt, yer went inter that fly-specked shop er yours an' shut the bloody door!"

Lucy went into an ague. To the more alarmist in her group she was about to expire. That memories of more than thirty years ago, memories of an insane indiscretion, should be brought out now! The wretched boilerman was still talking. It seemed everyone in Hall Street, from Liverpool Road to Riley Street, was straining to listen:

"P'haps *you* wus unbalanced when we wus courtin' up Bradder Wood and 'round Westport Lake."

Without a doubt, she wanted to die. Then from every corner of her body she summoned the last dregs of her energy:

"My man!" she shrieked, "I've never spoken to you in

my life – you're drunk!"

"No duck, I'm not drunk...an' I'll tell thee what....you're such a mean ole varmint you put me off women for life!"

Whether this was to the deprivation of womankind is a matter best left open.

The other ministers in the Pelham Cabinet were sharing much anticipatory delight at the thought of the tittle-tattle to come but their leader's glares, now flying among them, ensured that, for now, such thoughts were shelved. What chilled Lucy Pelham, as much as Fred's asseveration was the surly smile escaping the features of little Millicent Dean. And to think that after the 1948 Works Outing to Blackpool, she had arranged with Ewart Bromley for five more shillings a week to be paid to this viper. Who in the world could be trusted?

In the next second all eyes turned to the church door. A massive gasp and then silence as Frances appeared in her white wedding gown. Suddenly a lone cry could be heard by everyone:

"God bless yer, Frances duck!"

It was the signal for loud cheers from every member of that delighted crowd. There are moving moments in every town's history – moments when a great excited shudder possesses a town's whole body – as when its townsfolk rush into its streets crying a war is over. This was just such a moment for Burslem. Most of those cheering were strangers to Frances but this crowd could not gainsay the fact that the sight of her brought a lump to the throat of each one of them. Lest, after the trauma of preceding weeks, she be overcome, Philip held her around the waist to steady her. They both smiled at the crowd and then at each other.

Strictly, it is an exaggeration to say that everyone had cheered, for Lucy Pelham had delayed her own special moment. As the couple moved down the church steps under a storm of confetti and as her Cabinet switched on a succession of synthetic smiles Lucy moved forward.

"Good luck, my dear," she exclaimed, waving a gossamer handkerchief. It was an expression perfectly formed, for it contained a just-adequate strand of sarcasm.

Though Mrs Frances Hughes was a saintly person, she was still human. She had descried well enough the spite in Lucy's words. Coolly she looked at Lucy and made as if to throw her the bouquet, then she circled her arm about her head and threw it, decidedly, in the opposite direction. It was the perfect put-down and generated peals of laughter, all at the expense of Miss Pelham.

Though Fred Knapper would not have owned it so, he was a sensitive man and he too had marked Lucy's insult. It was down to him to right matters so he stepped in front of the couple, reached for Philip's hand and made as if to squeeze it from his arm:

"All the best, mate!", he yelled.

Then he turned to the girl he worshipped. If ever a man needed words, Fred did at that moment but his veneration and wonder blocked his thinking and the words wouldn't come. When they did they came in a rush:

"Yer need never want for vegetables, little sweetheart." he called. It was a sign of his overwhelming joy at knowing her.

"God bless you, Mr Knapper," she whispered.

"AND GOD BLESS YOU, ME DUCK!", he replied, and all the hollow must have heard him. Though he didn't know it, to deepen the meaning of that moment, his cap jumped off his head into his hand.

When the bridesmaids came fully into view, the Pelham cohort was thrown into heated speculation, for one of them was Gwen Dempster. That must make things awkward for Jack Dempster, Bromley's Manager. Did he know about this? More importantly, did Ewart Bromley know? There were bound to be repercussions, and so on. So preoccupied were they with their doom laden guesses and suggestions they failed to notice the second of the bridesmaids. Small though she was, the crowd did not fail to notice that the dimpled fists holding the posy belonged to Denise Gratton. Just a few steps behind her, in the entourage now filing from the church, an ashen-faced young mother was tearfully happy. When the group was being marshalled by the photographer, Sally Gratton saw Frances reach out and grip little Denise to her side. It was then that Billy Hogan and "Ludo" Dunning stepped from the crowd on the other side of the church doors and carried the collapsed Sally back into the church. People were caught up in the drama of the photographs so few noticed this.

At the reception, Elizabeth Hughes was still dabbing at her eyes. In the church she had cried on behalf of the bride's absent mother, now she was crying on her own behalf. After the wedding breakfast and the speeches, the presents were being reviewed. Frances caught her breath when she came to no less a gift than a reproduction mahogany secretaire bookcase. Billy Hogan, watched carefully by his wife, stepped forward to demonstrate that in order to gain access to the desk section it was necessary to pull out the deep drawers and press a button on either side. This caused the front to hinge down on brass quadrants. She looked past the elegant, curved astragals of the glazed bookcase section and saw a card with copper-plate handwriting on it. Philip unlocked the door and Frances broke down as she read: *"To Frances and Philip with love and best wishes for your happiness – all the 'Grange' potters"*.... it signalled that every shop floor worker had contributed to this costly gift and it also indicated what the daughter of the fiery Ewart Bromley had come to mean to them.

In spite of her husband's ministrations it took some time for Frances to recover, only to be moved to tears again in succeeding seconds. She looked at a beautiful wall clock in Viennese rosewood. There was an elegant, gilt decorative surround to its enamel dial. The accompanying card read: *"With our fondest love. Much happiness to you both, Aunt Hilda and Uncle Frank."*

In spite of her tears she turned to hug them both, knowing that they had doubtless earned the chilling resentment of her father. As Frank Hollinshead held his tearful niece, it was in keeping with his essential decency that he whispered: "Be sure darling that your Dadder loves you very much."

Gordon Bromley, a smart thirty-year old looking every inch the professional man smiled warmly at them both. He handed them an envelope and with a twinkle he said:

"We lawyers take a pretty instrumental view of things so I have no beautiful furniture for you but I hope you'll accept this."

Later they were to discover his cheque was for two hundred pounds. As they thanked him he fixed Philip with a friendly but firm gaze:

"She's very precious to us, Philip. Look after her won't you?"

Holding Frances tightly Philip said earnestly:

"I won't even let the wind blow on her."

"I'm sure that's true", said the cousin with sincerity.

The couple moved on to talk to their other guests. Despite the constant watchfulness of his wife, Billy Hogan had undertaken the same duties. He felt it incumbent upon himself to bridge the gap between the various social classes there present. He complimented himself upon his ability to treat with everyone, be they labourers or kings, without embarrassment or affection. This is why he fetched up alongside Gwen Dempster and one of Frances' University friends, and affected to be listening carefully. In order that the girlfriend, a stranger to the hollow, should go away with the best possible impression of the area and its culture, Gwen was explaining intensely details of the proposed visit of the Sadler Wells Ballet Company. All the poetry of their motion could be seen at the Theatre Royal, Hanley, throughout the following week. Billy was rocked by this:

"Ballit?", he queried "...is that folks runnin' rind on their toos?... I'm a bit septic."

Haltingly, they assured him such activity was indeed the basis of the whole business. He dashed off in search of another drink. While he wanted to contribute to making the reception a "family party", there were limits, even for a man of his knowledge and sensitivity.

As Frances continued to move among her guests she was approached by Winnie Hood, Philip's former mouldrunner. Winnie seemed rather guarded as she whispered that someone waited at the side door to the room and wanted to see her. Winnie was clearly embarrassed and disappeared among the guests. This caused Frances to approach the door cautiously. In the corridor beyond, a pretty girl with blonde hair waited. It was Vera Foskett who had occupied the adjacent jigger to Philip in the top flat shop at the Grange and who had caused such commotion in Frances' early days there. Tears filled Vera's eyes as she said:

"Hallo, Miss....Mrs....it isn't much but I wanted you to have this present."

"Oh, Vera – what a lovely thought....thank you. May I open it?"

Within a corrugated tube and slide was a mass of tissue paper. Within the tissue paper was a ceramic toby jug. It was made by a North Staffordshire firm which specialised in the manufacture of such items.

"It's really nice, Vera. I'll always treasure it."

Vera had more to say:

"Miss....I'm sorry I was rotten to you but...it's just my way I suppose. I'll hope you'll be happy an' I know you'll make *him* happy."

Frances kissed her cheek:

'Come in...join us Vera...and wish him happiness yourself.:

The girl was alarmed.

"Oh no...Miss...I couldn't..."

Then she blurted out:

"Oh, Miss Frances – you look like a queen!", and was gone.

Frances dried her own tears before returning to the guests.

When she got back it was to see Clive Beresford talking to her husband. The master potter grinned as she came towards him:

"Oh, Frances.....how radiant you look."

As she was thanking him for his compliment he turned to Philip:

"Am I allowed to kiss her?"

Philip nodded and smiled, then he put an arm around his wife:

"Mr Beresford, thank you for your wonderful gift.

"We were overwhelmed," added Frances.

He was dismissive:

"Nonsense...you've got to cook on something!"

Then, to help him banish the topic, he turned to Elizabeth Hughes standing nearby:

"I see a family likeness here, Philip. Could this be your mother?"

Philip hastened to make the introduction:

"Oh yes....yes....this *is* my mother."

"Ah, well spotted eh? I'm very happy to meet you Mrs Hughes."

The day was proving altogether too much for the grey-haired lady from Hanover Street.

"I'm happy to meet you, Mr Beresford," she managed to say.

Her daughter-in-law noticed that Elizabeth Hughes

wheezed in the close atmosphere. The veins stood out on her neck and her face was florid.

"I'm afraid we're all giving her a lot too much work and worry about..."

"Oh no....it's a lovely day....", protested Elizabeth.

"You know, Philip, you're a lucky stiff. A lovely wife and a lovely mother and here I am, a crusty old bachelor with years of loneliness in front of me. Seeing you with your women folk like this makes me think," Beresford smiled. Then he sighed:

"Well Frances – I must be going. I just happened to be in the locality and thought I'd pop in to give my very best wishes to you both. Philip - I do hope your break will be blessed with good weather. Come back refreshed. Goodbye, Mrs Hughes – forgive my gate-crashing won't you?"

When he had gone Elizabeth Hughes sighed:

"Isn't he a perfect gentleman?"

Her son and daughter-in-law smiled their agreement and Philip said:

"We owe him a lot, mother."

At the other side of the room, as they saw Beresford leave, "Ludo' Dunning turned to Fred Knapper:

"Who were that?"

Fred was amazed – that the fireman could not recognise the son of the most prosperous family in the area.

"Yer mean ter say yer don't know Clive Beresford?," Fred gasped.

"From Whitfield potbank?"

"Aye – an' th'other bank they've got up at th' neck end... well...e's Phil's boss nah!"

"Ludo" shook his head:

"Our Phil's a lad all right, i'n't he?"

Fred gulped down a chocolate éclair at one swallow then became conspiratorial: .

"He is that...an' dunner forget this....if thee and me an'

th' little un 'ere adna fixed 'im up with that house in York Street, Clive Beresford wouldna a bin able buy 'im a 'lectric stove fer put in it."

"That's rate!", said "Ludo" and Billy became thoughtful:

"Ah wunder what thee've done with their old stove?"

That night the three of them were still recalling the wonder of the day's events. The conversation was in danger of winding down at long last when Fred turned to the others as if electrified:

"Eh.....what's think?", he shouted, "ah forgot tell thee both till nah! Who dust think ah met outside church?"

In the next few minutes, Lucy Pelham's name was passed back and forth and the laughter became louder and heartier. Finally, as sleep began to claim them, they stirred and made for home.

"By....but we've supped some ale today lads," said Ludo.

"Aye..." protested Billy.... "but eet's all bin in a good cause!"

At that same instant, after several hours' motoring in their hire car (for motorways were yet to come) Mr and Mrs Philip Hughes were within an hour or so of their hotel in Somerset. They were extremely happy, with each other and the day's events. Of course, since it is not a perfect world they each had a negative thought obtruding into their contentment. Frances, of course, thought of her father whose absence from the wedding might mean their separation was hardening into estrangement. And Philip was thinking about Peter Bromley and the secret he still felt bound to keep from his adored wife.

Chapter Eighteen
The Testing Time

When Frances and Philip returned from honeymoon they set about making a home of the house on York Street. They were helped in this by the relatives of old widow Tunnicliffe who, despite the attempted intervention of Mr Claude Roebuck, had decided that the curtains and carpets in place there were so snugly tailored to the house it would be a pity to move them. Not only did they make the couple a gift of these items they even apologised for the fact that there was a small tear in the stair carpet on the sixth tread from the bottom of the flight. Philip thought they could mask it with tape until they were able to re-carpet the stairs and Frances agreed.

They were busy, purposive days for them both. Frances obtained a post as head of a laboratory at Tilestones Ltd, a large manufacturer of tableware, in Tunstall, a short distance away. They had acquired a second-hand Austin car in good condition. Frances drove to Tilestones each day, leaving Philip at Beresford's Whitfield Pottery on the way. She brought to her new role energy and drive as well as valuable knowledge of the salience of chemistry to ceramics production. Even so, she still had enough energy left over to tackle the cooking, sewing, cleaning and general home-making with enthusiasm. These tasks were important enough in themselves but they also helped to speed along the hours until Philip came home.

Philip would arrive home either from work or from evening classes at the Technical College. Under the smiling satisfaction of Clive Beresford, and the nodding wisdom of Dick Chidlow, the fledgling manager was finding his feet at the "Whitfield" while at the College he was coming to terms with strange, new knowledge. He had mastered the trade of platemaking, a trade carried on in the hollow for longer than anyone could remember. Now he was discovering that such terms as "deflocculation", "elutriation", "pneumatolysis" and "electrostatic precipitation" were linked to this same trade. He addressed himself to the meaning of these terms and their application to the day-to-day working of the "potbanks".

The first year of married life was one in which all the diverse feelings of Philip intensified. He developed a deep respect for Dick Chidlow. Whereas he might otherwise have conjectured that the man had achieved his eminence by experience, instinct and earthy common sense, he now realised Chidlow had helped the "Whitfield" obtain its standing by the application of sound scientific principles – those same principles he, himself, was now struggling to master.

He discovered that the firm had never experienced any

significant outbreak of "specking", "crazing" or "crooked flat" because, many years ago, Dick had paid for his own schooling at the Wedgwood Institute with the money he was able to save from his weekly wage as a dish maker.

Philip watched as the Whitfield Pottery speedily put on its new face. The production processes were being automated and new tunnel ovens were being built and yet, it was the old man with the young mind who was called upon to deal with the "experts". Dick Chidlow talked to them in their specialised language and Philip noted the experts invariably received some instruction in their own callings. Clive Beresford would make no move without him. In the building of a glost tunnel, the experts had suggested diatomaceous earth for insulation. Chidlow had shaken his head and growled "hot face". Clive Beresford had nodded and the tunnel had been duly lined with "hot-face" insulating brick.

The thought that someday he might be called upon to fill his master's boots made Philip swallow. He wasn't at all sure. In fact, at times he doubted himself. Also, there were many moments at College when he felt that the whole venture was beyond him and his faith in himself began to falter.

But when he returned to York Street Frances would see to it that this frame of mind did not last. On his return, the gorgeous blue eyes were always there to question him. He would explain his misgivings and softly she would talk them all away. They would look at the study notes together and she would explain "alpha cristobalite" and "beta tridymite" were not beyond his understanding, they only sounded fearful. And so, he would once again privately resolve to work harder, strive harder, try harder, to justify her abundant faith.

Here again his feelings intensified. He had cared for her deeply before the marriage but now, unreservedly, he allowed himself to become dependent on her. In fact, they were fast becoming a necessity to each other, thinking, feeling and acting as a duality. The only flaw in their happiness was that Ewart Bromley persisted in ignoring any letters, gifts or remembrances of her mother and brothers Frances sent to him. Yet again, Philip's feelings intensified, his sadness turning to rancour.

With the knowledge of Jack Foley, whose loyalty to his former major did not preclude his loving concern for Frances, it had been arranged that Mary Ellen Foley would call on Frances whenever she came to Burslem town for Saturday shopping. On her visits, the housekeeper would give Frances all the current news about her father. Philip was glad of this, for it seemed to ease his wife's anxiety and he knew that while his wife was unhappy about the situation he could never be happy either. This was why, with Christmas drawing near, and unknown to Frances, he called at Bradwell Grange once more. Bromley refused to see him but Philip told Frances nothing of this. Important news had led to the visit.

One night in mid-December they were walking back from the Hill Top Methodist Church having attended a performance of "Yeoman of the Guard". They had chosen to walk there and returning she said to him as they drew abreast of "The Big House" on Chapel Bank:

"Philip – we're going to have a baby."

He took hold of her and they kissed. One of the town's small boys, abroad in spite of the hour, whistled in admiration.

Philip knew what was in Frances' mind as the days had passed and that was when he had decided to visit Bradwell Grange. He was reluctant to advise her to write to her father with their news lest no reply came. He suggested they tell Mary Ellen Foley on her next visit to them and he told Dick Chidlow in the hope that the news would reach

Clive Beresford and subsequently Ewart Bromley at the next Manufacturers' meeting in the Association Chambers.

On the Tuesday immediately before Christmas Beresford confirmed Philip's hope for this outcome when they were at the factory gates:

"Hallo Philip - how are you?"

"Very well, Mr Clive – thank you."

"How's Frances?"

"She's fine."

"And what's this latest news of yours? I'm very happy for you both. I'm just dashing off to the Association Chambers but there is one thing – now that you're taking over more work from Mr Chidlow it mightn't be a bad idea if you were on the 'phone. You never know - when the new glost kiln is ready you might be called out at night so we'd better be able to reach you easily. See Mr Chidlow about the application going through, will you? Goodbye."

Philip smiled as he stared after his employer. Clive Beresford knew it would be a long time before he, a new clay manager, was given any responsibility for a glost tunnel kiln. In effect, he would have needed to be in post as the Works Manager. Yet this is not all that the managing director would know. He would realise that as Frances' pregnancy neared full-term she would find a telephone invaluable and an added safeguard when she was alone at York Street. And finally, Beresford knew that in those days of dire austerity and endless controls the only way in which telephones could be newly installed was if the instrument were required for business purposes of high priority. As Philip walked back into the firm he was still smiling.

A few days afterwards Philip watched anxiously as Frances prepared her Christmas gift for Ewart Bromley. He suggested she might also enclose a note about her baby. He thought that in conjunction with the news Clive Beresford would have passed to him by then her father might contact her and so end her heartache.....but Ewart made no contact nor sent any greeting. Although their Christmas was a happy one he sensed his wife's deep disappointment. Then, like all the others in the hollow, the couple looked to what the New Year might bring, hoping for some improvement in the quality of life in post-war Britain.

The New Year lost little time in producing a special shock. In the third week of February Sally Gratton, worn out by a weak heart, hard work and physical abuse, passed away in her sleep. Close to where, just a short time earlier, Tyrone Carroll had been laid to rest, they put Sally's body into the ground. Frances and Philip were immensely moved to hear old Florence Birks reading out for Sally's young children the sentiments attached to the wreaths, including one which read:

"God keep you, Sally – Top Shop."

From that day, the girls acquired the love and support of another woman. They would come to know her as "Aunt Frances".

The new baby was due to arrive in August and the Hughes' waited patiently. In the meantime, Frances coaxed and tutored Philip through his study notes and assignments. As they pushed on through his revision sessions she paid no heed to her own tiredness, holding him back when she felt he had not given some topic sufficient attention and pushing him gently when he hesitated through lack of confidence. Gradually he felt his grip on the mysteries tighten.

There was no shortage of visitors to York Street for in addition to Elizabeth Hughes, Margaret Hogan and Mary Ellen Foley, Gwen Dempster often busily hurried there, despite the ambivalent attitude of her father. Moreover, she let it be known with great pride that she was "knitting". Winnie Hood and Teresa Hogan also announced that they were "knitting" and when Frances looked at Sally Gratton's children across the tea table she mused sadly that had their mother lived, she too would have been "knitting".

As Frances' time drew near, Philip became anxious. He was walking up Hanover Street after a visit to his mother when a cry came from behind him:

"Hey! Phil!"

Instinctively, he knew the voice and turned to see that Billy Hogan was accompanied by his bosom pals, 'Ludo' and Fred. They caught up with him.

"How's missus?"

"Well enough thanks, Mr Hogan."

The elf squared himself as he always did before making a weighty pronouncement:

"Thay mustner werrit, Phil. Thee mother tells me thays bin werritin'. It dunner do any good. Way 'ad a bad time on it when our Vin was born and dust know what I used ter do?"

Philip could probably guess but shook his head, not wanting to break the elf's momentum:

"Ah used ter goo fer a jar or two an that wuz thunny road ter get me mind off things!"

Billy ignored the laughter of his companions for he had a bright idea:

"Whay dusner come with us nar?"

"Well, it's very good of you Mr Hogan – but I'm just off home to Frances and I've got swotting to do yet."

"Swotteen??", the trio chorused. The word was lost on them.

"Yes....you know.....for the examinations."

"Oh.....ah," nodded "Ludo" Dunning "the art o' potting at th' Institute."

"That's it: the exams are on Tuesday and Wednesday next week."

"Ludo" grinned:

"Yer can always come to me lad if you want to know how to fire ovens."

Hogan also grinned:

"Am' ah kin always show thee how ter write a bet ite."

Fred Knapper was serious:

"Dunner take a lot o' notice o' what they tell thee. Chemeecs anner natural."

They reached the edge of St. John's Square. Philip left the three of them outside the "Star" public house in Queen Street. As Philip walked on, Fred Knapper shouted:

"Yer'll 'ave a nice babbee. You wait an' see."

As the examinations became imminent, Frances watched Philip ever more closely. He doubted his own ability still and though he meant to hide it there was still much about his studies that troubled him. On the night before the first examination he looked at her:

"Frances, why are you so pale?"

"I'm not pale and I feel fine."

He took her hands:

"Are you worrying?"

"I'm only worrying for you, because I know you're tightening yourself up about the exams. Relax, Philip – you've got nothing to worry about. I've told you – you'll head the pass list."

He frowned:

"Every day for the last month you've kept telling me I'll head the pass list. I wish you wouldn't. You're giving me a mountain to climb. You don't realise there are people on the course with better educations and better backgrounds. But what does it matter anyway?......I just want you to be concerned about yourself."

"Yes – you're right....I'm sorry....I'm trying to build

your confidence and you're worried about my expectations. I want you to pass – and pass well – because you deserve the chance you've been denied, that's all. Forget things like education and background – there are no better potters on that course than you – just wait."

He kissed her and left for work the next morning learning on his arrival that Dick Chidlow wished for the two of them to have lunch together. During the lunch there was little or no discussion. Then when he expected the old potter to open the conversation he merely picked up his newspaper and began to read it intently. There were only five minutes left before the buzzer blew when suddenly Chidlow's eyes bored into the young manager:

"What werritin' about?"

"Nothing Mr Chidlow – of course I want Frances to be all right."

The old man ignored the answer and put his next question:

What's the most important thing to remember about potting problems, here or anywhere else?"

"Well....I suppose....to keep my head and to use my common sense....."

"It's just the same in exams, m'lad. Some'll fail tonight because they'll be that anxious to show what they know they'll go all round the Wrekin. Nail the point of the question and answer it. Don't flannel. Remember what my headmaster used to say: 'you must read every question at least once'".

"I see...yes."

"An' although it's a theory paper tonight, let 'em see you've got the practical ability to manage a potbank. That'll matter more to the examiners than a load o' tautology about cristobalite squeeze and crypto-crystalline structures."

Philip had to smile. Dick looked at him again:

"Now in your oral tomorrow night, practical ability'll be even more important...stands to sense. If they give thee a piece of ware with a cobalt-blue that's milky, don't start rambling about "opalescence due to devitrification" without telling 'em they want more alumina in the colour or the glaze. They want to know what you'd do to put it right on your own factory. Don't assume they don't want to know if they don't ask because they damn' well do!"

He was leaving the office when, once more, the Works Manager, looked up from his newspaper:

"An' don't forget to use your eyes. If they give thee a vase that's crooked, don't think there's got to be a technical explanation for it. Don't go on about there bein' too much flux on the body if you can see the thing's badly designed in the first place. The best body in the world won't keep a thing straight of its shape's rotten for potting."

Stepping back into the works, Philip was feeling relaxed and confident. In the meantime, Dick Chidlow had returned to his newspaper. That evening, the first examination over, Philip motored from Stoke back to York Street. Her fine eyes were anxious. Though Frances tried to hide it she was tense:

"How did it go?"

He took her by the shoulder:

"Will you sit down and stop worrying?"

His smile reassured her.

"Were you satisfied?"

"I think so."

"Do you want to show me the papers and talk it through?"

"Not unless you want me to..."

"I think I do....very much."

He sat and pulled her on to his knee, pressing her head against his shoulder. His fingers went through the silk of her hair:

"Frances...listen.....you look very tired and this is just not right. I certainly don't fancy burdening you with 'determination of grain size' and 'empirical formulae' tonight, honestly."

"But I've lookcd forward to your coming home and discussing it with me. In fact, I've been looking forward to it for a long time."

"I know you have....but you're tired out, sweetheart, and you're still turning out to work every day. And whatever we discuss won't make any difference now, will it? On top of that – if we bring out all the mistakes I've made, it won't put me in the best frame of mind for the oral tomorrow night. Got it?"

She screwed up her face in anguish:

"Oh Philip – you're hopeless!"

He laughed, kissed her ear and whispered:

"Be a good girl.....and go off to bed now."

A few seconds later he was alone. He took out the examination paper and sat in thought for a long time.

The following evening, he went to the Wedgwood Institute in Burslem to sit the Chemistry paper and to attend the oral examination. He had decided to leave the car at home that morning thinking that after a busy day at the firm the walk from the Whitfield Pottery to the Institute in Queen Street would freshen him up.

As nine o'clock drew near, a broad-shouldered, athletic-looking young man paced up and down in front of the Institute. At last, when the candidates were emerging, he pushed through the surge towards Philip:

"Phil!"

"....Vin....what's up?"

Seeing Philip's expression there was no need for preliminaries. The placer took hold of his arm:

"It's Frances, Phil.....she must 'ave 'ad a bit of a do. I went up to your house with your mother to carry some laundry. She sent for Dr Challinor and asked me to come down here for you."

Philip ran along Qucen Street past the Co-op Emporium

and towards Swan Bank. Vincent was at his shoulder.

"How long have you been waiting?"

"About half an hour."

"Half an hour! Why didn't you send out for me?"

As they raced on, up Moorland Road, Vincent was uncomfortable:

"Well, I was thinkin' about the exam n' that."

Philip called back:

"What the hell does *that* matter?"

The two of them sped on and when Philip burst through his front door he saw his mother's fingers fly to her lips. He was about to bombard her with questions when he heard a door close at the top of the stairs. A small, bent figure appeared in the hallway:

"Goodness – those stairs are steep," said Daniel Challinor.

"What's wrong, doctor?", asked Philip tensely.

"Are you the husband?"

He nodded.

"Nothing to worry about. She'll be all right. Her blood pressure's high. Keep her quiet for a day or two. She must rest – but she'll be all right. I told her early on her blood pressure was a bit high. We mustn't risk eclampsia."

Philip's great sigh caused the doctor to cock his eye towards him:

"Anything been worrying her?"

"Well....nothing....except that I've been taking some exams and I think she's been concerned for me but, perhaps more importantly, she's been working up to now."

"Ah, well there's two more months to go yet but she should stop work now. And you must keep her quiet for a day or two. Then I'll come in again to check. After that, all being well, friends and relatives can pop in again. G'night."

"Goodnight, doctor."

A thought had gone through Philip's mind when the doctor

had mentioned "relatives" but when his mother and Vin Hogan had left for home he went up to see Frances.

He sat on the edge of the bed and gathered her into his arms.

"How do you feel now?"

"Fine."

"I was worried sick. Don't give me any more shocks like that."

" 'Shocks'?....I fainted, that's all."

" 'That's all'!....mother didn't think so or she wouldn't have sent for the doctor."

"How did the Chem. Paper and the oral go?"

He was furious:

"For pity's sake Frances! The exam! What does it matter? Can't you think about yourself?"

"There's no need to lose your temper. You're too intense about the whole thing. I'm having a baby....and that's perfectly natural so don't get things out of proportion, Philip."

He lowered her head back onto the pillows.

"You must rest now.....and for the next few days. Mother will be back in the morning and er....I will have to stay late on the works....but I'll be back as soon as I can. Will that be all right?"

"Of course it will."

He kissed her.

At about seven the next evening he motored to Porthill and entered the grounds of Bradwell Grange. He heard the bell ring inside the house. Satisfied, he took his finger off the button. Mary Ellen Foley seemed glad but tense at seeing him. She was wiping her hands worriedly on a bright teacloth.

"Is Mr Bromley in?"

"He is, Mr Philip....but....I think he's engaged."

"Please ask him if he'll see me, Mrs Foley. Tell him it's

about Frances."

"Is she all right?"

Philip nodded to reassure her, then added:

"But I need to see him about her....it's important."

Uncertainly she went back into the hall and when she returned he knew the answer before she said:

"I'm sorry."

"Excuse Mrs Foley," he said quietly and crossed the hall then entered the library/drawing room.

Ewart Bromley goggled at him. Jack Dempster, his Manager, rose rather shamefacedly from his chair.

"Hughes, how dare you come in here? Well?!", Bromley roared.

"I'm not here on my own behalf. Frances isn't well and I think she'd face her confinement better if you and she were reconciled."

Bromley's eyes glinted:

"Oh, *you think so*, do you?"

The scorn in the man's voice made Philip feel violent but, for Frances' sake, he still controlled his reply:

"I've told you before – I want nothing from you and I'd rather be anywhere than talking to you right now. But Frances would be better in herself if the quarrel between you was patched up. I've come to ask if you'll see her - or at least write to her."

Obviously the master potter was going to relish his next words. To underline their importance he rose magisterially from his chair and pointed towards Philip:

"The relationship between my daughter and me is none of your concern, much as you'd like to think it is. Furthermore, the 'quarrel' – your word – will soon be patched up and by Frances herself! You say she isn't well but perhaps it's more than that Hughes – perhaps she's tired of you. That's the change you see in her no doubt. Your connection with her hasn't lasted as long as even I thought it would. What's more there's a home here for her, and the child when it comes. But don't think any namby-pamby talk about her confinement'll help you get your feet under the table. You can cart yourself off – and for good!"

He waved to the door but it was too much for Philip who now advanced to the nearest chair and gripped it. He thrust his face forward and his voice could be heard throughout Bradwell Grange.

"When are you going to get it through that thick skull of yours that the only thing you've got that's worthwhile is the love of your daughter? Would you continue seeing her worried because you think that somebody might steal the 'Grange' Pottery from you? Well let me tell you that 'Grange' Pottery or Bradwell Grange or anything with 'Ewart Bromley' stamped on it isn't in jeopardy as far as I'm concerned.

When Frances married me you let your shame be known far and wide. Has it ever occurred to you that the shame might have been on *my* side? The fact that my mother can't breathe has helped you get where you are – so don't let's talk about shame. You don't know any of the people who've put you where you are and you don't want to know them. And you imagine that I would want some of the money they've made for you? Well if I ever did, I hope the next food I took would choke me!"

Jack Dempster moved forward:

"Don't you think you'd better go now, Hughes?"

Philip flared around:

"It might be better for you if I did, wouldn't it Mr Dempster? Because you're really behind all this, aren't you? You've poked and pried and got Gwen to tell you every time I've met Frances. Then, all under the guise of 'loyal duty' and for the good of 'Grange' Pottery, of course, you made sure her father knew. He hadn't the gumption to see that you usually told him *after* we met. If he had he'd have seen through your game."

Dempster's face was ashen and his voice lacked conviction:

"What do you mean 'game'?"

"I mean you were out to make trouble for Frances. You dug a pit for her.....is that straight enough? You resented her being at the factory. That's the reason, for my money, why Bromleys has never had a clay manager. You wanted to run the whole show – in spite of the fact that you've never really bottomed a job in your life. That's why the place has no proper costing system and why *I* had to teach Frances to file tools and to make flat. When you saw we'd become friends, you thought you'd turn that to your advantage, didn't you?

Well, it hasn't done you much good has it? You're not a director yet and if he thinks as much about his precious firm as he says he does, I don't suppose you ever will be. You're a 'yes man' and suit Ewart Bromley because he hates anybody who stands up to him.....even supposing they might be right."

Philip found himself at the library door confronting them again:

"If you want to dismiss this visit as a case of a barbarian betraying his origins that's your privilege, Mr Bromley – but you'd better be sure of another thing – whether you choose to see Frances or not is up to you, but if you don't and she lets it get her down she might well have a difficult time with the baby. And if that happens, I'll come up here again and, as old as you are, you'll find yourself spitting teeth!"

At that instant, Foley appeared. Hearing the row he had dashed in from the garages. He advanced towards Philip who held up his hand:

"Jack – I've no quarrel with you – but don't come any further."

Though they heard the main door of the house close after him it was several seconds before the three men looked at one another.

As he drove down Porthill Bank, Philip was angry with himself. Things had gone horribly wrong. He had intended to ease his wife's distress but had only succeeded in making things worse. He could say her father's attitude left him with no alternative but that wouldn't wash. He had known full well the man was a bully and he should have allowed for it. He could still have tried reason instead of temper. Now, nothing short of a miracle could bring the two of them together again. One thing was certain – he would never tell her about his visit.

If there is any truth in the dictum that a true marriage is a union of minds then the lives of Frances and Philip offered evidence for it. Not only did their views on most things correspond closely but each also developed a powerful insight as to how the other would think and act in a given situation. For instance, though they had never discussed it Frances knew that he had recently been to see her father. And because there was no word from her father, she also knew that Philip's disappointment deepened.

Obviously she was bitterly sorry too, though more for her father than for herself. She knew that in his heart their separation made him suffer. She also knew that her absence would deepen his grief for his wife and sons. Yet, in spite of her pain for him she never doubted her place was by Philip's side.

One morning in early July she looked up at him as he was leaving for work:

"Do you think the result'll be here today, Philip?"

He sighed:

"Well, you've been asking every morning for the last two months practically, so I ought to say 'yes, it's possible'."

"I'm so excited for you. Why don't you wait for a few minutes? The first post'll be here soon."

"I can't wait and I want you to stop worrying about exam results. Think about yourself, Frances – it won't be long now. Have you had any more discomfort?"

"No."

"Will you be O.K. until my mother comes?"

"Philip Hughes, you're a fusspot – of course I will."

She held on to him:

"Philip, do you really love me?"

"I suppose so – because with your hair all over the place like that, I don't think anybody else would have you."

When she punched him, he held on to her for a little while longer.

"Now lie back and rest for a bit," he whispered, then made for the bedroom door.

She called to him:

"Philip?"

"Yes?"

"I do so love you."

He winked:

"Same here", then went clomping down the steep, dark stairway.

As he was opening his car door he saw the postman turning into Park Road from Moorland Road which was now filling with early morning traffic. By the time he was nearing the end of Park Road the postman had passed him.

"No point in chasing him now," he thought.

Then just as he reached the junction at Moorland Road his mother came around the corner. The long walk from Hanover Street had left her fighting for breath. Philip stopped the car and wound down the window:

"Are you all right? You look done in. You should've stayed with us last night, like we wanted you to...."

"I've got me own home to see to, haven't I?"

"Well, if you're sure you're O.K....."

"'course I am. Now you get off....it'll soon be snappin' time."

Through his mirror he watched her trudge along Park Road then he turned into Moorland Road and made for the town centre. Had he waited a little while longer he would have seen her stop and take a long rest. In the meantime, with her verbal dart about it nearing the breakfast break she had reminded him she had been used to going to the potbank before seven each morning. When he had started his managerial job she had quipped "I suppose that means you'll be going to work when the streets are aired."

When Philip got to the traffic lights at the top of Swan Bank he motored down to Queen Street and subsequently turned out of that street into Bournes Bank. He turned right under a sign which read "Ephraim Bracegirdle, Potter's Merchant". In ten more minutes he was examining his third box of sponges.

"Are they all like this, Mr Bracegirdle?"

"Every one the same, Mr Hughes and, as usual, 'Whitfield' has the first look at 'em."

"They're certainly better than we've had for some time. Things must be getting better in the Aegean."

The merchant smiled:

"Even Dick Chidlow ud find notheen up with them."

"We'll take six cases and while I'm here I'll look at some big bench sponges if I may."

"Over here, Mr Hughes."

The two men went to a wooden pen next to the entrance door to the warehouse, where Philip spent some ten minutes or so looking through the bigger sponges:

"Hm. These vary quite a bit more, don't they."

"Yes....they're not quite up to the potting sponges I must admit."

Philip was uncertain. Bracegirdle said:

"How many are you wanting?"

"About four dozen....six if they're up to scratch."

"Well I tell you what – will you leave me to pick the best out of 'em for you and we'll deliver what we've got along with your six cases....(?)"

The young man was nodding his head when the entrance door swung open. An agitated Clive Beresford stood there:

"Philip!"

The call filled him with foreboding and he immediately thought of his mother. Beresford took him by the arm and said to the merchant:

"You'll have to excuse us, Mr Bracegirdle."

The merchant could only stare at the closing door.

In the yard outside the warehouse Clive Beresford fingered his car keys nervously:

"Look, old chap – I've got some bad news for you. I'm afraid there's been an accident."

Philip's jaw sagged and he could hardly say:

"Is it....is it....my mother?"

The master potter's voice became especially tender:

"I'm afraid it's Frances, Philip."

"What....?"

"We had a 'phone call from your mother. I happened to be passing through the General Office when it was received.... so I came down here. They've taken her to the Haywood, because it's the nearest hospital. I think you ought to get up there now. I'll follow you if you like."

In a few minutes Philip was speeding up Moorland Road followed by Clive Beresford in his Sunbeam-Talbot. As Philip passed Park Road he glanced along its length. It would have been better had he not done so for the pavement at the far end was full of speculating neighbours. Reaching

Smallthorne they turned left along High Lane and were soon in the car park of the hospital. At its entrance Beresford laid a hand on Philip's arm:

"Philip – I look on Frances as a dear friend. You have absolute carte-blanche to get whatever help is necessary."

"Thank you, sir", he replied as he burst through the door. Not far from the doors he saw his mother sitting on a bench:

"Philip!"

About fifty people were waiting for attention on the long benches of the Outpatients Department which was also close by. Strangely, for a second or so, he seemed oblivious to his mother's call. Fifty heads had turned in unison towards him and there was a tension in their stares that made him afraid – it was as if they were waiting with grave concern for some outcome.

In the next second the starch of a nursing sister rustled its way towards him:

"Are you Mr Hughes?"

Mutely he nodded.

She conducted him and his mother to a side room and told them she would return very soon with "the surgeon". When she closed the door on them, Clive Beresford engaged her in conversation.

In the side room it was a long time before Elizabeth Hughes was able to tell the full story to her son, for the tears choked and muffled her words. She explained that having turned the key in the door at the house in York Street she had found Frances lying at the foot of the stairs. She had phoned for an ambulance and then phoned Whitfield Pottery to tell him, not knowing he had to make a visit on the way. Elizabeth had also come to the hospital in the ambulance. Frances had remained unconscious during the journey and was still unconscious when she was admitted.

It was an hour and a half later when the door of the

side room opened. The man in the gown seemed much too young to be a surgeon. Philip thought of him not much more than his own age. He looked kind and spoke softly:

"Mr Hughes, you'll know of course that your wife had a bad fall this morning. While she's obviously very poorly as a result of her injuries and has not recovered consciousness yet, we're not unduly alarmed by this. We haven't the facilities here to make a full examination but there doesn't appear to be any serious head injury though as I say we can't be sure yet. I believe your friend Mr Beresford is arranging for a neurosurgeon from the North Stafford to come here tomorrow. That seems the better option at the moment than to move her there. Unfortunately, we couldn't save the baby – a boy. I'm very sorry."

Philip was frozen with shock and grief. Barely audibly he asked:

"May I see my wife?"

The surgeon was hesitant:

"She's not ready to be moved to a ward yet, I'm afraid, and it's impossible to say when she will regain consciousness. I think if you go home now we can ring you immediately she comes around. As it is, there's very little you can do here at the moment."

"I'd like to stay if I may", was all Philip could whisper.

The surgeon nodded, repeated his regrets and left the room quietly. Soon the sister appeared and organised some tea for them both. Philip merely nursed the cup. He looked at his mother:

"You look done in. Let me run you home – then I'll come back here."

Elizabeth would have none of it:

"I'm not going home. I can't rest until I know she's all right."

So they stayed for the rest of the day, waiting and wondering.

They were given more tea but both of them refused the offer of food. When the evening shift came on, the new sister in-charge, whom Philip had known at school, told them they could visit Frances for a little while.

She looked extremely pale and both of them were alarmed to see her head was swathed in bandages.

"That looks a lot worse than it is. There has been some bleeding but it's from the scalp. The skull is perfectly sound."

They sat for two hours, just looking at her then Philip glanced across at his mother who seemed exhausted. He leaned across:

"Will you stay with us tonight, Mum?"

She nodded.

"Right. I'll run you down there."

He stood stupefied and looked at Frances for a long time. Then they left.

It was still warm and light on that July evening and three men were standing in the Market Place outside the ancient Lloyds Tavern. Fred Knapper sniffled as he said:

"Thay reckoned the babby'd got a mass o' black hair, same as her."

Before the other two could question his discovery of this intelligence, Billy Hogan was pointing:

"Hey! Did yer see who that was?"

They looked as the rear end of a Humber Super Snipe was disappearing behind the vast bulk of the Old Town Hall.

"Who?", asked "Ludo" Dunning.

"Ole Ewart – I bet he's off up th' Haywood."

They were right, for on hearing the news of Frances' accident Jack Foley had driven Ewart Bromley all the way from London. They were now on the last leg of their journey. A few seconds after Philip had turned his Austin down Hamil Road en route to his home the Humber passed that particular High Lane junction en route to the Haywood Hospital.

Philip's first action on reaching home was to look at the steep, dark staircase. There on the sixth step was the confirmation of his worst fears. The carpet's torn patch had now become a divot. When Frances had descended the stairs, seemingly in a rush, her foot had pierced the worn fabric causing her to stumble. He cursed himself knowing that each time he passed it he had promised himself to mask it with carpet tape until the whole carpet could be renewed. He now determined that it would be replaced immediately.

His mother went off to make them some tea and he went to the sitting room, looked out over the Park in the fading light and flopped onto a fireside chair. When his mother returned with the drink she begged him to eat but he refused. In turn he told her to provide something for herself and then go to bed. Before she went away she pointed to an envelope she had placed on the mantel-shelf. He glanced at it but decided the first thing he must do was to make the stair carpet safe, if only temporarily. Ten minutes later he had done this with a few carpet tacks.

He returned to the fireside chair then looked up to the mantel-piece and reached for the letter. It announced that he had passed the College's examinations in Preliminary and Ordinary Ceramics and that his marks justified the granting of a scholarship for the succeeding course in Advanced Ceramics. Now he saw the whole picture. Before his mother had arrived Frances had heard the snap of the letter box and rushed down the stairs in the hope that his results had arrived – and, of course, falling had not reached the envelope. He had not headed the pass-list as she had forecast but the scholarship marked him out as one of the industry's "up and coming" young men. He hoped she would be proud of him but, if not, it didn't matter for she could never be as proud of him as he was of her.

Grief has its stages. First the heart stopping *chill* when understanding is suspended, then the *stupor* when realisation dawns but the mind cannot function fully since it has no bearings yet and then the *letting go* when the tide of tears gives evidence of the torment. Philip's tears were now flooding forth.

He must have sat there for two more hours because midnight was near when the knock on the door made him stir. Jack Foley stood on the doorstep:

"The Major wonders if you'll see him..."

"Of course."

As Ewart settled into the second fireside chair, Philip offered to take his coat. He shook his head. Elizabeth Hughes, still fully dressed, reappeared.

"Will you have a cup of tea, Mr Bromley?", she enquired.

"I'd rather have something stronger," he said, in a low, tired voice.

As Philip poured him whisky, Elizabeth asked if she could prepare him some food. Again he shook his head but suggested, since Foley had been driving all day, he might welcome some. Elizabeth shepherded the chauffeur into the dining room leaving the two men together.

Alone, they looked at each other in silence. Philip thought Ewart looked old and about to collapse under the burden of his sadness. Ewart could see the marks of Philip's misery in the swollen redness of his eyes. Still they said nothing but at length, Philip said softly:

"I appreciate you coming here."

Ewart's mouth was dry and he could barely articulate but the sentiment was clear enough:

"I'm sorry for your loss."

Philip tried to be as calm and self-possessed as possible though the whole of his body and mind was staggering under the weight of his sorrow.

"Yes. Thank you. It was a bad job. Now we must hope and pray that Frances is all right. The doctor said he didn't think she was badly injured but a specialist is going to see her tomorrow. I just want her to come 'round...."

Ewart Bromley nodded. He was too choked with emotion to say anything so Philip carried on:

"It was a little boy.....we'd decided on his names..... Denzil Peter. A girl would have been Alice Elizabeth....."

He looked across the fireplace.....to where Ewart was sobbing. It seemed natural for the young warrior to go to the old warrior and lay an arm around him. A little later he poured another whisky for Ewart and left the room in search of Jack Foley, finding him seated with his mother in the dining room.

"Have you had enough to eat, Mr Foley?"

"Yes, thank you."

"I think Mr Bromley is going to be some time yet."

"That's good ", said the chauffeur.

The sentiment was not lost on Elizabeth Hughes who had begun afresh to dab at her eyes.

"Yes...but...he was saying you'd been driving all day. I was just wondering whether you'd like to go back to Porthill and turn in. I'll bring him up when he's ready to come."

Jack Foley's eyes opened wide:

"Oh, no. Thanks for the offer but I've got to stay with the Major. I'm not leaving him. I wouldn't sleep anyroad 'till I know Miss Frances is all right......I'm very sorry about the baby....I must stay with the Major."

Philip understood, acknowledging to himself the reason for the man's devotion to his master:

"O.K. Well the 'phone's there if you want to speak to Mrs Foley....I'll expect she'll be worried."

When the young man returned to the sitting room, his father-in-law seemed a little more composed. As Philip sat down Ewart looked at him steadily:

"You had a good pluck to come up to see me and say what you did. You said some things that weren't easy to listen to....but they showed what your feelings for Frances were. Even then I couldn't give credence to it.....but what I didn't want to believe then I can tell you now.....I can see that her place is with you....you..... and she....belong together."

The old potter put out his hand. Philip shook it:

"Let's hope she's spared to us...both of us....for a long time to come, Mr Bromley."

Later, when the Humber Super Snipe pulled away from the kerb in York Street Philip returned to his mother and finally persuaded her to go to bed. When he was sure of this, he returned to the Haywood Hospital.

"Mr Hughes? Mr Hughes?"

Someone was pushing gently at his shoulder. He opened his eyes – it was the nursing Sister who had been on duty when Frances was first admitted. A tall, slim scholarly looking man with wispy, white hair stood behind her.

"I'm sorry – I must have fallen asleep," Philip murmured.

"Little wonder," said the Sister. "Mr Hughes – this is Mr Mervyn Steen. He is a neurological specialist and would like a word with you."

They were in the small, private room where, on the previous day, he had waited long hours, with his mother, for news of Frances. He began to get up but the tall man said:

"No...don't get up - I'll draw up a chair."

The Sister disappeared and Mr Steen began:

"Clive Beresford asked me to look at your wife but in my preliminary examination I can't find anything that causes me concern. However, it will be important for me to have her under my care at the Infirmary. My Unit there has all the facilities for a thorough look at things. So as soon as she can be moved, which I'm told could be later today, with your permission we'll transfer her. How do you feel about that?"

"That's fine by me, doctor – whatever you think is best. I'd like to go with her if that's O.K."

"It looks to me as though you should be getting some sleep."

"No. I'm O.K. I'd prefer to go with her."

It was during the journey through the City that Frances recovered consciousness. Philip was overjoyed but it was clear that she was still disoriented so he stepped back to allow the nurse travelling with them to minister to her.

Five days later he was able to take her back to York Street. It was confirmed that she had made a full recovery though the specialist advised Philip that her psychological recovery would take longer. This proved to be the case for while Burslem rejoiced at her return, apart from fitful tears now and then, Frances was silent and withdrawn – disengaged, in fact, from the ordinary business of living. It was as if her grief was so deep it rendered her insensible.

Those were hard days for Philip to live through. He thought that renewed contact with her father would be of great comfort to her. Ewart could not do enough for her and was bemused to realise that while she was glad enough to see him, like Philip, he was kept at bay from her innate self. Both men became very worried – Ewart fearful lest his earlier lack of understanding may have caused the tragedy, Philip feeling that his very contact and courtship of her had led eventually to her present predicament. Elizabeth Hughes was also saddened. The open-hearted, loving daughter-in-law who had filled her with pride had become morose giving no more than monosyllabic answers, and usually negative ones at that, to every enquiry and effort made for her health and well-being. Elizabeth had told her son to be patient, but knew from her own disappointment how saddened he must be.

The problem continued for weeks, during which Frances had returned to the laboratory at Tilstones but seemed to have little appetite for the work there. One night as the first signs of winter were appearing they came home virtually at the same time. He could see she was cold and tired. He said:

"Go and sit down Frances. I'll make a hot drink for you. I'll get the meal tonight."

He guided her into the dining room and turned on the radio for her. In a few minutes he returned with the drink and smiled:

"What would you like to eat?"

She turned her head away from him. It was the most cutting response imaginable and he walked around her chair so she could see his face. Tormented, he said:

"Frances, please come back to me. I honestly don't know what to do."

Then he left the room for his hurt was intolerable.

He entered the sitting room and went over to the window, looking out of it and thinking. The vision came back again – of how happy and excited she was seeing the birds diving and swooping over the river bank that day in the café at Grasmere. Now she was sullen, impassive, unapproachable – almost ghost-like in her self-imposed exile.

He continued to look out, though seeing nothing, for now it was dark and not a vestige of the Park was visible. Suddenly, he felt an arm circle his waist. It was Frances. He held her while she sobbed, knowing that such sobbing could only have come from a broken heart.

At last, she said: "I've failed us, Philip."

He held her tightly:

"Frances, you could never fail at anything. I'm the one who failed. I should have seen to that stair carpet. That's why I thought you wouldn't speak to me."

"Oh no," she said and her hand went to his mouth to stop any more of his apology.

He held her tighter:

"Frances, listen to me – you never fail, you always succeed. You always succeed at making people love you. I'm your biggest success because you've made me care with a love that's truer and deeper than all the loves in the great love stories. Sweetheart, I don't have your religious faith but I do think there's someone up there in charge of things and we've been tested with this setback. There are bound to be other tests and other setbacks but we'll always come through Frances, because we know what we feel for each other and our love will always be enough."

Epilogue

Things were now settled. They would never forget the child they had lost but realised, mutually, that their future together called for all their loving attention and effort to be directed to each other and a wider world.

One matter had to be decided immediately: their connection with, or rather their severance from, the affairs of Ewart Bromley and Son Ltd (Grange Tableware). In Philip's case, the situation was quite clear: he was delighted that Frances was reconciled with her father and as Ewart now seemed a calmer, more reasonable individual, Philip had no difficulty in letting go of his resentment towards the man. However, a managerial position in his father-in-law's business was the last thing he wanted. He knew where his professional loyalties lay. Clive Beresford had been a great force for good in his life – in offering him his present job and in supporting him so readily at the time of Frances' accident. So his desire to stay at the Whitfield Pottery was absolute.

For Frances, things were more complex. The case for returning to "Bromleys" was underscored by countervailing forces of family feeling on the one hand and plain job satisfaction on the other. She knew her father badly needed help in the firm though even now she wondered whether he understood the true extent of his need. On the professional side however, she had been expensively trained as a scientist and this is where her inclinations as well as her capacities now lay. When she had returned to work, Tilstone's of Tunstall, impressed with her previous analytical skills, had announced the expansion of their laboratory facilities and offered her the post as its head with freedom to choose her own staff and develop, within the company's objectives, its programme of operations. She realised that work in applied science and intellectual engagements with other researchers within and beyond the firm, offered her the best chance of fulfilment. Accordingly, she told her father of this and, albeit reluctantly, he accepted her decision.

The couple settled into their home in Burslem steadily putting their stamp on it over the next two years. By this stage they had saved enough to consider ceasing to rent "York Street" and possibly purchasing a property of their own – in the country perhaps, a little to the north of the City. One night Philip was reading the "Sentinel" while Frances was sewing. He looked up:

"Here's a cottage at Mount Pleasant!"

He held open the newspaper for her to see. Mount Pleasant was a small hamlet very close to Mow Cop Castle (a folly someone had built in former times on a gritstone ridge a few miles from the Potteries). The folly was in the shape of a castle ruin. His best boyhood memories were of playing around the "Castle" and being, by turns, Buck Jones, Tom Mix and many another Hollywood cowboy. The hamlet was an idyllic spot in the lush countryside of Staffordshire, while the Cheshire Plain was viewable from the ridge itself. Now here was an opportunity to settle in this perfect spot.

As she scanned the details of the detached dwelling he watched her and waited.

"What do you think?"

She smiled.

"It sounds just perfect. Can we go to see it?"

"Yes, but we'd better be quick. There'll be loads of folks after it."

On the very next evening, they toured the one hundred and fifty year old dwelling. It was soundly built of local stone, with well-proportioned rooms, a graceful staircase and soundly-made hardwood doors and windows.

The kitchen-dining room was the heart of the house. It was supplemented by a pantry, a china cupboard, a wash house, a coal house, a w.c. and some outhouses for storage. There was a bright and airy parlour, three bedrooms and a fair-sized garden behind.

Philip's eyes took in the deep skirting boards with their attractive moulding. She fingered the beautifully curved newel post at the foot of the staircase.

"This place was built when attention to detail mattered. We could make it a palace, Frances."

When they had scrutinised every nook and cranny of the cottage, he looked at her:

"Well, what d'you think?"

Too happy to speak, she nodded with sheer delight. He lifted her off the floor as though she were weightless and kissed her.

The next day they were finalising details of the purchase.

They asked when the owner would be removing the Queen Anne sideboard they had seen in the kitchen and the washstand in "Modern Gothic" still in one of the bedrooms. The estate agent smiled at Philip:

"I see you know your furniture, sir. As a matter of fact the gentleman who owned the property has emigrated. His relatives have no interest in those items. They come with the cottage. We ought to have said so in the particulars. I'm sorry. We could move them if you wish."

Philip assured him that this would not be necessary and winked at Frances.

The purchase stretched their finances almost to the limit but some reserves gave them enough latitude to plan how the property might be furnished. They both felt it important to furnish so as to reflect the period when the cottage was built. This would mean scouring the auction rooms for good pieces.

"How do you fancy that, darling?", he wondered.

"Lead on, Sir Knight," she grinned.

In the months that followed, and in the years after that, they acquired a sofa and two armchairs, a carved bookcase, a rosewood needlework table, a corner cupboard for displaying china, two large oak and mahogany wardrobes, a heavy kitchen table and a set of small dining chairs in polished mahogany with plaited osier seats.

Mary Ellen Foley came to see the cottage. Prompted by Ewart a stream of materials began to arrive which the good lady suddenly found surplus to her needs. There was, for instance, the striped silk with which Frances made covers for the sofa and armchairs. There were the heavy damask curtains which she was able to cut down and remake for two of the larger rooms.

Often working until the early hours she embroidered cushions, runners, mats and a firescreen. In time, blinds of white Nottingham lace appeared at every window. Around the base of the oak beds (they had discovered in a clearance sale) she fitted charming valances. One day Philip came home in triumph on a haulier's cart. He and the carter brought a delightful dressing table into the cottage. Frances draped it, and its mirror, with starched and frilled muslin lined with coloured silk.

Yet if there was one task which epitomised their heart-and-soul effort to create the beautiful home the cottage became it was the restoration of the newel post which stood in the little hall at the foot of the staircase. It was coated with many layers of paint, the last being the chocolate brown of the wartime years. He pointed to it:

"If we clean that up, sweetheart, what's underneath'll be well worth seeing."

"While we're at it, I think we ought to clean up all the staircase and the handrail," she replied.

As it happens, the paint on the balusters and the handrail yielded quite readily to their assaults with solvents and wire wool. However, the covering of the newel post was stubborn and it was many weeks before it gave up the last flake of paint. Taking in the revealed grain of the post which had been enhanced by the superbly intricate work of the wood carver's tools, Philip touched it with his smarting, bleeding fingers.

"You can see why Chesterton talked about the harmony of wood."

Sucking her own blistered hands, she looked at the newel post. She felt they had uncovered its beauty because of their feelings for each other and in surviving Philip's death and her own death it would help their love to go on. It was a startling thought. It came without warning and moved her deeply. Then she told him what she was thinking.

They lived in their enchanted home for the next thirty or so years. Before they had acquired their second car, on most evenings of the week, one or other of the couple could be seen in Tunstall market-place waiting for the McIlroy 'bus which would take them to Mow Cop. The 'bus was the only one possessed by the McIlroy family but they had managed to retain their licence to operate the Tunstall – Mow Cop service in the face of competition from much bigger enterprises.

The 'bus was well past its prime and always resentful of the climb it had to make out of the hollow. From time to time it suffered from prolonged bronchial seizures. The driver, who by turns also acted as conductor, mechanic and raconteur, would curse it savagely for its contrary ways. In his desperation he would beg for evil spirits to descend and destroy "this load o' junk". Seemingly there was never anyone available to hear his imprecations for after its long periods of indifference the 'bus would always, quite suddenly, shudder into life.

Then somehow, muttering sullenly, the vehicle would manage to crest the rim of the hollow one more time. Even when the Hughes bought their car which took them, among other places, to Hardy country, Bronte country and Shakespeare country, Frances never wavered in her affection for the McIlroy 'bus and the pleasant social occasion a journey in it always provided. For its part, the 'bus always smiled in greeting when she struggled towards it with her shopping. Despite its breathing difficulties it would set off resolutely for the long hill climb, intent on doing its best because the pretty lady was on board.

The marriage of Frances and Philip transpired to be childless. This was deeply sad for both would have seen children as the greatest of blessings. Frances's deep religious convictions prompted her to pray continuously for the "precious gift of a child" even when, as she moved into middle age, she knew this was not going to happen.

While Philip did not share Frances' beliefs he was convinced that God existed. His tireless quest for enlightenment in literature, art, the applied sciences and philosophy made his attachment to the idea more and more firm. And if there was to be any hope for the world, the teaching of Christ was the touchstone. Here he agreed with Chesterton that the Christian ideal had not been tried and found wanting – it had been found difficult and never tried.

Yet though he was sad at God's decision about a child he did not dwell on it. Again, Chesterton had the word for it when he said that melancholy should be but an innocent interlude, a tender and fugitive frame of mind.

Frances saw things differently. Because no child appeared she felt a failure. Knowing how Philip loved children so, and would empty his pockets when a child came near, only increased her pain. She became quieter and would search his face to see what thoughts were written there lest disappointment might be among them.

After the evening meal on one occasion she turned to him suddenly:

"Philip?"

"Yes?"

"Do you love me?"

At first, he was flustered.

"....course I do," he murmured, ultimately.

"You never tell me."

The hint of bitterness in her expression conveyed her need for reassurance.

"Well.....I'm not given to affectionate language, Frances, I wasn't brought up on it. And if you judge me from what I do, you ought to know what my feelings are."

She was nervous of making her next comment:

"All the same....it would be nice to be told that I'm important to you....that you're not....disappointed."

"Frances....stop it," he whispered then, as if to atone for his enigmatic reply, he rose from his chair, went over to her and held her close.

A little later he left the cottage and walked over to the edge of the ridge. He often did this when the day was dying. This night especially he took in the crepuscular beauty of the land below him: over to the left the wonderful views of the Cheshire Plain and to the right the verdant scenes of Staffordshire. In a jungle of unspeakable stenches, thousands of miles away, he and others had fought for this land and its chocolate-box perfection. Many had not returned to see it again. Yet he felt that all of them would have shared his belief that their struggle had been well worth it, had they been spared to see it.

Then he began to ponder on Frances' questioning and her mounting anxiety. She had spoken of love. Love...what did he know of it? What did it mean to love her, as he most surely did?

He had to say that loving her was no longer like a fervent fire – it had been replaced by something deeper: she had become a necessity to him. His love was made up of higher superfine feelings that all his reading, all his study, had not yet taught him to articulate. This was of no help to Frances of course but he did not feel altogether defensive about his clumsiness. He remembered Proust had said that in a scene of parting, the person who truly loves is the person with nothing to say.

What he knew about her was that while her life was strictly separate from his own he needed her life force bound up with his own. If love was a sickness, as some had described it, then only she had the cure for his affliction. He, who up to meeting her had been so self-possessed, did not now mind being possessed by someone else....by Frances Bromley, a woman beautiful in body and soul. Her life had once been nothing to do with him but it had then become a life most intimately his, with love as the catalyst because it had changed two lives without being itself changed. But having changed their lives the catalyst, however powerful, could not re-change them, because their love would never change. This was a happy chance discovery thought Philip and it would have emerged sooner had he been more of a scholar, had he known more about the language of love.

As he thought about it, he also believed that love should be intertwined with personal integrity. He could never betray her but that was the only part of it. Being in love with her, seeking to make her happy, caring for her when she was sick, had produced for him a preferred version of himself. In his quest for his best self, his deep love for her had given him integrity and wholeness. His authentic self was the person who always wanted to be with her.

Shakespeare had said "Love is not altered when it alteration finds." This could be applied without question to his feelings for Frances. They had married with the unspoken assumption there would be children. Now it was clear they would be childless. He knew this worried her. It had also undermined her confidence in his love. So he resolved to do what, out of regard for her feelings and religious beliefs, he had baulked at doing. He would suggest they recognise what had never been brought into the open.....there would be no children. More, he would insist she believed that, for him, being with her was infinitely more important than being the head of the family he might have produced with some other woman.

"Love".....it was a very grand word, perhaps too grand. Maybe one should never use the word until one had deserved to use it.....until one had learned the behaviour of loving rather than declaring oneself to be "in-love". Possibly some people would never have fallen "in love" if they had never heard of "love".

All he knew was that the skills and senses of his life

would have been under-utilised if he had failed to love Frances. His endless longing for her approval had produced countless tokens of his love....they were there in the cottage behind him. And she herself had voiced the beautiful thought about the newel post: that it would survive their deaths and continue as a declaration of their love for each other.

As the light faded fast now, a cold wind began to crest the ridge. He walked back to the cottage, bent on telling her how much he loved her.

Apart from their sense of loss at being childless, their lives were happy and contented. However, there was a shock in store for them when, in 1962, it became known that Enoch Bromley and Son Ltd, Grange Tableware, could no longer meet its financial obligations. The Company was wound up with the loss of four hundred and eighty jobs. This was a great blow to Burslem, the first of many the town would sustain in years to come.

Already, world-wide competition was making the medium-sized firms producing tableware extremely vulnerable. Grange's output was of good quality but there was no premium for novelty in the shapes and decorations it had offered. Consequently the only competitive 'edge' left to it was in price. In this respect, the updating of its processes and capital equipment had been partial at best and its costing systems were still either outdated or incomplete. Ewart Bromley struggled to the last to save his family's business, but it had to be said that while its demise was largely a result of "market forces", his own lack of vision and aversion to risk taking played some part.

The measure of the man, however, can be gauged from the fact that he was a "captain" prepared to go down with his ship. His words to his local bank manager, a good friend, were:

"Do you think I'm the sort of weasel that'd hide behind the bankruptcy laws? The creditors will be paid with every penny I've got. My family's reputation is all that matters to me."

Being as good as his word entailed the disposal of his beautiful home, Bradwell Grange, but he was prevailed upon by Frances and others to provide himself with some sort of home from the proceeds. He took possession of a small house adjacent to Sparch Hollow on Wolstanton Marsh. Mary Ellen Foley had passed away two years before the Company was wound up. So he offered Jack Foley a place in his little house in exchange for his agreement to "see to things" day by day. The offer was gladly accepted.

In fact in Ewart's last years, Foley transpired to be a boon companion, recalling for the Major the battles they had fought in, the horrors they had endured and the men who had shared them and not returned. Ewart Bromley died in 1966 at the age of 72. Jack Foley followed him two years later.

It is, of course, purely conjectural but the extinction of the family business does raise the question – if Frances and Philip joined it, could they have saved it? Obviously, neither of them could inject further capital into it so it comes down to whether their brains and energy might have made a difference. As we saw earlier, her role at Tilstone's gave her much job satisfaction. It also allowed her adequate time to be a wife and home-maker. The pressures at "Bromleys" would have precluded this possibility and a job for which she had no heart would have taken over her life. As to the contribution she could have made in policy terms it would hardly have been sufficient to stem the burgeoning power of market forces. She also knew her father well enough to recognise his psychological insecurity – he would hardly have been willing to let her "steer" the business for, in the end, his opinion would always be the only one. And she had no stomach for the long fights that would probably have been necessary even for limited victories.

As for Philip, in addition to his loyalties to Clive Beresford and "Whitfield" it would have been beyond possibility for him to have joined his father-in-law since, after seven years' service with Beresford's of Burslem, he decided to leave management altogether.

One night in the cottage he had turned to his wife:

"What would you say, Frances, if I told you I wanted to return to the potter's bench?"

Mystified, she looked at him:

"This sounds mysterious......you mean, leave your present job...altogether?"

"Yes, that's it."

"Well, I'd wonder what your reasons were.....if you're really serious, that is....because you seem to have been doing so well."

"I'm concerned about the quality of our lives, sweetheart. We don't see each other as much as we should. I'm always rushed and preoccupied and when I am at home, as like as not, I've brought work with me. I chew over problems in my mind and that keeps me awake."

"I know. I hear you padding about often enough."

"I read in a magazine recently about heart attacks and what builds up to them. Stress and overwork are among the main causes and when victims are interviewed a typical comment is – I was under a lot of pressure and I always believed it would get better the next year, but it never did."

She frowned:

"Do you feel ill, Philip? Is that it?"

"No, I'm absolutely fine. You see – when I was

platemaking, no matter how physically tired I was, at the end of the day I could leave it – it was over. I can't do that in my present job – I have to live it. I don't know how long ago I picked up a book – the sort of book you read for enrichment I mean.

But these are the negative reasons, if you like. My positive reasons are because we should be living a fuller life – going to concerts, visiting the beauty spots, reading good literature, looking at paintings, seeing what the rest of the world has to offer. As it is, if we can get two weeks away together, we're lucky – and it's usually some place where I can be on tap. Time is going on, Frances, and we ought to be doing these things while we can enjoy them.

I'm grateful to you and to Clive Beresford and Dick Chidlow for how you've helped and supported me. I've done my very best in the job but it gives me less and less satisfaction. I'm sure, as well, that if you have to give up work, to have a baby for instance, I can earn enough at the bench to keep us on an even keel."

She smiled at him:

"You're a caution, Philip Hughes. Do you know that? Still, I suppose I always knew there was something different about you."

Having thought for a minute, she said:

"Don't do anything more at the moment. Think about it – we'll both think about it – for a couple of weeks or so – then let's discuss it again."

They did discuss it at a later stage, in more detail, and Frances said finally:

"If it's what you want, and it makes you happy, then I want it as well."

After he had kissed her, he shouted:

"Open your windows – and listen to this – I've got a girl in a million!"

Then whistling "Colonel Bogey", he picked her up and

marched around the room, carrying her in his arms.

The following day he asked to see Clive Beresford who was his usual urbane, charming self. His anxiety showed, however, when Philip explained that he wanted to resume working as a platemaker. Incredulous he asked why and Philip gave him the explanation he had outlined to Frances.

"Well, of course, I have to accept your reasons and in some ways I envy you – it'll be a much more relaxed life. But, you see, you seem to have taken everything in your stride. I have to say, Philip, you've done a wonderful job for us and will be very hard to replace. Remember too that Mr Chidlow is on the verge of retirement and we will need a Works Manager. Still, I hear what you're saying and thanks for telling me."

The master potter thought for the moment:

"So, what's the next step?"

"Well, I thought I'd look round for an opening in a "flat" shop somewhere and then give in my notice. I know there are no vacancies here at the moment but I don't think it would take me long to get fixed up, somewhere."

"I'm sure it wouldn't, but before you start looking around, let me think about it. Don't do anything until you see what we can offer you."

"Mm – right, Mr Clive." Bemused he left his employer.

Within two days he was summoned to Clive's office. Still thoughtful, the managing director looked at him:

"You haven't changed your mind, Philip?"

"No, sir."

"Well it so happens that in the last month or so we've been giving some thought to where we're going as a company. Competition is really hotting up now and though we may look big locally, in world terms we're really rather small. Now – when a small to medium-sized organisation like ours exists profitably side by side with larger firms, it doesn't try to put these giant international corporations out of business by apeing what they're doing. It slides down the cracks of the market by selling what is novel, what is distinctive. I hope we shall be a significant tableware manufacturer for some time to come – but there are too many of us producing basically the same shapes and the same patterns by the same processes. If we are to survive we simply must differentiate ourselves from competition."

Philip was intrigued:

"So if you diversify somewhat, do you see a role in that for me, Mr Clive?"

"Yes I do...and so does Dick Chidlow. He'll be retiring very soon and it's a pity we can't transfer you into his job.... but you've made your views clear on discontinuing your career in management and I respect them, so we won't revisit that issue."

Beresford leaned back in his chair, relaxed but watchful:

"We think you're the person to take charge of our research and development. We'll call it the "R & D Department" probably. You're a competent hands-on potter and you've been technically trained. That's a rare combination. We'll rig up the Department with a jigger for "flat", a holloware jolley, a potter's wheel and some turning equipment. What you don't know about throwing and turning, Dick would teach you. It's a wide remit because you'd have to work closely with designers on the practicability of their ideas, see to firing trials and even oversee the testing of new colours, glazes, processes even. Does that interest you?"

Philip was dumbstruck. If ever there was a perfect job for him, this was it. He could hardly voice his assent but ultimately managed to say:

"It's a wonderful opportunity. I'm really grateful!"

Clive smiled:

"Well, you can get started as soon as we've found a

replacement for you, which won't be easy."

Never one to leave "loose ends," he added:

"As far as the salary and the pension status are concerned, this is an important job, which won't be easy, even if it's one you can relax from at the end of the day, so we'll leave your present remuneration intact."

They shook hands and Philip's deep gratitude was evident to his employer – a man who had consistently been an enlightened boss and a true friend.

That night he raced home to tell Frances his news, at the end of which he began marching on the spot whistling "Colonel Bogey". He put out his arms horizontally and obligingly Frances vaulted into them so that the parade around the room could commence.

They stayed near Mow Cop until 1986. They were contented years for they had made courageous decisions about the type of work to which they were best suited. So their moral courage was rewarded by the rich and interesting lives they were able to lead as a consequence. There were, of course, sad patches. Ewart Bromley was already dead. Elizabeth Hughes was 70 years of age when she died in 1969. Both were missed and mourned but both had been content to see Frances and Philip so settled and happy, though silently they shared the couple's sadness that no child ever arrived for them despite the unrelenting prayers of Frances. Because of this her love and support of the Gratton girls and the Carroll children intensified.

In 1985, Frances had her first stroke. Philip was upstairs preparing for work. Hearing a clatter below he rushed down to find her unconscious on the floor of the kitchen-dining room. Soon afterwards an ambulance, siren blaring, was making its way through the crowded streets of the Potteries en route to the Infirmary.

When she recovered consciousness her right arm was stiff and devoid of feeling. At that stage, the medical staff counselled patience for in the coming days or even weeks she might regain the use of it. However, she did not do so and one day, while Frances was undergoing routine tests, Mr Stuart Morris, the neurologist caring for her, asked to see Philip.

He explained exactly how she had become a stroke victim: a lesion on the left side of the brain having produced the paralysis in her right forearm. Although Philip was now on the brink of retirement the couple had redeemed the mortgage on their property in 1980 and since then had saved a relatively small but "handy" reserve for contingencies. Philip made clear his anxiety that everything possible should be done to restore the use of the arm – he would provide the finance for any expert the neurologist might suggest.

The reply was that the effects of the stroke were not reversible and that future procedure would be to manage the stroke through the services of physiotherapists and other health care professionals. Philip's role would be to assist the work of the team in the Stroke Rehabilitation Unit as much as possible, especially by helping Frances though the mood disturbance, anxiety, depression and other clinical problems that might well arise.

"But is there nothing in the way of surgery that might help, Mr Morris? You find the best people available. I'll find the finance."

"No, no. Nothing like that is appropriate. What you should do is be guided by the stroke nurses and the physiotherapists about the equipment you could acquire to help her and the adaptations needed in the home so she can live as normally as possible."

There was a blank expression on Philip's face.

"Is there a problem, Mr Hughes?"

"Well, we live out at Mow Cop. I'm just wondering whether it might be sensible to move – perhaps nearer the hospital. It would be a big wrench, but if it's for the best...."

"It might be sensible to do that, but who can say? What she does need is adequate ground floor accommodation where you are free to make whatever modifications are necessary."

Philip thanked the specialist whom he instinctively trusted and, on the day he left the hospital with Frances he explained to her why he thought it best that they move from Mount Pleasant. She was crestfallen:

"Oh dear, I'd hate to give it up....after all these years."

"I know.....but it's for the best....."

He was too saddened himself to give her any reasoned analysis. In any event, since it hinged on her future health, he was careful not to sound too grave.

"But are you sure, Philip? It'll cost money and you've always said we mustn't cut into our reserves."

Philip laughed:

"Sweetheart, we didn't save the money to hoard it! We saved it for contingencies like this. Now, as it is, it might be wise to come back into the City – find a modern place, near the hospital perhaps, so we can cut down on your journeys. What d'you think? You're the important one in all this."

For a while, she was silent. He was careful not to interrupt her thoughts. Then her questions came quickly:

"Will you be short of money? Will it worry you? Are you sure you want to do it?"

"Of course. Neither of us is getting younger. Perhaps we're a bit too far out from the City now. Everything will be fine. O.K.?"

Surprisingly, their home at Mount Pleasant on which

they had lavished so much love and care proved difficult to sell. A combination of increasing travel costs, a tight mortgage situation, and the dwelling's lack of appeal to younger buyers meant they had to wait for an enthusiastic older buyer to appear. No one came.

Then one day the estate agent acting for them appeared with a firm offer. It was from a "business gentleman" who could complete the purchase immediately. They were buoyed up by the news until they heard the offer. It was at least twenty five percent below their asking price which this same agent had initially assured them was a true reflection of the property's real value.

About a week later, Philip was working in the garden at the rear of the house when he heard another ominous clatter. He ran into the house and found Frances kneeling in a pool of water. Using her left arm she was scooping into a saucepan, as quickly as she could, the vegetables he had prepared for her earlier. She looked up at him. Her cheeks were wet with tears.

"I'm sorry, Philip," she choked.

He put his arms under her shoulders and lifted her to him, whispering:

"Never you mind, m'duck. You're doin' champion."

As he sat her down he was thinking quickly. The bathroom and some of the domestic fittings had been adapted for her and they had also bought some appropriately designed items of new furniture. The social services department of the local authority had provided a home help too – a lady who did far more than she was paid for but, in the end, had to work to a schedule to cover the needs of other disabled people. However, Philip felt he had to do more, since Frances had reluctantly admitted that shoulder pain had now developed on the affected side of her body. He sat her down and made her a cup of tea.

"Look Frances, we've got to think about getting you

more help," he said.

"But I'm fine. That was just an accident."

"Listen – I know how much your independence means to you but you're right-handed. How can you suddenly expect to do everything with your left hand?"

"But I'm getting better. I've got to work......as part of my rehabilitation. That's what they said at the hospital."

"Yes – but they don't know about the shoulder pain yet and doing all the things you're set to do by the physiotherapist is a better way to rehabilitation than doing domestic chores. I want you to agree to having more help."

"Where?"

"Here, at home, every day."

"But we can't afford that. If we have to take a cut in our selling price we've got to be careful.....you said so."

We *can* afford help....it's a matter of first things first." The argument went on until Frances, with the utmost reluctance, agreed to have the services of a daily companion. It helped that the lady who came in each day was a kindly, selfless soul who transpired to be a good friend to Frances as well as a helper.

Philip also took Frances back to Mr Morris for further consultation. Morris believed that the shoulder pain was caused by poor recovery of the arm function. To abate it, he would ensure that his own staff took special care in the handling of the hemiplegic limb. Also, under the guidance of the physiotherapists, the use of arm supports and shoulder strapping would be provided. He agreed with Philip that extra care from the physiotherapists would be beneficial. Unknown to his wife, therefore, Philip agreed to finance this from his own resources.

The shoulder pain was reduced somewhat as a result of these extra measures and all was going tolerably well, but within a year of her homecoming, she had her second attack. This was when Philip decided to act. He accepted the lower offer for their home which had been made through the estate agent by the "business gentleman". He transpired to be a builder who, Philip assumed, would be buying the house for his own occupation. When Frances was about to be discharged from the hospital he arranged for her to enter a nursing home for a period while he concentrated on finding a new home for them near the hospital.

Before that, of course, they had to decide what furniture would be going to their new home, which would have to be smaller, from a care and maintenance standpoint, yet with one large enough interior space which could be adapted to his wife's needs. He had hoped to find a new home for them but in the end had to settle for one recently built which though near enough to the hospital was not in a very salubrious part of the City.

It became obvious, when he returned to Mount Pleasant, that very little of their furniture could go with them. He assessed things carefully - no more than one or two of the smaller pieces could be retained. Broken-heartedly, he advertised the rest for sale. This was not a successful move. Such members of the "admass" that visited the house dismissed the beautifully crafted furniture as being "too heavy", "too dark" or "too depressin'". The last of these visitors gave it all a withering look and, rhetorically, asked:

"It's not very 'contempry', is it?"

Having had enough of these "enquiries", he decided to turn over the problem to a firm specialising in house clearances. This firm's manager had a demeanour which Mr Claude Roebuck would have envied. Faced with such "unmarketable" pieces, this man pleaded dire poverty in "these difficult times", paid Philip an insultingly low sum, in cash, and arranged for the wonderful artefacts to be borne away in triumph. On the day they came for them, Philip left the key with his nearest neighbour and spent the day with Frances at the nursing home for he could not bear to see them go.

His disappointment intensified when he took a closer look at the house he had purchased. Since he had realised a significantly lower price on their own property than they had imagined and since he intended to retain a considerable sum for Frances' welfare, admittedly he had had to lower his sights. Even so, he considered that what their money had bought was poor value.

The house had been left in a dirty state by its former owners. But beyond that, though only a few years old, it was starting to look decidedly distressed. Cupboard doors wouldn't close properly and at the bottom of the kitchen fitments there were humps where the man-made timber had absorbed water from the floor. On the floor itself several of the vinyl tiles were lifting at the corners and one or two tiles were even disintegrating. The place was poorly ventilated as signalled by the colonies of dark spores on the badly emulsioned walls. When he tried to open a window to freshen the air it resisted all his efforts.

In his heart he thought this newly-built dilapidation a waste of their hard-earned money. In other times and circumstances he would never have looked it. It was a testament to shoddy building and a criminal lack of builder's after-care. Sloppy owners had made a bad situation worse. He knew he would never be able to meet his wife's eyes when he brought her to the house for those magnificent eyes would be brimming with tears. When he left the place that day to visit her he had a long struggle to lock the front door.

Had he known what was happening at Mount Pleasant that instant he would have been incensed. A bulldozer was ploughing its way through the stone cottage which had been their home.

In front of the cottage, a group of demolition men had lit a fire. They were feeding it with the wooden fixtures and fittings they had brought out of the cottage.

"Look at this, gaffer," said one of the workmen. He pointed to the beautifully carved newel post they had taken from the foot of the stairs.

"Burn it," ordered the foreman.

"But there's some workmanship in that. It'll be worth a bob or two."

The foreman was displeased by the delay:

"The rates for this job are low enough as it is. We'll never make any money if you faff about.....BURN IT!"

Then he pointed to the oak sign which Philip had so carefully carved and mounted over the cottage's front garden gate.

"An' burn that as well......"Potter's Cottage" .....it's a daft name for a place anyroad," he sneered.

In a sense he was correct. The sign would have been out of place for the site was to be developed to contain 3 "executive style" houses. A more appropriate name for the location would therefore have been: "Greed is good".

The second stroke was more far reaching in its effects because Frances became unable to speak and had great difficulty in keeping her balance. The neurologist had explained that this development was due to the original damage to the brain. It also became clear to Philip that although the services of a speech therapist would now be made available there was a limit to what socialised medicine could do for Frances. With the help of Mr Morris who could not, however, offer any guarantees that the strategy would work, Philip arranged to finance substantial extra care from the speech and physiological therapists.

It all resulted in no more than marginal progress in her speech. It was also clear that, despite her own efforts and those of everyone around her, she was becoming steadily more depressed.

Even so, Philip listened carefully to the speech and language therapists as they explained appropriate communication techniques to him. He was tireless in his efforts to help her, talking to her first about general topics, then specific issues, using photographs and newspapers as prompts and aids, and asking Frances about things that were important to her especially her religious faith. The sum total of his efforts and those of the professionals was, in the end, little or nothing.

"Come on, sweetheart....we mustn't let it beat us," he would say, as she struggled with the tasks that had been set for her. But, in the end, when the message in the still magnificent eyes was begging they stop, he would sigh understandingly and squeeze her arm. For him, the hardest thing to bear was the destruction of Frances as a person. The person he had met and loved, as girl and woman, had become a tired old lady who, because of the neurological damage she had sustained, was much given to weeping. The once shapely Frances Bromley had become amorphous. When he held her as she wept he would turn his face from her so she would not see his own misery.

She was now largely confined to a wheelchair and most days he wheeled her through the town centre of Stoke. On their journeys he noticed how the town, like the other Potteries towns, was changing. Its once busy note was becoming more and more muffled. Familiar landmarks looked sad and uncared for. Factory after factory was closing and many of the bottle-kilns were disappearing.

They were going through the town one day about eighteen months after her second stroke. Although largely unable to communicate he could always perceive how she tried to involve herself in the business of the walk. Using the "good" left arm she would point out things she knew would interest him – a bird landing on the pavement, the smile of a small child. He would always say something kind and encouraging to her and squeeze her shoulder with great tenderness.

On this day, however, she seemed uninterested in things around her. Then suddenly her head slumped forward. Philip had to move quickly to stop her falling from the chair. Using one hand to steady her and pushing the chair with the other he wheeled her into a nearby shop where anxious people 'phoned for an ambulance. In thirty minutes she was lying in a coma at the Infirmary.

For the next three days he sat by her bedside, refusing to leave and dozing occasionally when at last he had to yield to the urge to sleep. He would talk to her as she lay there, breaking off only when one of the hospital staff drew back the screens around the bed.

"It's all right, Mr Hughes," the Sister had said when she first interrupted him. "Keep talking to her. We may think she can't hear but nobody knows that for sure."

Philip took up his quiet talking again, hoping it was no soliloquy. He told her, among many other things of the places they would visit when she was well again. But on the fourth day he stopped for he realised he had been talking like some automaton, talking for the sake of it, talking so as not to say what he knew he must say. So when the morning visit of the staff was over he went back and looked down at her. He must tell her about Peter Bromley. He must answer truthfully all the questions she had put to him those many years ago when she had come to work at "Grange" Pottery.

When they had married, he had expected continuous questioning about Peter's death. This had never happened. He felt there were two reasons for this. Firstly, she had been notified by the authorities that her brother's name was featured among others on a memorial in a particular cemetery in the Far East. This meant he had no known grave. The second was that during the early years of their marriage, his sleep was continually riven by nightmares. Frances would wake him and after explaining that he had been crying out fearfully she would bring him fresh night clothes to replace the ones soaked with his sweat. One night he woke to find himself sitting on the edge of the bed, with her holding him while he rocked back and forth. After that, Frances never spoke of Peter. Doubtless it seemed to her that his name was somehow bound up with her husband's horrors. It was private grief she could not intrude upon.

Nevertheless it was a matter which lay rock-like upon their lives, unspoken but ever present. Now as she lay there stricken, Philip eased himself into the chair beside the bed. He took her hand, pushed back the thick, white hair from her forehead and began to talk. He talked without ceasing.

"Frances, there's something I've got to tell you. I should have told you all those years ago when you came to work with us. I said I didn't know what happened to Peter. That was a lie. I kept on lying. I've kept the truth from you ever since.

We were together....and he was wounded.....very badly. We were always retreating at first and when we did we took the wounded with us, either on mules or on our backs.

After Peter got hit though we were told that the wounded would have to be left, that we had a duty to get out alive and we wouldn't do that if we tried to take the wounded with us. We pleaded with our officers but they said no.....the wounded must be left."

Now he paused, but only for a second before continuing:

"You must understand, Frances, we were fighting a terrible enemy. Peter was unconscious but I've seen men die and I knew there was no hope. I looked at him. I didn't want him bayoneted....or mutilated.....because that's what they often did. The blood was pouring through his dressings. We couldn't stop it. I took his rosary out of his pocket and I wrapped it around both his hands......Then I shot him, Frances.

It's true, Frances. I killed him. I can only say he was

more than a friend to me. I loved him like a brother. And I've always believed I had to do it. Sweetheart.....I had to do it. It was wrong, but I had to do it.

I'm sorry I've lied to you all these years. I loved you Frances from the first, and I thought that if you knew you could only hate me. Please, please forgive me, Frances. You've got to forgive me."

Then he sat still and silent. Presently, and he would never be in any doubt about it, he felt the fingers of her left hand squeeze his own hand where he held it in hers.

"Oh Frances......Frances......I'm sorry. I'm sorry. I do love you!", he called to her, then every heart in that long and very public ward felt pierced by the sounds of a strong man weeping.

Though he had not been aware of it, the screens parted a few seconds later and someone hovered over Frances. Then the screens were closed again and he was left alone again quietly sobbing.

A little later, the screens parted yet again. There was an arm about his shoulder and a face came close. It was the Sister:

"Mr Hughes, Frances has gone now and we have to see to her. You need rest. Go with Nurse and she will look after you. If you wish you can come back later. She was a lovely woman. We are all very, very sorry."

A few days later, people all over Burslem and very many in other parts of the Potteries were waiting for the 'Sentinel' to arrive. They looked to the "Deaths" columns and there it was. They read it, re-read it, passed it among themselves and talked about it. Then they cut it from the newspaper and put away carefully among the memorabilia of their own families. The notice began:

"HUGHES. Of your charity please pray for the repose of the soul of Frances Mary, devoted and dearly loved wife of Philip William Hughes, who passed away, peacefully on 2nd

March 1987 after a long illness patiently borne. Fortified by the rites of Holy Mother Church......."

At her death she was 62 years old. Many people, potters, miners and others followed her to her resting place in Burslem Cemetery, quite close to where Tyrone Carroll and Sally Gratton lay. Michael and Luke Carroll were mischievous school boys when she came into their lives. Now strapping men with families of their own they felt privileged to be among her pall bearers. Two other "children" to whom she had been a surrogate mother were also there and they too had families by now.....apart from Philip, no-one was more stricken by the loss of this beautiful woman than Maureen and Denise Gratton.

A little while after the funeral, Philip moved back to Burslem, making his home in a terraced street off Dale Hall. When we next meet him the turn of the century is approaching.

He was exhausted. He had just struggled to the house with three shopping bags full of his weekly groceries. He no longer had a car. After finding it outside his former home near the hospital vandalised once too often, he decided to give up driving. As he approached his front door he instinctively looked up at the security light. It was smashed. A malicious game-playing had become established as the norm: as soon as the security light was repaired, wreck it.

Unlocking his door was a complicated business for he was continually adding new features to make it thief-proof. But the ingenuity of the robbers always proved too much for him. They still seemed able to enter his home at will, especially on days like today when he had drawn his pension from the post office. Once inside, he began the laborious business of locking all the security devices he had just unlocked. He straightened up. Tired or not, the house must be tidied now that he was back. He would make some tea then get everything into proper order. The standard he worked to was that of Frances in their cottage at Mount Pleasant. Everything always emerged from her cleaning activity neat, tidy and shining.

As he sipped his tea she stayed in his thoughts. Just then a banging began on the door, interrupting these thoughts. He could see the letter-box was being raised.

"Are yer there, yer stupid ole git?!"
Philip stood up and faced the door. The bellowing continued:

"My father's comin' ter get you! He'll soon sort you out. Yer a mis'rable ole swine!"
It was quiet for half a minute or so before he heard malignant laughter and feet padding away from the house. He walked to the door and anxiously unlocked it. Its entire surface had been smeared with a thick, tarry liquid. A little way down the path from the house he could see a paper hanger's brush lying in a pool of tar. This substance had obviously been taken from a site nearby where a road battered by juggernauts was being resurfaced.

He had recognised the threatening voice and the cackling, menacing laughter. They belonged to the leader of a group of rowdies he had seen throwing fireworks at a whining dog. He had burst through the cordon of its tormentors and carried the terrified animal away in his arms. Unable to find its owner he had walked with it to the People's Dispensary for Sick Animals some distance away. According to the barbarian codes of behaviour which now prevailed he should never have done this: it was an infringement of the group's freedom. His newly tarred door served him notice that he would have to pay for his actions.

Now, painstakingly, he cleaned up the door then, just

as assiduously, he cleaned up the house. Finally he cleaned himself up.

He was now well into his seventies but he was still a man of polished shoes, trousers with knife-edge creases and immaculate linen. The care which he had lavished on his work at the potbank extended to care for his own appearance. This had been reinforced by the Army. Thankfully, the Army had also lit within him the flame of relf-reliance. This was of great value now that Frances had gone.

Yet his smartness was not peacock-smartness, only what was reasonable. He had learned the importance of this from his father and had been astounded to see this affirmed in the Meditations of Marcus Aurelius:

"Manliness without ostentation I learnt from what I have heard and remembered of my father." Book 1.2

He remembered many other simple though profound ideas of this man, both emperor and philosopher, for instance:

"Put from you the belief that 'I have been wronged' and with it will go the feeling. Reject your sense of injury and the injury itself disappears." Book IV, 7.

What a miracle that he, a humble potter, should have become conversant with a conceptual framework provided by Marcus Aurelius. Since Frances' death, and doubtless as part of the grieving process, he had intensified his quest for self-improvement even to the extent of obtaining a Bachelor of Arts degree at the local university. How this had enriched his friendship with literature and the arts by sharpening his powers of observation and analysis seemed a wonder to him.

After the degree ceremony the 'scholarship' boy had walked to the grave of Mr Clare the old schoolmaster who had exhorted him to remember that life was "too short for anything but the best". The message he now had for his mentor was "I have kept the faith with you for the faith you had in me."

After the tidying up, he sat down for a little while and thought more about Marcus Aurelius. Of course, whereas the emperor frequently alluded to "philosophy" Philip appreciated that today it would be more accurately described as religion. Marcus had believed in a system of philosophy termed stoicism. It was a pantheistic creed. It held that God was immanent in all created things but had no separate existence outside them.

This was not Philip's view. For him, God existed very much as an entity. He was to be found very clearly in Thomas à Kempis's "Imitation of Christ" which might be thought of as the Christian counterpart to Marcus' thinking. Yet Philip was not yet quite at home with organised Christianity. His own faith was not mediated by either priest or prelate. It was a standpoint in which the intimate relationship of God and his created individual was paramount. It was a relationship of reasonableness, loyalty and love. Church rules didn't come into it, so far.

In this he differed from Frances whose whole life had been inextricably bound up with her Church and its liturgy, with its saints, novenas, feast days, hymns and, above all, its Holy Mass. Her long years of religious devotion had fuelled his deep love and respect for her. He had felt the same about her brother – he remembered how, whenever they were pulled back from the front line, Peter would brave an unaccompanied journey through miles of jungle to hear Mass.

These days Philip would go, quite often, to the church where Frances had worshipped. Just to sit there brought back the clearest memories of her - how she would rush in after work, prepare his meal, then dash out again in order to get to "Stations". Whenever he was in the church he would look around at the Stations of the Cross, the sequence of Christ's agonised steps to Calvary. He had long since recognised how emblematic they were – of Christ's journey, of Frances journey, of Peter's journey, of all the journeys of all the faithful struggling through life towards the goals of human perfectability and Heavenly reward. Surely Frances and Peter had gone to this reward by now. If not all was futile.

He stirred from his reverie and thought he would like to go the church right now and sit with his memories of them both. He combed his hair, carefully brushed his jacket and gave his already shiny shoes another rubbing with a soft cloth.

As he walked, ramrod-backed, from the house, three or four young men were lounging against a wall nearby. He also glimpsed two girls with them. They wore clothing which detracted from, rather than safeguarded, their modesty. The pair were grinning at the boys as if to challenge them into confrontation with Philip in some way or other. None of the boys responded openly except as he passed them, one whispered slyly:

"O.K. Colonel?"

Philip walked with sneering laughter following his steps. Whenever anyone had goaded him Frances' advice was against anger. She would say: "remember darling, to know all is understand all." To know all is to understand all. But who had troubled to understand those other young men who had accompanied him to the stinking swamps and stayed there? He strove not to give vent to his feelings, but it was hard. It was very, very hard.

On this particular day, nearing the town centre, he decided to detour slightly. Instead of going direct to the church he would visit the streets he had known as a young man. Arriving there he was astonished. The streets had vanished.

Down on the left, a huge shed had appeared. Over its main entrance was a large sign which said: "The Dungeon". The mock-gothic lettering of the sign was dripping red paint, connoting blood. The place looked evil and menacing. He stood stupefied until a young mother came by, with a baby in a pushchair and a toddler on her arm. She looked pale and tired.

"Excuse me," Philip apologised, "I don't want to hold you up, but is Hanover Street around here?"

"Used to be mister," she answered.

"And what's that place?", he wondered, pointing to the grim shed.

"A night club," she said.

Then she became animated:

"This used to be a respectable place. Full o' tidy workin' folks. Now it's a hell 'ole."

"I can't believe it," he murmured to himself.

"At the weekends they're drinkin' 'ere till the early hours of the morning. They come out on the pavement, shoutin', drinkin', fightin', buyin' drugs. An' some of the girls are worse than the men."

He fished in his pocket for coins to give to the children. She refused these at first but at his insistence took them and thanked him.

"You keep away from this place, mister", she called back as she hurried away.

He still could not believe what he was looking at. This had been home to consummately skilled mouldmakers, platemakers, slipcasters, enamellers, paintresses and gilders. Now there was not a sign they had ever lived here. There was only a giant shed for the making of money through the development of addictions in the young and the inculcation of hedonism, the doctrine that pleasure is the highest good. How far had we come from Mr Clare's dictum that "life's too short for anything but the best"?

With a heavy heart he walked on and, in a little while, crossed the square by the Old Town Hall. Why was it so quiet? Why did the famous pub where Josiah Wedgwood had met James Brindley to discuss the building of the Trent and Mersey canal look so sad and isolated?

He wandered around the streets off the Market Place where, not so long ago, busy family firms of drapers, bakers and cabinet makers had plied their trades. Now they too had gone, their premises being given over to "£1" shops, charity shops, antique shops, museums to tell the story of what had once taken place here, of the beauty that had once been created.

The most noticeable building he passed was the "Job Centre". He understood that thirty two thousand jobs had been lost hereabouts. The ceramics industry which, as late as 1975, had employed forty five thousand people, was reduced to thirteen thousand jobs today, with more redundancies to come. Many of the world famous old firms had gone. Nor was there any trace of the great ancillary industries of coal and steel, set up to supply and support the pottery factories. Some notable names had survived only by moving their operations to the Far East.

As he walked he continued his musing. The other day he had gone up to Mount Pleasant. He had not been put off by the obstacles and had finally found a vantage point from which he could look back towards the hollows.

He despaired. Virtually all the bottle kilns were gone and in their places was a colony of sheds in a variety of colours and sizes. The Victorians had been much maligned but they, at least, had left some notable and finely detailed buildings as their legacy. Now it was apparent that many of these had gone to make way for the march of the sheds.

What he now saw below him was a tectonic void, the negation of building as an art. The Clean Air Act had doubtless been a boon but some future landscape historian would conclude that while the Potteries had improved its appearance, after a fashion, in doing so it had lost its soul. Once beauty had been created down in the hollow, now all that was being created was money for a favoured few.

Today as his walk continued, two men with humpty-dumpty stomachs passed him.

"I dunno why I played such a rotten game – I'd only had six pints!", said one. The other laughed.

Why had the hedonistic calculus gripped the young so tightly, he wondered. Fifty years ago, thanks to the efforts of his own generation, Britain had had a unique opportunity to exercise moral leadership. Today other nations feared Britain's hooligan young. It was heartbreaking.

How much money had to be diverted from public health to fight the self-sown miseries alcohol and tobacco brought with them? "To know all is to understand all" is what Frances had said. It was true that some of today's young were struggling with the corroding indignity of unemployment, but so were the young of his own generation, with war and death and mutilation lying in wait for them.

Depressed by his own train of thought he finally arrived at the church. He sat down where she always sat, in an unobtrusive spot six rows from the back. Thinking of her, he remembered the line WB Yeats had written for his beloved Maude Gonne:

"One man loved the pilgrim soul in you."

Frances had been a pilgrim too. This had been her place of pilgrimage. He still marvelled that every visit here filled him with peace and contentment.

There were some parishioners cleaning the church today, keeping it as beautiful as ever. Near the altar there was the lady who always arranged the flowers. He had seen her often and had been impressed by her competence and sense of splendour. The impact of the flowers themselves seemed to him accentuated by the work of her hands.

As he looked at her, she turned and smiled at him quizzically. Then she gathered the dead flowers, before walking down the church towards him. As she moved along the bench to where he sat he saw how attractive she was. A little taller than Frances, her beauty was different from his wife's Celtic beauty. She had the fine bone structure of classical English beauties and her skin was remarkably soft and unlined. She reminded him of the heroines he had seen in the British films of fifty years ago.

"It's Mr Hughes, isn't it?........... Frances Hughes' husband?"

Her voice was gentle. Philip nodded self-consciously.

"I often see you in here", she smiled.

"Well, I drop in sometime when I'm passing", he murmured, thinking how shallow and inconsequential his words sounded.

"She was a lovely woman, Mr Hughes. She used to come to our prayer group. We do miss her."

He could only nod his thanks for this affectionate remembrance. Sensing his shyness, she smiled at him again.

"Listen, there's a missal in the sacristy nobody's ever claimed. I think it was hers. Would you like to look at it?"

"Yes, thank you".

"We have a break about this time. So stay with us for a cup of tea. A lot of the others knew Frances".

He watched her to go to the Sacristy and sighing, settled back in the bench for an instant. Then he looked up, to take in the splendour of the main altar. His gaze moved on - to the left and the Lady Chapel. This was when his eyes widened and his heart pounded. His chest tightened. He couldn't believe it... there was Frances!

It was true, she was there, smiling at him! Her beautiful face was plainly outlined in the front of the Chapel.

But now she had gone...... and this was when a great

sense of peace enveloped him. The pain and stiffness of his walk had vanished - miraculously – vanished. He felt buoyed up, happy and moving forward somehow as if he was starting a journey. Was he going to Frances? How could that be when he didn't know where she was?

"Frances?......... Frances?!......... Where are you now my darling?"

He had better start the journey.........now!........ because wherever she was – he had to find her! Frances where.....

THE END